AGGRESSION
BIOLOGICAL, DEVELOPMENTAL, AND SOCIAL PERSPECTIVES

THE PLENUM SERIES IN
SOCIAL/CLINICAL PSYCHOLOGY
Series Editor: C. R. Snyder

University of Kansas
Lawrence, Kansas

A Continuation Order Plan is available for this series. A continuation order will bring delivery of each new volume immediately upon publication. Volumes are billed only upon actual shipment. For further information please contact the publisher.

AGGRESSION

BIOLOGICAL, DEVELOPMENTAL, AND SOCIAL PERSPECTIVES

EDITED BY

SEYMOUR FESHBACH

University of California
Los Angeles, California

AND

JOLANTA ZAGRODZKA

Polish Academy of Sciences
Warsaw, Poland

PLENUM PRESS • NEW YORK AND LONDON

Library of Congress Cataloging-in-Publication Data

Aggression : biological, developmental, and social perspectives /
   edited by Seymour Feshbach and Jolanta Zagrodzka.
       p.   cm. -- (The Plenum series in social/clinical psychology)
   Includes bibliographical references and index.
   ISBN 0-306-45497-1
   1. Aggressiveness (Psychology) 2. Aggressiveness (Psychology)-
-Cross-cultural studies. 3. Psychology, Comparative.   I. Feshbach,
Seymour. II. Zagrodzka, Jolanta. III. Series.
   [DNLM: 1. Aggression.   WM 600 A2657 1996]
BF575.A3A466 1996
155.2'32--dc21
DNLM/DLC
for Library of Congress   96-38783
                                                                  CIP

ISBN 0-306-45497-1

© 1997 Plenum Press, New York
A Division of Plenum Publishing Corporation
233 Spring Street, New York, N. Y. 10013

Printed in the United States of America

CONTRIBUTORS

CLAUDIO BARBARANELLI, Department of Psychology, University of Rome, Via dei Marsi 78, 00185 Rome, Italy

LEONARD BERKOWITZ, Department of Psychology, University of Wisconsin, Madison, Wisconsin 53706

KAJ BJÖRKQVIST, Department of Psychology, Abo Akademi University, 65100 Vasa, Finland

PAUL F. BRAIN, School of Biological Sciences, University College of Swansea, Singleton Park, Swansea SA2 8PP, Wales, U.K.

GIAN VITTORIO CAPRARA, Department of Psychology, University of Rome, Via dei Marsi 78, 00185 Rome, Italy

LEONARD D. ERON, Department of Psychology, University of Michigan, Ann Arbor, Michigan 48109-1109

NORMA D. FESHBACH, Department of Education, University of California, Los Angeles, 405 Hilgard, Los Angeles, California 90095-1521

SEYMOUR FESHBACH, Department of Psychology, University of California, Los Angeles, 405 Hilgard, Los Angeles, California 90095-1563

ELZBIETA FONBERG, Department of Neurophysiology, Nencki Institute of Experimental Biology, Pasteur Street 3, 02093 Warsaw, Poland

NANCY GUERRA, Department of Psychology, University of Illinois, Chicago, Box 4348, Chicago, Illinois 60680

ROBERT HINDE, MRC Group, Cambridge University, Madingley, Cambridge, CB3 8AA, England

L. ROWELL HUESMANN, Research Center for Group Dynamics, Institute for Social Research, University of Michigan, Ann Arbor, Michigan 48106-1248

MARIA INCATASCIATO, Department of Psychology, University of Rome, Via dei Marsi 78, 00185 Rome, Italy

YORAM JAFFE, Department of Psychology, University of Southern California, University Park, Los Angeles, California 90089

PIERRE KARLI, Faculté de Médecine et Institut de reserche sur les Fondements et les Enjeux des Sciences et des Techniques, Université Louis Pasteur, Strasbourg, France

ARI KAUKIAINEN, Department of Psychology, University of Turku, Arwidssoninkatu 1, SF–20 500, Turku, Finland

LUCYNA KIRWIL, Institute of Social Prevention and Resocialization, University of Warsaw, 20 Podchorazych Street, 03420 Warsaw, Poland

KIRSTI LAGERSPETZ, Department of Psychology, University of Turku, Arwidssoninkatu, 1, SF–20 500, Turku, Finland

PÄIVI MYÖHÖNEN, Department of Psychology, University of Turku, Arwidssoninkatu 1, SF–20 500, Turku, Finland

CONCIETTA PASTORELLI, Department of Psychology, University of Rome, Via dei Marsi 78, 00185 Rome, Italy

ANNARITA RABASCA, Department of Psychology, University of Rome, Via dei Marsi 78, 00185 Rome, Italy

MAJID B. SHAIKH, Department of Neurosciences and Psychiatry, New Jersey Medical School, 185 South Orange Avenue, Newark, New Jersey 07103-2757

ALLAN SIEGEL, Department of Neurosciences and Psychiatry, New Jersey Medical School, 185 South Orange Avenue, Newark, New Jersey 07103-2757

JOLANTA ZAGRODZKA, Department of Neurophysiology, Nencki Institute of Experimental Biology, Pasteur Street 3, 02093 Warsaw, Poland

PREFACE

This book is dedicated to our friend and colleague, Professor Adam Fraczec. Professor Fraczec has achieved international distinction for his work in the area of aggressive behavior and has achieved prominence in Poland for his leadership role in advancing psychology in that country. He has devoted his scholarly interests to studying the role of cognitive, emotional, and personality mechanisms in the development and regulation of interpersonal aggression. Professor Fraczec introduced the study of human aggression into Polish psychology and stimulated other psychologists to undertake the study of this hitherto neglected area of inquiry.

From the very beginning of his scientific activity, Adam Fraczec recognized the importance of international cooperation in science. However, penetrating the Iron Curtain presented many difficulties, but despite these obstacles, he succeeded in building bridges between psychologists in the East and the West. In addition to visiting Western research sites and inviting Western psychologists to Poland, he and his research group played a major role in a cross-cultural study of television viewing and aggressive behavior. He is the author and coeditor of some 60 publications including the edited volumes *Aggression and Behavior Change* (with S. Feshbach), and *Studies on Determinants and Regualtion of Interpersonal Aggression* (with H. Zumkley).

Professor Fraczec has been an active member of the Polish Psychological Association, serving as a member of its executive board. He has also served on the executive board of the International Association of Experimental Psychology and as a member of the council of the International Society for Research on Aggression. He was elected as president of that society for the years 1991-92.

This volume reflects Professor Fraczec's cross-national orientation to scientific studies of aggressive behavior. No less important than the original data presented are the similarities and differences in the perspectives provided by investigators working in different cultural settings. An additional significant feature of the volume is the inclusion of studies of aggressive behavior in infrahuman species, providing an opportunity to consider continuities and discontinuities between animal and human aggression.

The first three chapters by Karli, Zagrodzka and Fonberg, and Shaikh and Siegel address differences in areas of the brain and neurochemical processes mediating offensive and defensive aggression in animals. The next chapter, by Brain, on alcohol and aggression, links animal and human studies. The ensuing section, consisting of chapters by Björkqvist, Kirwil, Caprara and his associates, and Feshbach, Feshbach, and Jaffe, addresses issues in the development of aggression. These include processes mediating modeling, concordance and disconcordance between parental attitudes toward aggression and developmental changes in aggression, the relation between aggression and subsequent adjustment and school achievement, and gender differences in the relationship between aggressive and depressive tendencies.

The chapters in the third part examine features of aggressive behavior in a broader social context. Eron, Guerra, and Huesmann consider the contribution of poverty, ethnicity, and aggressive normative beliefs to aggressive behavior; Lagerspetz explores the values of Punk culture and the ambiguous place of aggression in that culture; and Hinde addresses the institution of war and its questionable relation to individual aggressiveness.

The final part consists of a chapter by Berkowitz in which he broadens the frustration–aggression relationship to that of noxious affect–aggression and considers the role of automatic mechanisms in the evocation of aggression. The final chapter by Feshbach is an effort to interrelate and integrate the contributions to the volume. Each of the contributions is seen as bearing on one or more of the following issues: the different functions of aggression and corresponding mediating mechanisms; alternatives to frustration as a primary antecedent of aggression; revisions of the concept of frustration; and consideration of the conditions under which frustration and symbolic aggressive stimuli elicit aggression.

SEYMOUR FESHBACH
JOLANTA ZAGRODZKA

CONTENTS

Chapter 7

Chapter 8

PART III. SOCIAL INFLUENCES ON AGGRESSION

Chapter 9

Chapter 10

Kirsti Lagerspetz, Ari Kaukiainen, Päivi Myöhönen,
and Kaj Björkqvist

Chapter 11

Robert Hinde

PART IV. THE FRUSTRATION–AGGRESSION HYPOTHESIS:
A THEORETICAL REVISION AND AN OVERVIEW OF THE ROLE OF
BIOLOGICAL, DEVELOPMENTAL, AND SOCIAL INFLUENCES

Chapter 12

Leonard Berkowitz

Chapter 13

Seymour Feshbach

PART I

BIOLOGICAL INFLUENCES ON AGGRESSION

CHAPTER 1

CONCEPTUAL AND ETHICAL PROBLEMS RAISED BY THE STUDY OF BRAIN-BEHAVIOR RELATIONSHIPS UNDERLYING AGGRESSION

PIERRE KARLI

INTRODUCTION

For the neurobiologist who studies brain mechanisms supposed to be involved in aggressive behavior, conceptual as well as ethical problems arise from the fact that research dealing with brain-behavior relationships is both a research endeavor like any other and one that clearly differs from many others. It differs in that the data obtained, the interpretation they are given and the generalized conception of brain-behavior relationships that is derived from them, contribute to shape our vision of man, his "nature", his being and his evolution. Conversely, this vision of ourselves, of our supposed "nature", is bound to somehow orient-unconsciously, or more deliberately—the way in which we con-

PIERRE KARLI • Faculté de Médecine et Institut de reserche sur les Fondements et les Enjeux des Sciences et des Techniques, Université Louis Pasteur, Strasbourg, France.

Aggression: Biological, Developmental, and Social Perspectives, edited by Seymour Feshbach and Jolanta Zagrodzka. Plenum Press, New York, 1997.

struct the conceptual framework within which we elaborate our working hypotheses and interpret the results obtained when verifying them. It matters all the more to be fully aware of these reciprocal relationships between *personal convictions* and actual *scientific endeavor* since our basic interest lies in a deeper understanding of the biological determinants of our own personality and behavior, even though our experimental analysis is carried out—for obvious ethical reasons—on the brain of some animal species. The true weight and the real influence of our personal convictions clearly appear when, on the basis of one and the same array of available facts (but, admittedly, with selective emphasis put on some of them), some feel entitled to deliver, with regard to human aggression and violence, a "message" of necessity and fate, while others are led to deliver one of freedom, responsibility, and hope.

THE SPECIFIC ROLE OF THE HUMAN BRAIN

Quite obviously, brain-behavior relationships cannot be extrapolated from any animal species to man in the way one would rightfully extrapolate data concerning heart or liver physiology, or even elementary brain mechanisms, because the human being can by no means be reduced to his biological identity and functioning. In the life course of a human being, there progressively emerge, coexist and closely interact the three facets of the human "trinity": man is a biological individual, a social actor, and a reflecting and deliberating subject. Each of these facets carries on a dialogue with its own environment: the organism's material environment; the actor's social milieu; the subject's inner world. Since the three facets with their respective dialogue obviously share one and the same brain, it follows that the latter takes on the role of mediator in the threefold dialogue which evolves across the life course.

This threefold dialogue consists in three evolving sets of appropriate—that is adapted and adaptive—*interactions* which basically aim at the satisfaction of specific sets of needs or desires. The three distinct—but closely interacting—dialogues are governed by distinct sets of norms, and they can be related, within the human brain, with three major levels of integration, organization and adaptation that process in different ways different kinds of information. But, whatever the concrete objective, the prevailing norms and the kind of information being processed, any interaction eventually comes down to "getting at something" or "getting away from something". In either case, aggression is one of the available means of action that may appear—and prove—to be a highly effective behavioral strategy.

THE "NEURAL SUBSTRATE" OF AGGRESSION

Let us briefly outline the *functions* taken on by the brain in its role as the mediator of the threefold dialogue carried on by the human "trinity". The biological individual obviously needs an adequate mode of brain functioning in order to preserve his physical integrity and maintain the homeostasis of his internal milieu. Both the biological significance of the stimulus or situation that elicits the behavior and the behavioral strategy itself are to a large extent genetically pre-programmed, so that the overt behavior merely fits in with the present moment and its basic biological meaning. As for the social actor, brain functions are to be brought into play that allow him to experience positive—and avoid negative—social emotions in his manifold interactions with a particular and changing environment. In and through these interactions, the behavior acquires its historical dimension, and in turn reflects and dynamically shapes an individual life-history. Finally, the reflecting and deliberating subject requires a mode of brain functioning that accomplishes more complex cognitive and affective elaborations based on a number of internalized—and continuously reshaped—frames of reference so that the subject's behavior can be in keeping with—and make sense in—a more conscious, well considered, and deliberate personal plan.

Within the brain, it is essentially at the mesencephalo-diencephalic level that behavior is organized and controlled to ensure the satisfaction of the individual's basic biological needs and the defense of his physical integrity. At this functional level, two neuronal systems have an important part in orienting the individual's basic attitude and overt behavior: an appetence and reward system (running from the mesencephalic tegmentum through the lateral hypothalamus to a number of forebrain structures) which orients the behavior towards objects likely to lead to the satisfaction of some primary need; and a more medially-located, periventricular, aversion and defense system the activation of which promotes defense behaviors (flight, "defensive" aggression, immobility) that aim at putting an end to an aversive experience generated by some dangerous or otherwise unpleasant situation. Since aggression is an effective "instrument" both to "get at" and to "get away from" ("appetitively-motivated" or "aversively-motivated" aggression), it is not surprising that, right from the start, animal studies (stimulation and lesion experiments) pointed to the lateral hypothalamic area on the one hand, and the medial hypothalamus and periaqueductal gray on the other, as being essential components of the "neural substrate" of aggression.

Only a few experimental data can be given here (for more details, see Karli, 1981, 1991; Siegel and Brutus, 1990). Electrical stimulation applied to lateral hypothalamic sites was found to elicit intermale aggression as well as mouse-killing behavior in the rat and quiet-biting attack (on a rat) in the cat; conversely, lateral hypothalamic lesions were shown to abolish both mouse-killing behavior and territorial fighting in the rat. A more "defensive" and "affective" kind of aggression can be elicited from medial hypothalamic and periaqueductal stimulation sites, whereas a destruction of the dorsal part of the periaqueductal gray suppresses the spontaneous occurrence of such behavior. I shall give one example to illustrate the relations between the prevailing emotional state and the overt behavior that expresses it. Initiation of mouse-killing behavior is due to the rat's *neophobia* and it can be considered to be aversively-motivated; by repeating and reinforcing itself (in particular, through its getting associated with feeding on the killed mouse) the killing-behavior progressively turns into an appetitively motivated one. This helps to understand why it is that one and the same periaqueductal gray stimulation has different effects depending on whether it is applied to a rat that has been given an opportunity to become familiarized with the strange species or to an experienced killer-rat. In a previously non-killing animal, the periaqueductal stimulation induces both an intense aversive emotion, repeated attempts to jump out of the cage and, eventually, an *instrumental* killing behavior: the latter behavior can rightfully be considered to be instrumental, since the rat is no longer induced to kill the mouse once he has learned to "switch-off" the stimulation by merely pressing a lever. In the experienced killer-rat, the same stimulation appears to produce a "motivational conflict": this aversion-inducing stimulation sharply interrupts an ongoing—and appetitively motivated—killing behavior (Karli et al., 1974; Karli, 1981, 1991). Owing to the fact that a twofold (GABA-and opiate-mediated) moderating influence tonically lowers the levels of activity and reactivity of the periventricular aversion and defense system, one can experimentally manipulate the functioning of an aversion-moderating GABA-ergic transmission and thereby produce an emotive biasing of the brain's input-output relationships that clearly affects the individual's general attitude and overt behavior. Thus, unilateral injection—into the periaqueductal gray—of a GABA agonist (which facilitates GABA ergic transmission, thereby reinforcing the moderating influence exerted on the induction of aversion and defense) was found to provoke an enhanced *approach* responding to ipsilateral tactile stimulation together with a clear facilitation of *offensive* behaviors. Conversely, unilateral injection of a GABA antagonist (with opposite local effects) was found to provoke enhanced *withdrawal* and *escape* responding to any contralateral tactile stimulation together with an increased tendency to display *defensive* behaviors (see Karli, 1989a; Schmitt and Karli, 1989).

The major role played by a strong appetence (urge to get at) or a strong aversion (urge to get away from) in determining the *offensive* or *defensive* use of an aggressive strategy is further evidenced by the fact that the probability that such a strategy be used is closely correlated with the individual's degree of emotional responsiveness. For instance, lesions of the septum were repeatedly shown to increase markedly the rat's reactivity and, at the same time, to facilitate shock-induced fighting as well as initiation of mouse-killing behavior. The two behavioral effects are closely linked to one another, since the probability of initiation of mouse-killing behavior was found to decrease in the measure that the septal lesion-induced hyperreactivity gets attenuated over time. This probability remains high for months if the septal lesion is carried out at an early age (7 days, for example), in which case it induces a *lasting* hyperreactivity (Eclancher and Karli, 1979). It must be emphasized that a septal lesion which markedly increases the probability of the killing behavior in the naive—and "neophobic"—rat is without any effect in rats which were previously familiarized with mice. Thus, Blanchard and her colleagues (1979) are certainly right in considering that the destruction of the septum induces a more marked defensive attitude ("hyper-defensiveness") in response to signs of threat rather than any increased "aggressiveness".

A BASIC CHANGE IN SCOPE

The actual bringing into play of the above-mentioned mesencephalo-diencephalic neural substrate depends on functional relationships with the amygdaloid nuclear complex. For instance, a naturally existing differential predisposition of the cat to respond offensively or defensively to a variety of environmental threats was found to be correlated with both intrinsic functional properties of the amygdala and synaptic transmission properties between the amygdala and the ventro-medial hypothalamus. Moreover, by experimentally manipulating the latter transmission properties, one can modify, in a foreseeable way, the cat's natural predisposition (Adamec, 1991). The amygdala is also implicated whenever the affective significance of a stimulus or situation is modified through the shaping influence of experience, as can be exemplified with the following experimental facts. Various brain manipulations were shown to result in an initiation of mouse-killing behavior only in those rats that had not had prior experience with mice, and a bilateral lesion of the medial amygdala was found to abolish this aggression-preventing effect of a prior familiarization with mice (Karli, 1981; Vergnes, 1981). Similarly, bilateral lesions of the cortico-medial amygdala markedly attenuated the behavioral repercussions usually induced by the aversive experience of defeat, namely a decreased probability that an aggressive strategy be used again (Koolhaas 1984).

In any mammalian species except man, aggression can be—and in some instances must be—used as an effective behavioral strategy that allows to "get at" or "to get away from" something in order for the individual to meet his basic biological needs and to master his interactions within a biologically-determined social system. In the case of such an individual, the linearly organized neural structures which realize this potentially existing strategy can be described as "the neural substrate of aggression". But the mere existence of this substrate should never lead us to consider that the brain generates an endogenous "aggressiveness" thought to act as a unitary causal reality, or the closely related universal "aggression instinct" postulated by Konrad Lorenz (1967). Moreover, things change essentially as regards the human species. Especially in our so-called developed countries, the human being is—or should be—only very exceptionally constrained to resort to an aggression in order to survive and/or to defend his physical integrity as well as that of his offspring. As a social actor, his interactions take place in a culturally determined social system with its specifically human aspirations, projects, values, and norms. He strives to satisfy his personal *interests* which evolve as a relational construct that develops in—and through—the dialectical relations between his own needs and desires and the people thought to be capable of satisfying them (see van der Wilk, 1991). The social actor's life-history generates a meaning of its own that is no longer genetically and rigidly pre-programmed, owing to the specifically human interpretation and symbolization of the experienced events. And as a reflecting and deliberating subject, man is capable of consciously shaping the way in which he gets engaged in—and contributes to orient—the events he experiences: he can choose, in particular, to resort to prosocial rather than to aggressive strategies.

If the neurobiologist is interested in brain-behavior relationships that prevail in the human, and hopes that the data obtained in animal studies will have relevant explanatory virtues, he must take full account of the outlined shift from genetically-determined cause-consequence relationships which prevail for the biological individual to culturally—and historically—determined relationships between means and ends which reflect and shape the social actor's interactions with others. This obvi-

ously leads to a fundamental change in scope (Karli, 1989b). When reflecting on human aggression, the neurobiologist can no longer start
from a given behavioral output (some "model" of aggression) to analyze
the various brain structures, processes and mechanisms that appear to
be involved in the bringing about of such an output, and then "explain"
the observed aggression on the basis of the thus analyzed—and somehow reconstructed—experimental data (thereby specifying some of the
biological "roots" of aggression). If a social actor resorts to an aggressive
strategy in the face of a given situation, the problem is primarily one
of social cognition and social emotions which depend on both the individual's life-history and a given socio-cultural context. More concretely,
two related questions await an answer: why did he perceive, interpret
and experience that situation in such a way that aggression appeared
to be the appropriate strategy, most likely to help to cope with the situation or, rather, with the social actor's personal relation to that particular
situation; why did he eventually resort to this kind of behavioral strategy
(with two major more precise questions coming in here: what about the
individual's history of reinforcement with respect to aggression; and
what about processes such as correct risk assessment, true attachment
experience, reliable social support, that could have helped to hold the
potential aggressor back)? Once multidisciplinary studies have uncov-
ered and analyzed the major—endogenous and exogenous—factors and
processes which contribute to determine the probability that, in the face
of a particular situation, a given individual will eventually resort to an
aggressive way of coping with it, then—but only then—can we fruitfully
analyze all the brain processes and mechanisms that either generate or
merely process the various components of a highly complex "causal
field" with its overt behavioral outcome.

This change in scope by no means minimizes the significance of
neurobiological studies for a deeper understanding of the determination
of human aggressive behavior. Quite the contrary, such a biological perspective can more easily be reconciled with the psychosocial perspectives
that are elaborated in the study of human aggression. Many relevant
individual features can be fruitfully subjected to neurobiological investigation, such as: the level of overall emotional responsiveness, as well
as the more specific sensitivity to the aversive character of threat, provocation, or frustration; the proneness to impulsive responding; the generation, individual degree and behavioral repercussions of anxiety; the
individual "behavior style" shaped early in life; the affective state of *social comfort* and the *affiliative* behaviors that both generate and reflect it;
the way of recording—and referring to—the life-history, especially the
history of specific and relevant reinforcement; the changes in both cog-

nitive and affective significance that may result from processes or events such as familiarization, success or defeat, and punishment. Quite clearly, the conceptual framework and the concrete results thus obtained are in keeping with studies that aim at clarifying the role played—in the generation of human aggression—by personality factors such as "irritability" and "emotional susceptibility" (Caprara et al., 1983; Caprara and Pastorelli, 1989), "weak self-control" with a marked dependence on situational cues and internal impulses (Pulkkinen and Hurme, 1984), and cognitive structures ("scripts") for social behavior' which both determine and result from social interactions with their outcome expectancies (Huesmann and Eron, 1989).

FROM THE ETHICAL POINT OF VIEW

In other words, the human brain should no longer be considered as a *generator* of possibly—or even inevitably—occurring aggressive behavior (with improper emphasis on some humoral factor or even single gene thought to be specifically implicated), but rather as the *mediator* of a dialogue which may take on an aggressive form for reasons that can only be truly clarified through joint multidisciplinary efforts. Such a perspective has two further related advantages. First, it fully recognizes the importance of the historical dimension of life. In animal and man alike, the individual life-history contributes to shape the phenotypic expression—in brain structures and processes—of genetically-coded information. But only in man does this history greatly contribute, in addition, to shape the development—in close interaction with brain maturation—of personalized psychodynamics and cognitive structures, as well as the continuous updating of the internal representations of a specific sociocultural environment with its values, aspirations, models and myths. Second, to consider the brain as a mediating organ also gives full recognition to the fact that there are not just one-way relations between brain functioning and ongoing behavior, but that the brain undergoes—in return—the shaping influence of the multifaceted experience that derives from that behavior. And this shaping influence of experience does not just concern the *content* of the conditioned associations and of the more complex representations carried by the brain, but also the brain *mechanisms* themselves that are involved in the constitution, storage, and remodeling of that content. A number of experimental data clearly indicate that the role played by the brain in the process of socialization, in the development of a social identity and in its overt expression in social interactions, is one of a "two-way mediation across the life-course" (Karli, 1995).

The transition from conceptual to ethical considerations comes here quite naturally. Since it was mostly on improper biological or naturalistic grounds that "messages" of necessity and fate which promote—unconsciously, or more deliberately—the evil myth of "the beast within", were and still are delivered. This can best be exemplified by peremptory statements in Konrad Lorenz's well-known book *On Aggression* (1967), where he stresses "*the destructive intensity of the aggression drive, still a hereditary evil of mankind*"; and there he sees "*man as he is today, in his hand the atom bomb, the product of his intelligence, in his heart the aggression drive inherited from his anthropoid ancestors, which this same intelligence cannot control*". Even more suggestive is the change the title of the book underwent when it was published in French: the original title "*Das sogenannte Böse. Zu einer Naturgeschichte der Aggression*" was changed into "*L'agression. Une histoire naturelle du mal*" (1969). In other words, a shift was carried out—apparently without the author's opposition—from a "*natural history of aggression*", a scientifically well-founded notion, to a "*natural history of evil*", an abusively inferred notion that confirms the pessimistic vision of man characteristic of ideologies like that of the "*social darwinism*".

Konrad Lorenz's point of view is but one milestone in a long—and still continuing—history of misconceived "explanations" of human aggression and violence, again and again closely tied up with some supposedly typical and inherited biological feature. Let us briefly consider a few significant episodes of this history (for more details, see Karli, 1991, 1994). In the first half of the 19th century, Gall maintains that the human brain comprises twenty-seven distinct organs and that their growth allows one to evaluate—through mere palpation of the skull— several "*intellectual and moral dispositions*" of a given individual. Examining the skulls of a number of murderers of his time, he notices that the areas 4 and 5—which he locates behind the right ear—are specially developed, and he considers that this peculiar expansion indicates an obvious propensity for brawl and murder. In the second half of last century, Lombroso succeeds in imposing his well-know theory of the "*born criminal*" who is predisposed to criminal acts by his physical constitution. Examining in thousands of criminals and delinquents the morphological features of the skull, of the brain and of the physiognomy, he "*discovers*" the marks of criminality, the particulars that are beyond any doubt—he claims—those of the "*born criminal*".

FINAL COMMENT

In our century, the achievements of genetics are taken into account: one no longer relates aggressiveness and criminality to some inherited morphological mark, but to some component of the genetic material itself. In 1965, Jacobs and his collaborators report that a supernumerary Y chromosome was found in a population of subjects treated in institutions (who displayed both a degree of mental deficiency and a propensity to violence or crime) in a higher proportion than in the general population. This publication gave then rise to a number of studies on what quickly became, for some, the *"crime chromosome"* or the *"supermales genetically programmed for violence"*. And yet, all serious research carried out later on leads to the conclusion that it is abusive to consider that the supernumerary Y chromosome *"predisposes"*, or even *"urges"* a subject towards crime, and that it is useless or even dangerous (since it generates anxiety and injustice) to proceed with this kind of *"stigmatization"*. Owing to the great progress of molecular biology, the culprit is now searched for at the level of the genes. In 1984, John Glover suggests that genetic engineering methods could be used to eradicate from *"human nature"* its *"more harmful and dangerous side"*, that is, *"the human instinct of aggression and self-destruction"*. In 1990, Daniel Koshland, editor-in-chief of *Science*, begins a leading article by referring to a recent hostage-taking with murder, which he relates to an *"irrational output of a faulty brain"*. He then goes on to express his conviction that molecular neurobiology will provide us with new tools that will prove more efficient in the struggle against violence than a number of social measures which can hardly be more than *"Band-Aid remedies"*.

In the face of this persistent promotion of wrong ideas, one cannot help wondering why human aggressiveness is considered an inevitable and unalterable biological fate, and why the myth of the *"beast in man"* has always been—and continues to be—so common. At least four reasons may be put forward.

- First of all, these notions provide us with a convenient alibi or scapegoat: not only do they *"explain"* any aggression, they also excuse it. How could we prevent, in spite of our obvious goodwill, the *"beast"*—which is claimed to be an integral part of our *"nature"*—from manifesting itself from time to time?
- The idea that some genetically controlled brain region *"generates"* aggressiveness as an endogenous driving force understandably appeals to the authorities who are given the difficult task of struggling against aggression and violence. For one can thus try either

to destroy the aggression generator by means of psychosurgery or to hinder its functioning by means of some *"anti-aggressive"* molecule, looking forward to the time when genetic engineering will allow one to eradicate evil at its root.

- In order to reinforce an ideology, its promoters readily project it into Nature so as to recover it in a naturalistic form, henceforth more convincing and more constraining as it is now based on some alleged *"Law of Nature"*.

- A scientific discipline will inevitably build up a narrow and mutilating vision of man's *"nature"* whenever it claims to totally *"explain"*—on its own—the being and evolving of man. Some biologists working on the human genome seem to be convinced that the expected results will allow us to finally understand in what consists our humanity.

From an ethical point of view, it is certainly not immaterial to realize that in the absence of any *"aggressiveness generator"* within the brain, one cannot act on such an *"aggressiveness"* in any highly selective way. Every brain manipulation (psychosurgery; psychopharmacology; eventually genetic engineering) is bound to modify—in a more or less marked and possibly irreversible way—the subject's personality. Since the dignity of man is intimately linked to the broadening and preservation of his personality, we must fight against *"ordinary"* aggression and violence (not to be confounded with a rare *"pathological"* aggressiveness which is a clinical sign—among others—of some brain lesion) with means other than direct brain manipulation, namely an education that leads to cognitive, affective and moral maturity, the promotion of social change and the development of measures of social defense.

REFERENCES

Adamec, R. E. (1991). Partial kindling of the ventral hippocampus: Identification of changes in limbic physiology which accompany changes in feline aggression and defense. *Physiology and Behavior, 49,* 443-453.

Blanchard, D. C., Blanchard, R. J., Lee, E. M. C., & Nakamura, S. (1979). Defensive behaviors in rats following septal and septal-amygdala lesions. *Journal of Comparative and Physiological Psychology, 93,* 378-390.

Caprara, G. V., & Pastorelli, C. (1989). Toward a reorientation of research on aggression. *European Journal of Personality, 3,* 121-138.

Caprara, G. V., Renzi, P., Alcini, P., D'Imperio, G., & Travaglia, G. (1983). Instigation to aggress and escalation of aggression examined from a personological perspective: The role of irritability and emotional susceptibility. *Aggressive Behavior, 9,* 345-351.

Eclancher, F., & Karli, P. (1979). Septal damage in infant and adult rats: Effects on activity, emotionality, and muricide. *Aggressive Behavior, 5,* 389-415.

Glover, J. (1984). *What sort of people should there be? Genetic engineering, brain control and their impact on our future world.* Harmondsworth: Penguin Books.

Huesmann, L. R., & Eron, L. D. (1989). Individual differences and the trait of aggression. *European Journal of Personality, 3,* 95-106.

Jacobs, P. A., Brunton, M., Melville, M. M., Brittain, R. P., & McClemont, W. F. (1965). Aggressive behavior, mental subnormality and the XYY male. *Nature, 208,* 1351-1352.

Karli, P. (1981). Conceptual and methodological problems associated with the study of brain mechanisms underlying aggressive behavior. In P. F. Brain & D. Benton (Eds.), *The Biology of Aggression* (pp. 323-361). Alphen aan den Rijn: Sijthoff and Noordhoff.

Karli, P. (1989a). Studies on neurochemistry and behavior. In R. J. Blanchard, P. F. Brain, D. C. Blanchard & S. Parmigiani (Eds.), *Ethoexperimental Approaches to the Study of Behavior* (pp. 434-450). Dordrecht: Kluwer Academic Publishers.

Karli, P. (1989b). Is the concept of "personality" relevant to the study of animal aggression? *European Journal of Personality, 3,* 139-148.

Karli, P. (1991). *Animal and Human Aggression.* Oxford University Press.

Karli, P. (1994). Du "criminel-né" au "chromosome du crime" (From the "born criminal" to the "crime chromosome"). In E. Heilmann (Ed.), *Science ou justice? Les savants, l'ordre et la loi.* (pp. 88-100). Paris: Editions Autrement.

Karli, P. (1995). The brain and socialization: A two-way mediation across the life course. In D. Magnusson (Ed.), *The Life-span Development of Individuals: A Synthesis of Biological and Psychosocial Perspectives.* Cambridge University Press (in press).

Karli, P., Eclancher, F., Vergnes, M., Chaurand, J. P., & Schmitt, P. (1974). Emotional responsiveness and interspecific aggressiveness in the rat: interactions between genetic and experiential determinants. In J. H. F. van Abeelen (Ed.), *The Genetics of Behavior* (pp. 291-319). Amsterdam: North-Holland.

Koolhaas, J. M. (1984). The corticomedial amygdala and the behavioral change due to defeat. In R. Bandler (Ed.), *Modulation of Sensorimotor Activity during Alterations in Behavioral States* (pp. 341-349). New-York: Alan Liss.

Koshland, D. E. (1990). The rational approach to the irrational. *Science, 250,* 189.

Lorenz, K. (1967). *On aggression.* London: Methuen.

Lorenz, K. (1969). *L'Agression. Une histoire naturelle du Mal.* (Aggression. A natural history of Evil). Paris: Flammarion.

Pulkkinen, L., & Hurme, H. (1984). Aggression as a predictor of weak self-control. In Human Action and Personality, Jyväskylä studies in Education, *Psychology and Social Research,* no. 54 (pp. 172-189). University of Jyväskylä, Finland.

Schmitt, P., & Karli, P. (1989). Periventricular structures and the organization of affective states and their behavioral expression. *Brain, Behavior and Evolution, 33,* 162-164.

Siegel, A., & Brutus, M. (1990). Neural substrates of aggression and rage in the cat. *Progress in Psychobiology and Physiological Psychology, 14,* 135-233.

Vergnes, M. (1981). Effect of prior familiarization with mice on elicitation of mouse-killing in rats: Role of the amygdala. In Y. Ben-Ari (Ed.), *The Amygdaloid Complex* (pp. 293-304). Amsterdam: Elsevier.

Wilk, R. van der (1991). Interests and their structural development: Theoretical reflections. In L. Oppenheimer & J. Valsiner (Eds.), *The Origins of Action* (pp. 159-173). New York: Springer.

CHAPTER 2

IS PREDATORY BEHAVIOR A MODEL OF COMPLEX FORMS OF HUMAN AGGRESSION?

JOLANTA ZAGRODZKA AND ELZBIETA FONBERG

INTRODUCTION

The explosion of violence and crime in the contemporary world stimulates scientists to investigate intensively social, psychological, as well as biological aspects of multiple forms of human aggressive behavior and their complex mechanisms.

Although the relevance of animal models to human behavior is often questioned, an accepted vast amount of data (including neurophysiological, pharmacological, and biochemical ones) confirmed the similarity of the mechanisms of aggression in humans and other species (King, 1961; Delgado et al. 1968, Mark & Ervin, 1970; Lagerspetz, 1981, Schubert & Siegel, 1994). One needs to be very careful when projecting observations from animals and animal models to human life, especially when such a complicated, multiply determined behavior as aggression, is considered. The degree of complexity in human aggressive behavior is much higher then in case of other mammals. First, it is not limited to

JOLANTA ZAGRODZKA AND ELZBIETA FONBERG • Department of Neurophysiology, Nencki Institute of Experimental Biology, Pasteur St. 3, 02093 Warsaw, Poland.

Aggression: Biological, Developmental, and Social Perspectives, edited by Seymour Feshbach and Jolanta Zagrodzka. Plenum Press, New York, 1997.

direct physical attack, it might be manifested in many ways (for example, verbal or symbolic) and, as it is realized by norms' transgression, is associated with the development of intrapsychic regulators and with the process of socialization.

Nevertheless, experiments on animals and animal models of aggression can be useful, especially in studying basic mechanisms that underlay the expression and control of aggressive behavior. Lagerspetz (1981) has pointed out to several reasons for using animal experiments in the research on aggression. Some fundamental questions concerning neuroanatomical and neurochemical substrates of aggression cannot be answered without techniques that employ brain lesions, brain stimulations, and chemical and pharmacological manipulations. These cannot be carried out using humans as the object of study. Moreover, research on animals, because of their less complex nervous system on the one side, and less complicated social structure on the other, offers the opportunity of investigating the causes and mechanisms of aggressive acts in a simpler, more clear form.

The commonly stressed non-unitary nature of aggression led investigators to propose a number of different classifications of potentially injury-causing behaviors. They are based on various criteria such as stimulus situations that elicited attack (Moyer 1968), anatomical substrates and behavioral pattern (Flynn 1967), utility of the behavior to the animal (Brain 1981), neurophysiology (Fonberg 1979) and psycho-social mechanisms (Feshbach 1964, Fraczek 1992). The most widely cited is still Moyer's classification that offers eight categories: predatory aggression, intermale aggression, fear-induced aggression, irritable aggression, maternal aggression, territorial defense, sex-related aggression and instrumental aggression. This classification, although very extensive and demonstrative, possesses some difficulties in that there is an obvious overlap between categories. Our main objection concerns, in particular, "instrumental aggression" as a separate category, since an instrumental component can be found in all of the remaining categories of the Moyer's classification. We also think an additional class, i.e., pathological or frustrative aggression-characteristic for humans, but also present in various situations in other species (widely described by ethologists) should be included. Fonberg (1979) has incorporated this form of aggression in her three model categorization of types of aggression. This classification is based on the presence of emotional, emotional-instrumental or purely instrumental mechanisms as the basis of aggressive motivation. Emotional aggression may be either primary (evoked by excitation of the so called "rage centers" within the brain) or secondary (mediated by primary activation of the other motivational systems like sexual, alimentary, fear, pain etc.). One can say that secondary emotional aggression is simply the instrumental one, because the behavioral pattern of aggression serves as an instrumental act to, for example, the obtaining of food or a sexual partner. The differentiation between these categories, however, seems to be important, because secondary emotional aggression involves innate patterns of behavior as well as learned instrumental acts.

The problem with Fonberg's classification though, is that the third category (purely instrumental) concerns only some extreme cases in humans such as paid murderers, state executioners or military personnel. However, in this last case, hate for the enemy (invader), and patriotic emotional feelings or frustration may be also present. In animals, in natural circumstances it is also difficult to find the examples of pure instrumental aggression. Usually special training is necessary for police or guard dogs or animals used for racing, the circus, fighting contests, etc. It seems therefore that many forms of aggressive behavior in human beings as well as in other species belong to the secondary emotional aggression category.

PREDATORY AGGRESSION

One of the examples of this category might be predatory behavior. It should be noted however, that the classification of this particular behavior is still a matter of controversy. Ethologists consider predation as food getting, a behavior that belongs to the alimentary system (Lorenz & Leyhausen 1973, Manning 1972, and others). On the other hand, undoubtedly it does fit with the commonly accepted definition of aggression as behavior that is oriented toward the injury of a target. In neurobiology, predatory attack is usually regarded as a class of aggressive behavior and very often is used as a model of aggression in cats and rodents (Flynn, 1967; Ursin, 1981; Brain, 1981; Schubert & Siegel, 1994).

Our studies on various aspects of predation in spontaneously killing cats have shown that this behavior is based on a complex motivational system, independent of, although linked to alimentary and aggressive mechanisms. It involves moreover, a strong hedonistic component (Fonberg & Zagrodzka, 1980).

PREDATORY BEHAVIOR AND FEEDING

Predatory attack, at least in carnivores, is a means to secure food. Our studies however, have furnished the evidence that alimentary motivation is not necessary to drive the predatory behavior. The experiments we have conducted, were designed as close to the natural circumstances as was possible under the laboratory conditions. Such an approach, in contrast to intracranial and pharmacological manipulations eliciting attack, enables one to study the behavior in its full complexity i.e., at the motivational and executory levels. Only cats pre-selected as spontaneous mouse-killers were used in the experiments. They were confronted with the a live white mouse in a big experimental compartment. The predator-prey interactions were videotaped for 20 min. and registered according to the ethogram chart prepared on the base of Leyhausen's description of cat's predatory behavior (Leyhausen, 1975). As a rule, the following behavioral parameters were noted: (1) latency of cat's first approach to the mouse; (2) latency of killing; (3) latency of consuming the prey; (4) duration of consumption. The construction of the experimental compartment made it possible for the mouse (and also the cat) to escape from the aggressive attacks; allowed the cat to display the full pattern of predatory behavior as chasing the prey, running for it, jumping etc.

We have studied the effects of a number of neurophysiological parameters on the cat's behavior in this environmental context. Our lesioning studies have shown that destruction of the ventromedial part of amygdala results in total inhibition of the predatory behavior. At the same time, food intake (standard laboratory meal) remained unchanged, except for the first few days after the surgery (Zagrodzka & Fonberg, 1978). Moreover, during a meat-mouse choice test, cats with ventromedial amygdala lesions consumed meat from the bowl, ignoring the mouse, whereas before the surgery they always preferred the mouse, leaving the food bowl intact. In contrast, lesions placed in the dorsomedial part of the amygdala did not abolish predatory attack in any of its components, but food intake was significantly decreased after the surgery. As to the hypothalamus, we have found that destruction of the ventro-postero-medial region of this structure did not impair mouse-killing, while mouse-consumption was totally inhibited. In the same animals intake of the standard food was only transiently diminished (Fonberg & Serduchenko, 1980). Therefore the lesion eliminated the motivation for natural reward which, for predatory behavior, is eating the prey, leaving, nevertheless, the predatory drive unchanged. In our pharmacological studies, amphetamine, a drug of well known anoretic properties, did not prevent cats from killing the mice. However, the cats left most of them unconsumed. (Zagrodzka & Jurkowski, 1988). Also, scopolamine treatment did not inhibit predatory motivation either in terms of interest in the mouse or in killing it, although prey consumption as well as food intake were totally suppressed due to the abolishment of the sensory-motor control of jaw movements (Zagrodzka & Kubiak, 1991).

It is evident therefore that disconnection of the killing-eating link does not affect predatory motivation. Thus, the motivational system for predatory behavior may function independently from feeding mechanisms. This is in agreement with the results of Flynn and his coworkers. They have shown that hypothalamic points in which stimulation evokes quiet biting attack behaviors (i.e. predatory ones) in cats that spontaneously do not kill mice are different from the points that produce eating (Flynn, 1967; Flynn et al. 1970). It seems however, that neural substrates for alimentary and predatory behaviors are in close anatomical vicinity. We have found that lesions of the lateral hypothalamus impair both, feeding and predatory activities i.e., food intake, instrumental reactions reinforced by food, mouse-killing and mouse-eating (Brudnias-Graczyk & Fonberg, 1987).

The fact that after surgical or pharmacological manipulations which eliminate seemingly the most important biological goal of predation, i.e., food reward, the animal is still interested in the prey; chases it, attacks and finally kills it, indicates that some other reinforcing values of the predatory act should be taken into consideration.

HEDONISTIC COMPONENT OF THE PREDATORY BEHAVIOR

Since P. T. Young (1941) who first attempted to scientifically verify Spencer's idea of pleasure as one of the guiding principles in evolution and adaptive behavior, it well known that hedonistic responses exist in animals and they are an important basis for many motivational processes. It has been shown that the predatory act itself may serve as a reinforcement in the learning of difficult tasks (Roberts & Kiess, 1964). Also, our experiments on cats with lesions in the ventro-posterior hypothalamus demonstrated that animals after operation are still fully motivated to catch and kill the prey, preserving their domination in predatory competition and not allowing other cats to take the killed mouse. They, however, did not eat the prey. Therefore, the reinforcement has been associated only with the aggressive act, neither with food getting nor rewarding taste of the prey (Fonberg & Serduczenko, 1980; Fonberg & Zagrodzka, 1982; Brudnias-Graczyk & Fonberg, 1987). Our other experiments with the use of imipramine seem to confirm the existence of a hedonistic component in predatory motivation. Imipramine is used in the human clinic as an efficient remedy for the treatment of depression, which is characterized by anhedonia (Wise, 1982). We have found that imipramine facilitates predatory behavior in spontaneously non-killing cats (Zagrodzka et al., 1987) as well as in the cats with suppressed predatory attack after ventromedial amygdala and lateral hypothalamus lesions (Fonberg, 1980). It has been shown also that imipramine facilitates intracranial selfstimulation and alleviates the abolishment of this reaction resulting from lesions of some brain structures (Horowitz et al., 1962). Therefore, assuming that predatory behavior possesses a hedonistic value similar to self-stimulation, it might be supposed that imipramine-enhancing central noradrenergic functions act on the positive reward system eliciting predatory motivation and leading to effective attack. Although, the biochemical basis of positive reinforcement mechanisms is not fully recognized (Stellar & Stellar, 1985), noradrenaline is considered as one of the biochemical substrates of reward (Stein, 1975; Cytawa & Trojniar, 1979, Morley et al., 1988). Moreover, we have found that imipramine used in the predatory competition test, results in an increase of predatory motivation in previously submissive cats (never trying to get a mouse in the presence of their partner) to the level sufficient for the competition and even to obtain the dominant position (Zagrodzka et al. 1985). These results support again the involvement of a hedonistic component in predatory behavior, which might be released under the influence of imipramine.

PREDATORY BEHAVIOR AND AGGRESSION

Predatory behavior is not commonly regarded as aggression (Barnett, 1969; Plotnik et al. 1971) as it has been previously noted. No one can deny however, that in order to obtain prey, the killing act that is purely aggressive, is necessary. On the other hand, predatory behavior is easy distinguishable from affective aggression because of its typical behavioral pattern (it is characterized by a quiet stalking attack with biting directed to the neck of the prey and a lack of vocalization and other signs of autonomic system arousal, in contrast to affective display of offensive or defensive attack) and because it is mediated by different neural mechanisms on the level of amygdala and hypothalamus as well as the midbrain (Flynn et al., 1970; Bandler, 1984, Siegel & Pott, 1988). There still remains the question, however, whether and/or to what extent neurophysiological mechanisms of predatory behavior that are included in the aggressive system are partially overlapping or are quite independent. We have found (Fonberg et al. 1985) that ability to perform a fast and effective predatory attack is not related to the level of affective aggression. The experiments were performed with the use of the predatory competition test, elaborated in our laboratory. Cats, selected before as good-killers, with established short latency of attack, were yoked in pairs and each pair was submitted to a predatory test with only one mouse present at time. We wanted to elicit high level of predatory motivation due to competition, and, as a consequence, social conflict that allows one to observe affective aggression, i.e., defensive and offensive behaviors in both partners.

It has been found that the level of affective aggression displayed during the process of forming the hierarchy within each pair does not determine the dominance in the situation of predatory competition. Low levels of affective aggression were not correlated either with the efficiency of predatory attack or the dominant position in the competitive task (Fonberg et al., 1985, Fonberg, 1988). These results suggest that the aggressive component in the predatory behavior of cats is limited only to the instrumental act of killing. It might be supposed that the stimulus specific for this form of aggressive behavior, e.g., a prey object, evokes excitation of specific emotional-motivational mechanisms without exciting the rage system within the brain; that is, without involving the neural substrates for affective aggression. This is in agreement with the fact that the effective sites for centrally elicited predatory and affective aggression differ, although located along the same amygdala-hypothalamus-midbrain axis. Predatory attack can be produced by stimulation of the region of lateral and perifornical hypothalamus (Wasmann & Flynn, 1962; Siegel & Pott, 1988), the ventral tegmentum (Bandler et al. 1972) and ventral aspect of the midbrain periaqueductal gray matter (Bandler, 1984; Shaikh et al., 1986). Affective aggression might be evoked from stimulation of sites located in the medial preopticohypothalamus and dorsal aspect of the midbrain periaqueductal gray (Wasmann & Flynn, 1962; Bandler, 1984; Fuchs et al., 1985). The major role of the amygdala is considered to be a modulatory one. According to our results however, the lesion of the ventromedial part of this structure selectively abolishes predatory motivation in spontaneously killing cats (Zagrodzka & Fonberg, 1978). On the other hand, it has been found that electrical stimulation of the amygdala does not produce predatory attack (Fonberg & Flynn, 1978), but stimulation of some sites within the amygdala (including lateral, central and basolateral nuclei) facilitates hypothalamically elicited predatory attack, while stimulation of some others (medial, central, basomedial nuclei) inhibits it (Siegel & Brutus, 1990). It is of interest that the above mentioned parts of the amygdala influence electrically evoked affective aggression in an exactly opposite manner (Siegel & Brutus, 1990).

The research of John Flynn and his group has shown that excitation of brain sites eliciting predatory attack, produce significant alterations in sensory-motor functions. The major executory components of predatory attack, i.e., visual tracking of the prey, paw striking, jaw opening and jaw closing are a consequence of specific stimulation-induced changes in visuomotor and somatomotor mechanisms (MacDonnell & Flynn, 1966; Bandler et al., 1971; Bandler et al., 1972; Bandler, 1984). It has been suggested that the same centrally mediated sensory-motor alterations occur during natural predatory behavior (Bandler, 1984), and are a precondition for the expression of particular executory acts of effective prey-killing. This process is activated by some emotional-motivational factors, apparently other than rage or anger. Biological needs, such as alimentary drive may be one of them. However as we have shown, predatory behavior occurs without an alimentary component as well. Also the hedonistic value of the attack and of play with the mouse and, as we have found in our meat-mouse preference experiments (Fonberg & Zagrodzka, in preparation), the highly rewarding taste of the prey, seem to be very important as a motivational base for predatory behavior. According to Fonberg (1979), secondary emotional aggression may be provoked directly by excitation of specific motivational systems without producing rage. Predatory attack seems to be a good example here.

DISCUSSION AND CONCLUDING REMARKS

Contrary to Delgado's (1979) opinion that feline predatory behavior has no equivalent in humans, we believe that spontaneous predatory behavior in cats may serve as a useful model for investigating and understanding the mechanisms of, at least, some forms of human aggression. The innate predisposition of homo-sapiens as a hunter, inherited from our ancestors, is only a marginal aspect of the mechanisms underlying human aggressive behavior.

It seems that most of the interpersonal aggressive acts observed in everyday life, similarly to predatory behavior, are not based on the rage arousal. So called "reactive-emotogenic aggression" (Fraczek, 1992), based on the emotion of anger, is often observed in early child development as a natural reaction to nociceptive stimuli. This kind of aggressive reaction may be considered as a prototype of affective aggression (see also Fonberg's classification "primary emotional

aggression," Fonberg, 1979). In the process of development and socialization, the expression of anger becomes transformed and controlled,
even suppressed in many cases and therefore this type of aggression,
in its pure form, occurs relatively rarely. As Lagerspetz (1981) denotes,
in the infra-human world, it is easier to find examples of affective aggression, but with progressive phylogenesis, instrumental aggression
becomes prevalent due to social learning and cognitive assessment of
life situations.

Predatory behavior seems to share some common features with
human task-oriented (instrumental) aggression. Task-oriented aggression is defined as noxious stimulation directed toward the achievement
of other non-injurious goals such as social approval, money, dominance and many other life needs and values (Berkowitz, 1981). As we
have mentioned earlier, it would be very difficult to find an example
of pure instrumental aggression that does not involve an emotional
component, because every goal is associated with a particular kind of
motivation and emotion. It might be supposed therefore that task-oriented aggression is based on both instrumental and emotional mechanisms (see also Fonberg, 1979). In the case of predatory behavior,
emotional components are associated with primary biological needs
(prey as a source of food) and hedonistic values (the pleasure of play
and attack, the highly rewarding taste of the prey, the pleasure of the
efficacy of the aggressive act and reaching the goal). According to our
results, alimentary reinforcement is not necessary to evoke and sustain
predatory motivation.

It might be supposed therefore that the act of chasing, and finally
killing the prey being rewarding, might become functionally autonomous. In this respect, predatory behavior resembles human intrinsic
aggression in which "organism's satisfaction appears to be intrinsic to
the aggressive act itself" (Feshbach, 1979). The reinforcement may be
associated with the infliction of pain or with the performance of an
aggressive response. The derivation of satisfaction from eliciting pain
or discomfort in others is considered as a typically human phenomenon. But there are data on various infra-human species confirming that
performance of the aggressive act itself has a rewarding value (Lagerspetz, 1969; Perachio & Alexander 1974). Our pharmacological experiments with imipramine and the experiments with ventro-posterior
hypothalamus lesioned cats, cited above as well as the data of Roberts
and Kiess (1964) show that the instrumental act of killing also, in the
case of predatory behavior, is reinforcing as such. The question arises
however whether the "satisfaction" from the performance of killing
act is reinforced by the canalization of rage arousal or by activation

of the instrumental reward system. Our pharmacological results, as well as the lack of affective aggressive display during mouse-killing, indicate that, at least in the case of predatory behavior, the reward system is involved. It might be supposed that, even in humans, while the affective, "reactive-emotogenic" aggression is associated with the emotion of anger and so called "rage system" in the brain, intrinsic aggression, "aggression for pleasure" (Fraczek, 1992) is based on reward mechanisms.

Predatory behavior in social situations in which the prey object serves as a competition-evoking stimulus, also seems to be a good model for studying the mechanisms of dominance. The tendency to dominate is one of the main motives of human aggressive behavior, but the nature of dominance is still far from being fully understood. One of the widely discussed problems in this field is whether the aggressive rank and other measures of dominance are related. Our research on predatory competition in cats (Zagrodzka et. al 1983, Fonberg et al. 1985, Zagrodzka et al., 1985, Fonberg, 1988) showed that aggression is not indispensable to gain and keep the dominance status. This is in agreement with some other data indicating lack of correlation between the level of aggression and other measures by which dominance can be assessed in primates (Kaufmann, 1967; Bernstein, 1970). The predatory competition model is also useful in the research on basic neurobiological mechanisms underlying dominance. We have found for example, that lesions placed in dorsomedial amygdala selectively abolish predatory dominance. Lesioned cats fully preserved their predatory abilities when tested alone, but in the presence of the previously submissive partner they seemed completely indifferent toward mice, permitting the partner to catch, kill and eat the prey (Zagrodzka et al., 1983). Very recently, the predatory competition model has been used to investigate neurochemical substrates of dominance (Krotewicz & Romaniuk, in press).

Concluding, feline predatory behavior, in spite of the fact that it is species-specific, is based on the mechanisms similar to at least two types of aggression, i.e., task-oriented and so called "aggression for pleasure" that are common for humans and other animals. Our feline studies suggest the possibility that facets of the aggressive act in humans may be intrinsically rewarding; that is, they may not have to be reinforced by food, sex or some external reward, or mediated by anger, in order for the individual to gain satisfaction or pleasure. This possibility, suggested by our animal model studies, warrants systematic follow-up and analyses at the human level.

REFERENCES

Bandler, R. J. (1984). Brain mechanisms of aggression as revealed by electrical and chemical stimulation: suggestion of a central role for the midbrain periaqueductal grey region. *Progress in Psychobiology and Physiological Psychology, 13,* 67-154.

Bandler, R. J., Chi, C. C., & Flynn, J. P. (1972). Biting attack elicited by stimulation of the ventral midbrain tegmentum of cats. *Science, 177,* 363-366.

Bandler, R. J. & Flynn, J. P. (1971). Visual patterned reflex present during hypothalamically elicited attack. *Science, 171,* 817-818.

Barnett, S. A. (1969). Grouping and dispersive behaviour among wild rats. In S. Garratini & E. B. Sigg (Eds.), *Aggressive behaviour* (pp. 3-14). Amsterdam: Excerpta Medica Found.

Berkovitz, L. (1981). The Concept of Aggression. In P.F. Brain & D. Benton (Eds.), *Multidisciplinary approaches to aggression research* (pp. 3-15). Amsterdam: Elsevier.

Bernstein, I. S. (1970). Primate status hierarchies. In L. A. Rosenblum (Ed.), *Primate behaviour. developments in field and laboratory research,* vol 1. New York: Academic Press Inc.

Brain, P. F. (1981). Differentiating types of attack and defence in rodents. In P.F. Brain & D. Benton (Eds.), *Multidisciplinary approaches to aggression research* (pp. 53-77). Amsterdam: Elsevier.

Brudnias-Graczyk, Z. & Fonberg, E. (1987). Comparison of the effects of lateral and ventro-posterior hypothalamic damage on the predatory behavior of cats. *Acta Neurobiologiae Experimentalis, 47,* 189-198.

Cytawa, J. & Trojniar, W. (1979). The pleasure system of the brain and its neurotransmitters. *Polish Journal of Pharmacology and Pharmacy, 31,* 283-292.

Delgado, J. M. R. (1979). Neurophysiological mechanisms of aggressive behavior. In S. Feshbach & A. Fraczek (Eds.), *Aggression and behavior change: biological and social processes.* (pp. 54-65), New York: Praeger Publishers.

Delgado, J. M. R., Mark, V. H., Sweet, W. H., Ervin, F. R., Gerhardt, W., Bach-y-Rita, G. (1968). Intracranial radio stimulation and recording in completely free patients. *Journal of Nervous and Mental Desease, 147,* 329-340.

Feshbach, S. (1979). The regulation and modification of aggression: commonalities and issues. In S. Feshbach & A. Fraczek (Eds.), *Aggression and behavior change: biological and social processes.* (pp. 271-286), New York: Praeger Publishers.

Feshbach, S. (1964). The function of aggression and the regulation of aggression drive. *Psychological Review, 71,* 257-272.

Flynn, J. P. (1967). The neural basis of aggression in cats. In D. C. Glass (Ed.), *Neurophysiology and emotion* (pp. 40-60), New York: Rockefeller University Press.

Flynn, J. P., Vanegas, H., Foote, W. & Edwards, S. (1970). Neural mechanism involved in a cats' attack on rat. In R. W. Whalen, R. Thompson, M. Verzano, & V. M. Edinberger (Eds.), *The neural control of behavior* (pp. 135-173). New York: Academic Press.

Fonberg, E. (1979). Physiological mechanisms of emotional and instrumental aggression. In S. Feshbach & A. Fraczek (Eds.), *Aggression and behavior change* (pp. 6-53), New York: Praeger Publishers.

Fonberg, E. (1980). Manipulation of various aspects of emotional behavior by amygdalar lesions and imipramine treatment. *Advantages in Physiological Sciences. Brain and Behavior, 17,* 487-494.

Fonberg, E. (1988). Dominance and aggression. *International Journal of Neuroscience, 41,* 201-213.

Fonberg, E., Brudnias-Stepowska, Z. & Zagrodzka, J. (1985). Various relations between the predatory dominance and aggressive behavior in pairs of cats. *Aggressive Behavior, 11,* 137-149.

Fonberg, E. & Flynn, J. P. (1978). Patterns of Aggressive Behaviour Evoked by Hypothalamic and Amygdalar Stimulation. XIV Conference of Polish Physiological Society, *Annales Academiae Medicae Lodzensis,* 19, 16.

Fonberg, E. & Serduchenko, V. M. (1980). Predatory behavior after hypothalamic lesion in cats. *Physiology and Behavior,* 24, 225-230.

Fonberg, E. & Zagrodzka, J. (1980). Bases motivacionales de la conducta de los predatores. Phronesis, Revista de Neurologia. *Neurocirurgia y Psiquiatria,* 1, 45-47.

Fonberg, E. & Zagrodzka, J. (1982). Complex mechanisms of the predatory behavior. In K. Lissak & P. Molnar (Eds.), *Motivation and the neural and neurohumoral factors in regulation of behavior* (pp. 45-59), Budapest: Academia Kiado.

Fraczek, A. (1992). Socialization and Intrapsychic Regulation of Interpersonal Aggression. In A. Fraczek & H. Zumkley (Eds.), *Socialization and aggression.* Berlin: Springer-Verlag.

Fuchs, S. A. (1985). The organization of the hypothalamic pathway mediating affective defense behavior in cat. *Brain Research,* 330, 77-92.

Horovitz, Z. P., Chow, M. Carlton, P. L. (1962). Self-stimulation of the brain by cats: effect of imipramine, amphetamine and chlorpromazine. *Psychopharmacologia,* 6, 455-463.

Kaufmann, J. H. (1967). Social relations of adult males in free-ranking band of rhesus monkeys. In S. A. Altmann (Ed.), *Social Communication among Primates.* Chicago: University of Chicago Press.

King, H. E. (1961). Psychological effects of excitation in the limbic system. In D. I. Scheer (Ed.), *Electrical stimulation of the brain* (pp. 477-486). University of Texas Press.

Krotewicz, M. & Romaniuk, A. (1995). Social interactions in cats: regional brain monoamines distinction in dominant and submissive cats. *Acta Neurobiologiae Experimentalis.* (in press)

Lagerspetz, K. M. J. (1969). Aggression and aggressiveness in laboratory mice. In S. Garattini & E. B. Sigg (Eds.), *Aggressive behaviour* (pp. 77-85). Amsterdam: Excerpta Medica.

Lagerspetz, K. M. J. (1981). Combining aggression studies in infra-humans and man. In P. F. Brain & D. Benton (Eds.), *Multidisciplinary approaches to aggression research* (pp. 389-401). Amsterdam: Elsevier/North-Holland, Biomedical Press.

Leyhausen, P. (1975). *Cat Behavior. The predatory and social behavior of domestic and wild cats.* New York: Garland STPN Press.

Lorenz, K. & Leyhausen, P. (1973). *Motivation of Human and Animal Behaviour* (pp. 144-246). London: Van Nostrand Reinhold Company.

MacDonnell, M. & Flynn, J. P. (1966). Control of sensory fields by stimulations of the hypothalamus. *Science,* 152, 1406-1408.

Manning, A. (1972). *An Introduction to Animal Behaviour.* London: Edward Arnold.

Mark, V. H. & Ervin, F. R. (1970). *Violence and the brain.* New York: Harper and Row.

Morley, M. J., Shah, K., Bradshaw, C. M., Szabadi, E. (1988). DSP$_4$ and Herrnstein's equation: further evidence for a role of noradrenaline in the maintenance of operant behaviour by positive reinforcement. *Psychopharmacology-(Berlin),* 96(4).

Moyer, K. E. (1968). Kinds of aggression and their physiological basis. *Communications of Behavioral Biology Part A,* 2, 65-87.

Perachio, A. A. & Alexander, M. (1974). Neurophysical approaches to the study of aggression. In R. E. Whalen (Ed.), *The Neuropsychology of aggression* (pp. 65-86). New York: Plenum Press.

Plotnik, R., Mir, D. & Delgado, M. R. (1971). Aggression, noxiousness, and brain stimulation in unrestrained rhesus monkeys, In B. E. Eleftheriou and J. P. Scott (Eds.), *The physiology of aggression and defeat* (pp. 143-221). New York: Plenum Press.

Roberts, W. & Kiess, H. O. (1964). Motivational properties of hypothalamic aggression in cats. *Journal of Comparative and Physiological Psychology*, 58, 187-193.

Schubert, K. & Siegel, A. (1994). What animal studies have taught us about the neurobiology of violence. *International Journal of Group Tension*, 24, 237-265.

Shaikh, M. B., Barrett, J. A. & Siegel, A. (1987). The pathways mediating affective defense and quiet biting attack behavior from the midbrain central gray of the cat: an autoradiographic study. *Brain Research*, 437, 9-25.

Siegel, A. Brutus, M. (1990). Neural substrates of aggression and rage in the cat. *Progress in Psychobiology and Physiological Psychology*, 14, 135-233.

Siegel, A. Pott, C. B. (1988). Neural substrate of aggression and fight in cat. *Progress in Neurobiology*, 31, 261-283.

Stein, L. (1975). Norepinephrine reward pathways. In J. K. Cole & T. B. Sonderegger (Eds.), *Nebrasca Symposium on Motivation* (pp. 113-159). Lincoln University of Nebrasca Press.

Stellar, J. R. & Stellar, E. (1985). *The neurobiology of motivation and reward.* Springer-Verlag New York, Inc.

Ursin, A. (1981). Neuroanatomical basis of aggression. In P. F. Brain & D. Benton (Eds.), *Multidisciplinary approaches to aggression research* (pp. 269-293). Amsterdam: Elsevier.

Wasman, M. & Flynn, J. P. (1962). Directed Attack elicited from hypothalamus. *Archives of Neurology*, 6, 220-227.

Wise, R. A. (1982). Neuroleptic and operant behavior: The anhedonia hypothesis. *The Behavior and Brain Science*, 5, 39-88.

Young, P. T. (1941). The experimental analysis of appetite. *Psychological Bulletin*, 38, 129-164.

Zagrodzka, J., Brudnias-Stepowska, Z. & Fonberg, E. (1983). Impairment of social behavior in amygdalar cats. *Acta Neurobiologiae Experimentalis*, 43, 63-77.

Zagrodzka, J. & Fonberg, E. (1978). Predatory versus alimentary behavior after amygdala lesions in cats. *Physiology and Behavior*, 29, 523-531.

Zagrodzka, J., Fonberg, E. & Brudnias-Graczyk, Z. (1985). Predatory dominance and aggressive display under imipramine treatment in cats. *Acta Neurobiologiae Experimentalis*, 45, 137-149.

Zagrodzka, J. & Jurkowski, T. (1988). Changes in aggressive behaviour of cats treated with amphetamine. *International Journal of Neuroscience*, 41, 287-296.

Zagrodzka, J. & Kubiak, P. (1991). Scopolamine-induced alterations in predatory pattern in cats. *Acta Neurobiologiae Experimentalis*, 51, 29-36.

Zagrodzka, J., Kubiak, P., Jurkowski, T. & Fonberg, E. (1987). The effect of imipramine on predatory behaviour and locomotor activity in cats. *Acta Neurobiologiae Experimentalis*, 47, 123-135.

CHAPTER 3

THE ROLE OF SUBSTANCE P RECEPTORS IN AMYGDALOID MODULATION OF AGGRESSIVE BEHAVIOR IN THE CAT

MAJID B. SHAIKH AND ALLAN SIEGEL

INTRODUCTION

It is well established from studies conducted both in animals [1, 4-6, 11, 25, 53, 61] and humans [13, 17, 19, 21, 30, 34, 43, 57, 59] that the temporal lobe plays an important role in the regulation of aggression and violence. Particular attention has been given to the varied functions of amygdala in regulating aggressive processes. While experimental evidence indicates that, in general, activation of amygdaloid nuclei does not result in the direct elicitation of aggressive responses in animals [50], it is very clear from the literature that amygdaloid nuclei can powerfully modulate aggressive behavior induced by electrical stimulation of the hypothalamus or midbrain periaqueductal gray (PAG) [42, 52].

Utilizing brain stimulation procedures in the cat, it has been demonstrated that different nuclei of the amygdala differentially modulate

MAJID B. SHAIKH AND ALLAN SIEGEL • Department of Neurosciences and Psychiatry, New Jersey Medical School, 185 South Orange Avenue, Newark, New Jersey 07103-2757.

Aggression: Biological, Developmental, and Social Perspectives, edited by Seymour Feshbach and Jolanta Zagrodzka. Plenum Press, New York, 1997.

two forms of aggressive behavior [5,6,11,47]. Specifically, we know from these studies that the central amygdaloid nucleus suppresses defensive rage behavior [47], a form of aggression characterized by marked vocalization and sympathetic signs. In contrast, facilitation of this form of aggression is induced by stimulation of the medial amygdaloid nucleus [6, 49]. It has been further shown that stimulation of the same nuclei have just the opposite effects upon predatory attack behavior [5, 11], a form of aggression characterized by the stalking and biting of a prey object. Thus, stimulation of the central nucleus results in facilitation of predatory attack behavior and suppression of defensive rage. With respect to the medial amygdaloid nucleus, stimulation causes suppression of predatory attack and facilitation of defensive rage.

Recent studies conducted in our laboratory have utilized a combination of experimental methodologies which include brain stimulation, behavioral pharmacology, neuroanatomy and immunocytochemistry to gain a better understanding of the neural mechanisms regulating amygdaloid control of aggressive behavior in the cat [18, 42, 47, 49]. In the present chapter, we sought to focus upon an analysis of the mechanisms underlying medial amygdaloid control of defensive rage and predatory attack in the cat. Evidence is presented that supports the view that substance P receptors within the ventromedial hypothalamus play a critical role in medial amygdaloid modulation of both forms of aggression.

METHODS

In the studies described below adult cats of either sex whose weights ranged between 2.0 and 4.0 kg., were employed in these studies. All animals had free access to food and water throughout the experiments. The stereotaxic surgical procedures were carried out under sodium pentobarbital (40mg/kg) or Isofluorene (1%) anesthesia. Details of the methods have been described previously [29, 47-49]. Under aseptic conditions, stainless steel guide tubes (17ga and 10 mm long) were mounted according to the stereotaxic atlas of Jasper and Ajmone-Marsan [22] and cemented over holes drilled through the skull overlying medial hypothalamus, lateral hypothalamus and medial amygdala.

Cannula-electrodes were lowered vertically through the guide tubes into the medial and lateral hypothalamus as well as medial amygdala for the elicitation and modulation of defensive rage and predatory attack behavior. These cannula electrodes were also utilized for intracerebral administration of substance P receptor antagonist, CP 96,345, and substance P analog, [Sar^9, Met (O$_2$)^{11}]-SP or for microinfusion of a retrograde axonal tracer, Fluoro-Gold.

DEFENSIVE RAGE AND PREDATORY ATTACK BEHAVIOR

Defensive rage behavior was initially described by Ranson and co-workers [3, 20, 40]. This behavior is characterized by a number of sympathetic signs such as piloerection, salivation, retraction of the ears, baring of teeth, unsheathing of claws, increased heart rate, growling, hissing and a paw strike aimed at a moving object such as an awake rat, cat, or even an experimenter [2, 15, 44-51]. This form of aggressive behavior can be evoked under natural conditions when the cat is threatened by another animal [28]. In the laboratory, stimulation-induced defensive rage behavior can be elicited in the absence of any threatening stimulus.

Predatory attack behavior occurs under natural conditions [28] and which can be elicited by electrical stimulation of the lateral perifornical hypothalamus [6, 11, 45, 47] or ventral PAG [44]. Predatory attack behavior is characterized by an initial stalking and approach to the prey object, usually an anesthetized rat (in the laboratory conditions), followed by biting of its neck

ELICITATION OF DEFENSIVE RAGE AND PREDATORY ATTACK BEHAVIOR

One week after surgery the cat was placed in a wooden observation chamber (61×61×61 cm) with a clear plexiglas door. After lowering the cannula-electrodes (27 ga, 51 mm long) into the medial/lateral hypothalamus, stimulation was applied at 0.5 mm steps in freely moving cat to identify sites from which defensive rage or predatory attack behavior could be elicited. Electrical stimuli (biphasic, rectangular, pulses, 0.3-0.7 mA, 62.5 Hz, 1 ms per half cycle duration) were generated by 2 Grass S-88 stimulators connected to the cat in series with constant current isolation units (Grass PSIU6). A Tektronix 5000 series oscilloscope was used to monitor peak-to-peak current. The cannula-electrode was cemented in place with dental acrylic when defensive rage or predatory attack was consistently elicited within 15 sec of stimulation. Then, response latency values were measured with the aid of a stop watch with an accuracy of 0.1 sec. The time required to elicit a hissing response after the onset of electrical stimulation was defined as the response latency for defensive rage behavior. The hissing component was used as the principal measure of defensive rage behavior since it is elicited on each trial, even in an impoverished environment [15, 16, 44, 56]. The response latency for predatory attack was defined as the duration of time between the onset of stimulation until the cat's teeth made contact with the neck of anesthetized rat.

MEDIAL AMYGDALOID MODULATION OF DEFENSIVE RAGE AND PREDATORY ATTACK BEHAVIOR

The following procedures were employed to identify sites in the medial amygdala from which modulation of defensive rage and predatory attack behavior could be obtained. A stimulating electrode was lowered through the guide tube into the medial nucleus of amygdala. Then, electrical stimulation was applied as the electrode was further lowered in 0.5 mm steps concurrently with stimulation of defensive rage or predatory attack sites within the medial and lateral hypothalamus. Parameters for amygdaloid stimulation were identical to those used for the hypothalamus with the exception that current strength applied to the medial amygdala was maintained at 0.1 mA (i.e., a subthreshold current level for elicitation of seizure activity). Stimulation was limited to a maximum duration of 15 sec. At each step, paired trials of single (hypothalamus) and dual (amygdala + hypothalamus) stimulation were arranged in an A-B-B-A manner to avoid any order effects, with A representing single and B dual stimulation. Response latencies following single stimulation of an attack site in the hypothalamus were then compared with those following dual stimulation of both an attack site in the hypothalamus and a potential modulating site in the medial amygdala. At a site where dual stimulation clearly facilitated defensive rage or suppressed predatory attack, the amygdaloid electrode was cemented in place with dental acrylic. Parameters for stimulation of the hypothalamus during dual stimulation procedures, both before and after drug delivery, were kept constant. EEG recordings as well as behavioral observations indicated no signs of seizure activity.

DRUGS AND DRUG ADMINISTRATION

In these studies a highly selective, non peptide substance P NK_1 receptor antagonist, CP 96,345 (Pfizer, Groton, CT) was peripherally (i.p.) as well as intracerebrally administered separately into the medial hypothalamic sites from which defensive rage behavior could be elicited. Intracerebral microinfusions of CP 96,345 were made at dose levels of

0.05, 0.5 and 2.5 nmoles/0.25 ul, utilizing a 0.5 ul SGE syringe. CP 96,345 was peripherally administered at three separate doses of 0.05, 2 and 4 mg/kg. A substance P agonist, [Sar^9, Met(O$_2$)^{11}]-substance P (Sigma, St. Louis, MO), was microinjected into the medial hypothalamus at dose levels of 0.5, 1.0 and 2.0 nmole/0.25 ul. Drugs were dissolved in sterile water and pH adjusted to 7.4. Moreover, saline was injected into the medial hypothalamic defensive rage sites as vehicle control. All doses were administered in a randomized and counterbalanced manner.

For testing the effects of NK$_1$ antagonist upon medial amygdaloid modulation of defensive rage behavior, 10 paired trials of single (hypothalamic) and dual (hypothalamic + amygdaloid) stimulation were given prior to drug administration. In the second phase of this study, the NK$_1$ antagonist, CP 96,345 was administered peripherally or intracerebrally followed by a determination of response latencies for defensive rage during paired trials of single and dual stimulations over a 180 min postinjection test period.

In the second study, where the effects of intracerebral administration of CP 96,345 upon medial amygdaloid modulation of predatory attack behavior were tested, 5 paired trials of single and dual stimulation were given prior to drug infusion into the medial hypothalamus. Response latency values were again determined for paired trials over a 180 min postinjection time period. In the next phase of this study, the effects of microinjection of a substance P agonist into the medial hypothalamus upon predatory attack behavior were determined. Here, 10 trials of single stimulation of the lateral hypothalamus alone were given prior to drug administration. Response latency values for predatory attack behavior were again determined at 5, 60, 120 and 180 min, postinjection.

NEUROANATOMICAL STUDIES

These studies combined immunocytochemical and retrograde labeling procedures were employed to test the hypotheses that the medial amygdala: (1), contains neurons that react positively for substance P; (2), directly project to the medial hypothalamus and (3), are associated with the facilitation of defensive rage and suppression of the predatory attack behavior.

Following completion of the pharmacological investigations, a fluorescence retrograde axonal tracer—Fluoro-Gold (Fluorochrome Inc., Englewood, CO) was microinjected into the medial hypothalamic sites from which defensive rage could be elicited to identify the loci of labeled cells within the medial amygdala. An SGE syringe was lowered through the cannula electrode to microinject Fluoro-Gold (8%, dissolved in sterile water) in a volume of 0.5 μl over a period of 20 min. Postinjection survival times ranged from 5 to 14 days. Two days prior to perfusion, colchicine (2.5 μg/μl) was microinfused bilaterally into the amygdala. All animals were then perfused transcardially under deep anesthesia (sodium pentobarbital 45 mg/kg) with phosphate-buffered saline (pH = 7.4) and Zamboni's fixative or 4% paraformaldehyde at 4°C. Sections were cut (40 μm thick) on a freezing microtome and alternate sections were mounted on gelatin-coated slides, and covered slipped with DPX mountant or Permount for immunocytochemical analysis and cresyl-violet staining. Cresyl-violet sections were utilized to identify the electrode tips and injection sites.

Procedures for immunocytochemical analysis were employed to identify substance P-positive cells within the medial amygdala. Details concerning these procedures are described elsewhere [18,49]. In brief, sections were reacted with the primary rabbit antisera for substance P (Instar Corp., Stillwater, MN) for 48-72 hours at a dilution of 1:1000 in a cold room. The sections were reacted with secondary antibody (goat-antirabbit serum IgG at a dilution of 1:40) (Organon Technika, West Chester, PA) for 75 min at room temperature. Finally, sections were washed in buffer, mounted and coverslipped. Cells which reacted positively for substance P and cells double-labeled for Fluoro-Gold and substance P were identified and photographed under fluorescent illumination.

RESULTS

As shown in Figure 1, defensive rage sites were distributed within the ventromedial nucleus and adjoining regions of the medial hypothalamus. Sites from which predatory attack behavior was elicited by electrical stimulation were located within the lateral hypothalamus. Figure 1 also indicates the distribution of amygdaloid sites from which facilitation of defensive rage and suppression of predatory attack was obtained.

EFFECTS OF PERIPHERAL ADMINISTRATION OF SUBSTANCE P ANTAGONIST UPON AMYGDALOID-INDUCED MODULATION OF AGGRESSIVE RESPONSES

(A) Defensive Rage

This phase of the study was designed to test the hypothesis that substance P is associated with the facilitatory pathway from the medial

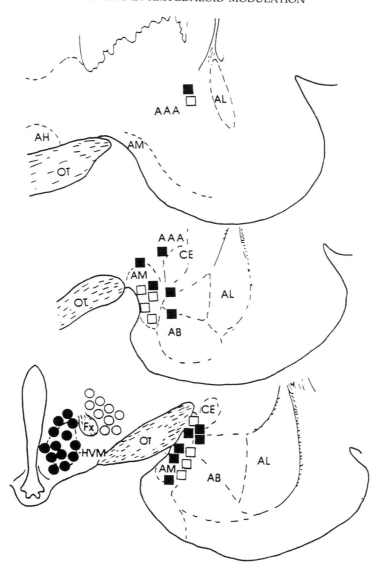

FIGURE 1. Maps indicate sites within (1) medial and lateral hypothalamus from which defensive rage (closed circles) and predatory attack (open circles) were elicited respectively; and (2) amygdaloid sites from which facilitation of defensive rage (closed square) as well as suppression of predatory attack behavior (open squares) was obtained. Abbreviations: AAA, anterior amygdaloid area; AB, basal nucleus of amygdala; AL, lateral nucleus of amygdala; AM, medial nucleus of amygdala; CE, central nucleus; Fx, fornix, HL, lateral hypothalamus; HVM, ventromedial hypothalamus; OT, optic tract.

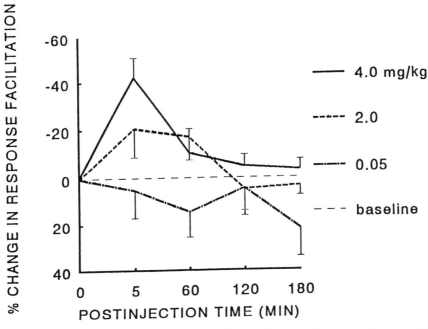

FIGURE 2. Graphs indicate that peripheral (i. p.) administration of substance P antagonist, CP 96,345 blocks facilitatory effects of medial amygdaloid stimulation upon defensive rage behavior in a dose and time dependent manner. For this and for subsequent figures "baseline" constitutes the level of facilitation or suppression observed after dual stimulation of the medial amygdala and medial or lateral hypothalamus prior to drug delivery and is given a value of 0% change. Vertical bars indicate S.E.M. for this and for subsequent figures (From Shaikh et al., [49]).

amygdala to medial hypothalamus as a neurotransmitter. Here, an NK_1 receptor antagonist, CP 96,345, was peripherally (i.p.) injected to determine its effects upon amygdaloid facilitation of defensive rage behavior. Prior to drug administration, dual stimulation of the medial hypothalamus and amygdala resulted in 30-40% decreases in the response latencies. These values were defined as "baseline" and then transformed to a value of '0'% change in order to depict the effects of drug administration upon amygdalaoid facilitation of defensive rage. In this phase of the study, 3 doses of substance P antagonist were administered. As shown in Fig. 2, drug administration resulted in a significant decrease of amygdaloid facilitation of defensive rage behavior in a dose- and time-dependent manner. A 42% decrease in facilitation was obtained as early as 5 min following infusion of the highest drug dose (4 mg/kg) and declined after this time period, reaching baseline levels at the period of 120-180 min, postinjection. The two lower doses (2 and 0.05 mg/kg) did not significantly block the medial amygdaloid facilitatory mechanisms of defensive rage behavior.

EFFECTS OF PERIPHERAL ADMINISTRATION OF THE SUBSTANCE P ANTAGONIST UPON DEFENSIVE RAGE BEHAVIOR ELICITED BY SINGLE STIMULATION OF THE MEDIAL HYPOTHALAMUS

This experiment was conducted in the absence of medial amygdaloid stimulation to determine whether or not blockade of substance P receptors would alter the response threshold or latency for the expression of defensive rage behavior. Moreover, CP 96,345 was administered at a dose level of 4 mg/kg (i.e., a drug dose found to be most effective in blocking the facilitatory effects of medial amygdaloid stimulation upon defensive rage behavior). It was observed that peripheral administration of this drug completely failed to alter response thresholds or latencies for defensive rage elicited by the single stimulation of the medial hypothalamus (Fig. 3). These results provided evidence that blockade of substance P receptors has no effect upon the occurrence of defensive rage behavior elicited by single stimulation of the medial hypothalamus. Collectively, the findings of this experiment suggest that the release of substance P is episodic rather than tonic.

(B) Predatory Attack Behavior

This experiment was designed to test the hypothesis that substance P is involved in medial amygdaloid-induced suppression of predatory attack behavior elicited from lateral hypothalamus. In this experiment the same paradigm as described above for determining the effects of medial amygdaloid stimulation upon defensive rage behavior was employed. Here, CP 96,345 was peripherally (i.p.) administered and its effects upon suppression of predatory attack (induced by dual stimulation of medial amygdala and lateral hypothalamus) were determined. At a dose level of 2 mg/kg (i.e., the highest drug dose employed in this study), CP 96,345 blocked amygdaloid suppression of predatory attack behavior only at the period between 5-60 min postinjection (Fig. 4). Administration of a lower dose (1.0 mg/kg) did not significantly alter the suppressive effects of dual stimulation at any of the postinjection time periods tested.

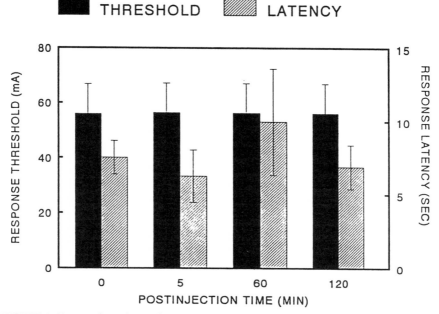

FIGURE 3. Bar graphs indicate that peripheral (i.p.) administration of CP 96,345 at a dose level of 4 mg/kg failed to change response latency and threshold values for defensive rage behavior in the absence of medial amygdaloid stimulation. Mean values shown at the "0" on x axis constitute preinjection baseline values (From Shaikh et al., [49]).

EFFECTS OF INTRACEREBRAL MICROINFUSION OF SUBSTANCE P ANTAGONIST UPON AMYGDALOID-INDUCED MODULATION OF AGGRESSIVE RESPONSES

(A) Defensive Rage

In this phase of the study, three doses of CP 96,345 were microinfused into medial hypothalamic sites from which defensive rage was elicited and its effects upon amygdaloid facilitation of defensive rage behavior were determined. It was observed that microinfusion of drug resulted in a highly significant overall blockade of the facilitatory effects of medial amygdaloid facilitation of defensive rage behavior over three epochs of time, postinjection (Fig. 5). At the maximum dose level (2.5 nmole) of CP 96,345 utilized in this experiment, an 84% blockade of amygdaloid facilitation of defensive rage was observed for the period

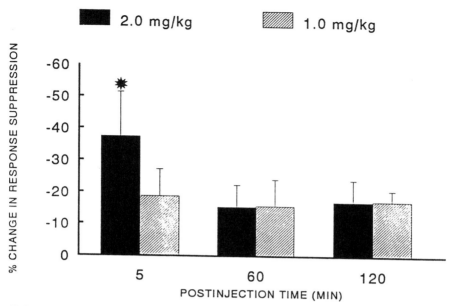

FIGURE 4. Bar graphs indicate that peripheral (i.p.) administration of CP 96,345 at the maximum dose level (2 mg/kg) blocked the suppressive effects of medial amygdaloid stimulation upon lateral hypothalamically elicited predatory attack behavior (*P < 0.001) (From Shaikh et al., [49]).

of 5-60 min postinjection. At the 180-240 min postinjection, period, mean response latencies returned to baseline levels observed with dual stimulation prior to drug administration. At a lower dose level of 0.5 nmole, microinfusion of CP 96,345 resulted in a 40% decrease in amygdaloid facilitation of defensive rage at the 5-60 min postinjection period. This blockade of facilitation of defensive rage declined after that time period and reached baseline values at the 120-180 min period. The lowest drug dose (0.05 nmole) did not significantly alter the facilitatory effects of dual stimulation at any of the postinjection time periods tested.

(B) Predatory Attack Behavior

This experiment was designed to test the hypothesis that medial amygdaloid-induced suppression of predatory attack behavior was mediated in part, at least, through a substance P pathway that terminates in the medial hypothalamus. Prior to drug administration, dual stimu-

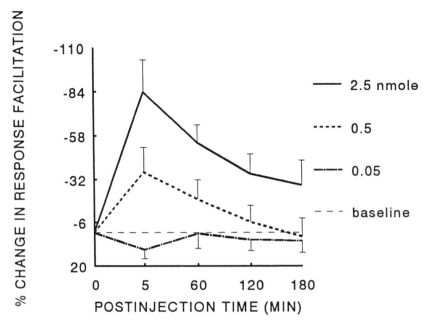

FIGURE 5. Graphs indicate that microinjections of CP 96,345 into medial hypothalamic sites from which defensive rage was elicited blocked facilitatory effects of medial amygdaloid stimulation (From Shaikh et al., [49]).

lation of the medial amygdala and lateral hypothalamus resulted in a 30-50% suppression of predatory attack behavior as indicated by an increase in response latencies. Again, as previously shown in Fig. 4, this baseline response was depicted in Fig. 6 as the common "0" point on the y axis. Here, three doses of CP 96,345 were microinfused into the medial hypothalamus and the drug effects upon amygdaloid suppression of attack behavior were determined. As shown in Fig. 6, drug administration resulted in a significant blockade of the suppressive effects of amygdaloid stimulation in a dose and time dependent manner. With respect to the maximum dose level (2.5 nmole) utilized in this experiment, the suppressive effects of dual stimulation were significantly blocked over time. At this dose level, amygdaloid suppression was reduced by 94% within the 5-60 min postinjection period. The magnitude of drug induced blockade of amygdaloid suppression was reduced to 28% when tested at the 60-120 min postinjection period. At the 5-60 min

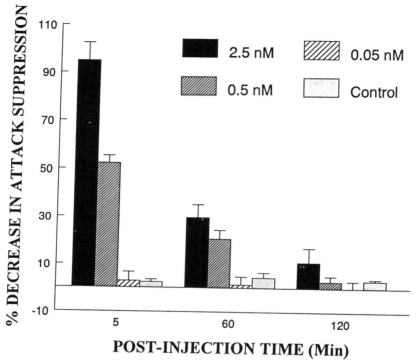

FIGURE 6. Graphs indicate that intracerebral microinfusions of CP 96,345 into the medial hypothalamus blocked the suppressive effects of medial amygdaloid stimulation upon predatory attack behavior elicited from the lateral hypothalamus in a dose and time dependent manner (From Han et al., [18]).

postinjection period, a 50% reduction of amygdaloid suppression of predatory attack behavior was observed following microinfusion of CP 96,345 at a 0.5 nmole dose level. Beyond this period, response latency values returned to predrug levels. However, CP 96,345 failed to alter the suppressive effects of dual stimulation upon predatory attack when administered at a dose level of 0.05 nmoles.

EFFECTS OF MICROINFUSION OF SUBSTANCE P INTO THE MEDIAL HYPOTHALAMUS UPON PREDATORY ATTACK BEHAVIOR

This experiment tested the hypothesis that activation of substance P receptors in the medial hypothalamus would mimic the effects of me-

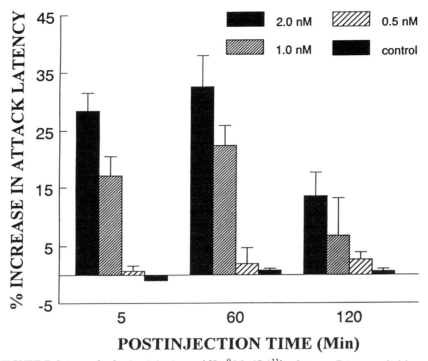

FIGURE 7. Intracerebral microinjections of $[Sar^9,Met(O_2)^{11}]$-substance P into medial hypothalamus resulted in a dose and time dependent increases in the latency values of predatory attack behavior elicited from electrical stimulation of lateral hypothalamus in the absence of medial amygdaloid stimulation (From Han et al., [18]).

dial amygdaloid stimulation by suppressing predatory attack behavior. Here, three doses of $[Sar^9,Met(O_2)^{11}]$-substance P (2.0, 1.0, 0.5 nmole), when microinfused into the medial hypothalamus, resulted in a dose and time dependent suppression of predatory attack behavior elicited from the lateral hypothalamus. Maximum suppression (32% increase in latencies) was observed at the highest dose level of substance P at the 60-120 min postinjection period. Response latencies reached baseline at the 180-240 min postinjection period (Fig. 7). At a dose level of 1.0 nmole, a 22% increase in response latencies was observed at the 60-120 min postinjection period and returned to baseline at the 120-180 min postinjection period. The lowest dose of substance P (0.5 nmole) employed in this experiment did not alter response latencies for predatory attack.

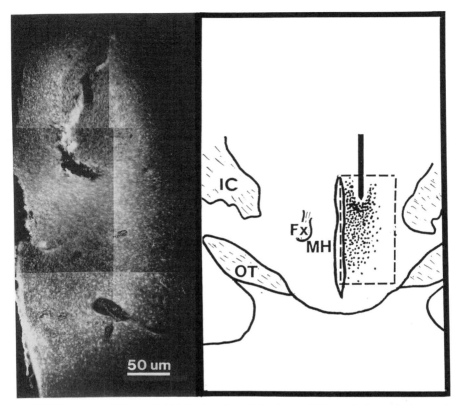

FIGURE 8. A typical Fluoro-Gold injection site within the medial hypothalamus is depicted in a microphotograph and line drawing. The position of the cannula electrode is depicted by a vertical line extending upward from the injection site on the right side of the figure. Grains represent the distribution of Fluoro-Gold within the medial hypothalamus (From Shaikh et al., [49]).

NEUROANATOMICAL ANALYSIS

This phase of the experiment was designed to provide anatomical evidence in support of the existence of a substance P pathway between the medial amygdala and medial hypothalamus. A typical Fluoro-Gold microinjection site within the medial hypothalamus from which defensive rage had been elicited is shown in Fig. 8. The vast majority of retrogradely labeled cells were identified within the medial nucleus of amygdala with some clusters of retrogradely cells situated in the basal

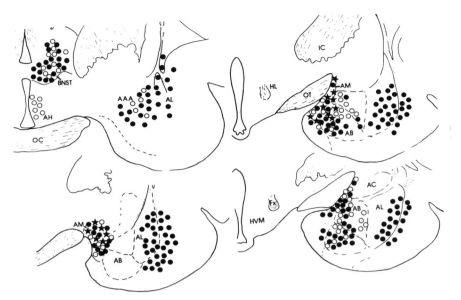

FIGURE 9. Maps illustrate distribution of: substance P immunoreactive cells (closed circles), retrogradely labeled neurons with Fluoro-Gold (open circles) and neurons labeled for both substance P and Fluoro-Gold (stars) within amygdala, bed nucleus of stria terminalis and preoptic region. Note that distribution of double-labeled neurons was confined to the medial nucleus of amygdala (From Shaikh et al., [49]).

nucleus and anterior amygdala as well as bed nucleus of stria terminalis. Analysis of the immunocytochemical data revealed the presence of substance P immunoreactive cells located principally within the medial, basal and lateral nuclei of amygdala. Neurons double-labeled for both substance P and Fluoro-Gold were identified principally within the medial nucleus of amygdala (Figs. 9 and 10).

DISCUSSION

Previous studies as well as the findings described in this chapter clearly indicate that the medial amygdala powerfully facilitates defensive rage and suppresses predatory attack behavior in the cat. Our recent findings further reveal that modulation of defensive rage and predatory attack behavior is mediated through a substance P pathway that projects directly to the medial hypothalamus. The underlying mechanisms involve the release of substance P into the medial hypothalamus from axon

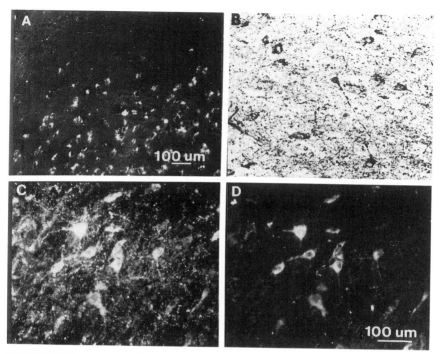

FIGURE 10. Fluorescence photomicrographs indicating the presence of (A) retrogradely labeled neurons within medial nucleus of amygdala following a microinjection of Fluoro-Gold into a medial hypothalamic defensive rage site; (B) neurons within medial amygdala which positively immunoreacted for substance P; and (C,D) neurons double-labeled for both Fluoro-Gold (C) and substance P (D) (From Shaikh et al., [49]).

terminals of the stria terminalis which originate from neurons situated in the medial amygdala.

Several lines of evidence are offered in support of these conclusions. Firstly, peripheral administration of a substance P antagonist resulted in a dose- and time-dependent blockade of the modulatory effects of medial amygdaloid stimulation upon defensive rage and predatory attack behavior. This finding indicated that substance P receptors are involved in the regulation of these two forms of feline aggressive behavior. However, it did not indicate where in the brain substance P might act to regulate aggressive behavior. Therefore, the second experiment was designed to specifically identify the sites in the forebrain where substance P interacts with receptors to mediate the modulatory properties of the medial amygdala upon hypothalamically elicited aggressive reactions.

The results of this group of experiments demonstrated that intracerebral microinjections of a substance P antagonist into the medial hypothalamus blocked the facilitatory effects of medial amygdaloid stimulation upon defensive rage behavior elicited from the medial hypothalamus. The findings further demonstrated that the suppressive effects of medial amygdaloid stimulation upon predatory attack elicited from the lateral hypothalamus are blocked by the infusion of the substance P antagonist into the medial hypothalamus.

Other evidence in support of the substance P hypothesis was the observation that predatory attack is suppressed following microinfusion of a substance P receptor agonist into the medial hypothalamus. Finally, a combined neuroanatomical and immunocytochemical analysis revealed the presence of substantial numbers of cells within the medial amygdala that were labeled for both substance P and Fluoro-Gold. These findings are consistent with other studies which have demonstrated the presence of substance P positive cells within the medial amygdala in other species [12, 32, 36, 54, 55] as well as the existence of high concentrations of substance P NK_1 receptors within the medial hypothalamus [18, 27, 31, 41]. It is of interest to note that NK_2 and NK_3 receptors are not known to be present in the medial hypothalamus [8, 10, 27, 31, 35], which further points to the likely importance of substance P NK_1 receptors within the medial hypothalamus.

Another finding of interest was that peripheral administration of CP 96,345 blocked the facilitatory effects of the medial amygdala upon defensive rage behavior but failed to change the threshold or latency values for defensive rage elicited from the medial hypothalamus in the absence of amygdaloid stimulation. This finding suggests that the medial amygdala facilitates defensive rage in a phasic and not in a tonic manner. The mechanisms responsible for its phasic effects may include amygdaloid inputs from thalamus and cortex, particularly areas associated with visual [33, 39, 58], auditory [26] and olfactory functions [23, 24]. In addition, the amygdala also receives projections from the prefrontal cortex [38], dopaminergic cell groups of the brainstem [9, 14], hypothalamus [7, 15, 37] and hippocampus [60]. These inputs may serve to activate the medial amygdala and its output pathways to the hypothalamus, and, in turn, regulate the mechanisms within the hypothalamus that mediate aggressive forms of behavior.

The present studies have suggested that the anatomical substrate subserving substance P-induced facilitation of defensive rage behavior involves a monosynaptic projection from the medial amygdala via the stria terminalis to the medial hypothalamus. The question must then be asked how inputs to the medial hypothalamus can control predatory attack elicited from the lateral hypothalamus. Recent experiments in our laboratory have, in fact, suggested that a short GABAergic (inhibitory) pathway, which arises from the medial hypothalamus, projects directly to the lateral hypothalamus. In this manner, activation of the medial amygdala can directly excite neurons in the medial hypothalamus. Excitation of the medial hypothalamus thus serves to drive the mechanism regulating defensive rage behavior while, at the same time, inhibit the predatory attack mechanism within the lateral hypothalamus by virtue of the short inhibitory interneuron.

ACKNOWLEDGMENTS: The studies presented in this chapter were supported by NIH Grant NS07941-26 and by a grant from the Harry Frank Guggenheim Foundation.

REFERENCES

1. Adamec, R. E. (1990). Role of the amygdala and medial hypothalamus in spontaneous feline aggression and defense. *Aggress. Behav., 16,* 207-222.
2. Bandler, R. (1984). Identification of hypothalamic and midbrain periaqueductal grey neurons mediating aggressive and defensive behavior by intracerebral microinjections of excitatory amino acids. In R. Bandler (Ed.), Modulation of sensorimotor activity during alterations in behavioral states, *Modulation of Sensorimotor Activity* (pp. 369-391). New York: Alan R. Liss, Inc.
3. Bard, P. & McK. Rioch, D. (1937). A study of four cats deprived of neocortex and additional portions of the forebrain. *Bull. Johns Hopkins Hospital, LX no. 2,* 73-124.
4. Bard, P. & Mountcastle, V. B. (1948). Some forebrain mechanisms involved in expression of rage with special reference to suppression of angry behavior. *Ass. Res. Nerv. Ment. Dis., 27,* 362-399.
5. Block, C. H., Siegel, A., & Edinger, H. (1980). Effects of amygdaloid stimulation upon trigeminal sensory fields of the lip that established during hypothalamically-elicited quiet biting attack in the cat. *Brain Res., 197,* 39-55.
6. Brutus, M., Shaikh, M. B., Siegel, A., & Edinger, H. (1986). Effects of experimental temporal lobe seizures upon hypothalamically elicited aggressive behavior in the cat. *Brain Res., 366,* 53-63.
7. Cechetto, D. F., Ciriello, J., & Calaresu, F. R. (1983). Afferent connections to cardiovascular sites in the amygdala: A horseradish peroxidase study in the cat. *J. Autonom. Nerv. Syst., 8,* 97-110.
8. Dam, T. V., Martinelli, B., & Quirion, R. (1990). Autoradiographic distribution of brain neurokinin-1/substance P receptors using a highly selective ligand [^{3}H]-[Sar^9,$Met(O_2)^{11}$]-substance P. *Brain Res., 531,* 330-337.
9. Deutch, A. Y., Goldstein, M., Baldino, F. J., & Roth, R. H. (1988). Telencephalic projections of the A8 dopamine cell group. In P. W. Kalivas & C. B. Nemeroff (Eds.), *The Mesocorticolimbic Dopamine System,* (pp. 27-50). New York: New York Academy of Science.

10. Drapeau, G., D'Orleans-Juste, P., Dion, S., Rhaleb, N. E., Rouissi, N. E., & Regoli, D. (1987). Selective agonists for substance P and neurokinin receptors. *Neuropeptides, 10,* 43-54.
11. Egger, M. D. & Flynn, J. P. (1963). Effects of electrical stimulation of the amygdala on hypothalamically elicited attack behavior in cats. *J. Neurophysiol., 26,* 705-720.
12. Emson, P. C., Jessell, T., Paxinos, G., & Cuello, A. C. (1978). Substance P in the amygdaloid complex, bed nucleus and stria terminalis of the rat brain, *Brain Res., 149(1),* 97-105.
13. Falconer, M. A. (1973). Reversibility by temporal-lobe resection of the behavioral abnormalities of temporal-lobe epilepsy. *New Eng. J. Med., 289(9),* 451-455.
14. Fallon, J. H. (1981). Histochemical characterization of dopaminergic, noradrenergic and serotonergic projections to the amygdala. In Y. Ben-Ari (Ed.), *The Amygdaloid Complex* (pp. 175-183). North Holland: Elsevier.
15. Fuchs, S. A. G., Edinger, H. M., & Siegel, A. (1985). The organization of the hypothalamic pathways mediating affective defense behavior in the cat. *Brain Res., 330,* 77-92.
16. Fuchs, S. A. G., Edinger, H. M., & Siegel, A. (1985). The role of the anterior hypothalamus in affective defense behavior elicited from the ventromedial hypothalamus of the cat. *Brain Res., 330,* 93-108.
17. Gedye, A. (1989). Episodic rage and aggression attributed to frontal lobe seizures. *J. Ment. Deficien. Res., 33(5),* 369-379.
18. Han, Y. C., Shaikh, M. B., & Siegel, A. (1994). Role of substance P in medial amygdaloid suppression of predatory attack behavior in the cat. *Soc. Neurosci., (Abs.),* 20.
19. Hermann, B. P., Schwartz, M. S., Whitman, S., & Karnes, W.E. (1980). Aggression and epilepsy: Seizure-type comparisons and high-risk variables. *Epilepsia, 22,* 691-698.
20. Hess, W. R. & Brugger, M. (1943). Das subkorticale zentrum der affektinen abwehrreaktion. *Helv. Physiol. Pharmac. Acta, 1,* 33-52.
21. Hood, T. W., Siegfried, J., & Wieser, H. G. (1983). The role of stereotactic amygdalotomy in the treatment of temporal lobe epilepsy associated with behavioral disorders. *Appl. Neurophysiol., 46,* 19-25.
22. Jasper, H. H. & Ajmone-Marsan, C. A. (1954). *Stereotaxic Atlas of the Diencephalon of the Cat.* Ottawa: National Research Council of Canada.
23. Kelley, A. E., Domesick, V. B., & Nauta, W. J. H. (1982). The amygdalostriatal projection in the rat: An anatomical study by anterograde and retrograde tracing methods. *Neuroscience, 7(3),* 615-630.
24. Kevetter, G. A. & Winans, S. S. (1981). Connections of the corticomedial amygdala in the golden hamster. II. Efferents of the "olfactory amygdala". *J. Comp. Neurol., 197,* 99-111.
25. Kluver, H. & Bucy, P. C. (1939). Preliminary analysis of functions of the temporal lobes in monkeys. *Arch. Neurol and Psychiat, 42(6),* 979-1000.
26. LeDoux, J. E., Ruggiero, D. A., & Reis, D. J. (1985). Projections to the subcortical forebrain from anatomically defined regions of the medial geniculate body in the rat. *J. Comp. Neurol., 242,* 182-213.
27. Lew, R., Geraghty, D. P., Regoli, D., & Burcher, E. (1990). Binding characteristics of [^{125}I]Bolton-Hunter [Sar^9,Met(O$_2$)^{11}]-substance P, a new selective radioligand for the NK$_1$ receptor. *Eur. J. Pharmacology, 184,* 97-108.
28. Leyhausen, P. (1979). *Cat Behavior: The Predatory and Social Behavior of Domestic And Wild Cats.* New York: Garland STPM Press.

29. Lu, C.-L., Shaikh, M. B., & Siegel, A. (1992). Role of NMDA receptors in hypothalamic facilitation of feline defensive rage elicited from the midbrain periaqueductal gray. *Brain Res., 581,* 123-132.

30. Martinius, J. (1983). Homicide of an aggressive adolescent boy with right temporal lesion. A case report, *Neurosci. Biobehav. Rev., 7,* 419-422.

31. McLean, S., Ganong, A. H., Seeger, T. F., Bryce, D. K., Pratt, K. G., Reynolds, L. S., Siok, C. J., Lowe, III & Heym, J. (1991). Activity and distribution of binding sites in brain of a non-peptide substance P (NK$_1$) receptor antagonist. *Science, 251,* 437-439.

32. McLean, S., Skirboll, R., & Pert, C. B. (1985). Comparison of substance P and enkephalin distribution in rat brain: an overview using radioimmunocyto-chemistry, *Neuroscience, 14,* 837-852.

33. Mehler, W. R., Pretorius, J. K., Phelan, K. D., & Mantyh, P. W. (1981). Diencephalic afferent connections of the amygdala in the squirrel monkey with observations and comments on the cat and rat. In Y. Ben-Ari (Ed.), *The Amygdaloid Complex,* (pp. 105-120). North Holland: Elsevier.

34. Monroe, R. R. (1978). *Brain Dysfunction in Aggressive Criminals* (1 pp.). Lexington, Mass.: Lexington Books.

35. Mussap, C. J., Geraghty, D. P., & Burcher, E. (1993). Tachykinin receptors: A radioligand binding perspective. *J. Neurochem., 60,* 1987-2009.

36. Neal, C. R., Swann, J. M., & Newman, S. W. (1989). The colocalization of substance P and prodynorphin immunoreactivity in neurons of the medial preoptic area, bed nucleus of the stria terminalis and medial nucleus of the amygdala of the Syrian hamster. *Brain Res., 496,* 1-13.

37. Ottersen, O. P. (1980). Afferent connections to the amygdaloid complex of the rat and cat: II. Afferents from the hypothalamus and basal telencephalon. *J. Comp. Neurol., 194,* 267-289.

38. Ottersen, O. P. (1982). Connections of the amygdala of the rat. IV: Corticoamygdaloid and intraamygdaloid connections as studied with axonal transport of horseradish peroxidase, *J. Comp. Neurol., 205,* 30-48.

39. Ottersen, O. P. & Ben-Ari, Y. (1979). Afferent connections to the amygdaloid complex of the rat and cat. I. Projections from the thalamus. *J. Comp. Neurol., 187 (2),* 401-424.

40. Ranson, S. W., Kabat, H., & Magoun, H. W. (1935). Autonomic responses to electrical stimulation of hypothalamus, preoptic region and septum. *Arch. Neurol. Psychiat., 33,* 467-477.

41. Regoli, D., Drapeau, G., Dion, S., & Couture, R. (1988). New selective agonists for neurokinin receptors: pharmacological tools for receptor characterization. *Trends Pharmacol. Sci., 9,* 290-295.

42. Schubert, K. & Siegel, A. (1994). What animal studies have taught us about the neurobiology of violence. *Internat. J. Group Tensions, 24,* 237-265.

43. Serafetinides, E. A. (1965). Aggressiveness in temporal lobe epileptics and its relation to cerebral dysfunction and environmental factors. *Epilepsia, 6,* 33-42.

44. Shaikh, M. B., Barrett, J. A., & Siegel, A. (1987). The pathways mediating affective defense and quiet biting attack behavior from the midbrain central gray of the cat: An autoradiographic study. *Brain Res., 437,* 9-25.

45. Shaikh, M. B., Brutus, M., Siegel, A., & Siegel, H. E. (1985). Topographically organized midbrain modulation of predatory and defensive aggression in the cat. *Brain Re., 336,* 308-312.

46. Shaikh, M. B., Dalsass, M., & Siegel, A. (1990). Opioidergic mechanism mediating aggressive behavior in the cat. *Aggress. Behav., 16,* 191-206.

47. Shaikh, M. B., Lu, C. L., & Siegel, A. (1991). An enkephalinergic mechanism involved in amygdaloid suppression of affective defense behavior elicited from the midbrain periaqueductal gray in the cat. *Brain Res., 559,* 109-117.

48. Shaikh, M. B., Schubert, K., & Siegel, A. (1994). Basal amygdaloid facilitation of midbrain periaqueductal gray elicited defensive rage behavior in the cat is mediated through NMDA receptors. *Brain Res., 635,* 187-195.

49. Shaikh, M. B., Steinberg, A., & Siegel, A. (1993). Evidence that substance P is utilized in medial amygdaloid facilitation of defensive rage behavior in the cat. *Brain Res., 625,* 283-294.

50. Siegel, A. & Brutus, M. (1990). Neural substrates of aggression and rage in the cat. In A. N. Epstein & A. R. Morrison (Eds.), *Progress in Psychobiology and Physiological Psychology* (14th Ed.) (pp. 135-233). San Diego, CA: Academic Press.

51. Siegel, A. & Pott, C. B. (1988). Neural substrates of aggression and flight in the cat. *Prog. Neurobiol., 31,* 261-283.

52. Siegel, A. & Schubert, K. (1995). Neurotransmitters regulating feline aggressive behavior. *Revs. in the Neurosc., 6,* 47-61.

53. Stoddard-Apter, S. L. & MacDonnell, M. F. (1980). Septal and amygdalar efferents to the hypothalamus which facilitate hypothalamically elicited intraspecific aggression and associated hissing in the cat. An Autoradiographic study. *Brain Res., 193,* 19-32.

54. Swann, J. M. & Macchione, N. (1992). Photoperiodic regulation of substance P immunoreactivity in the mating behavior pathway of the male golden hamster, *Brain Res., 590,* 29-38.

55. Swann, J. M. & Newman, S. W. (1992). Testosterone regulates substance P within neurons of the medial nucleus of the amygdala, the bed nucleus of the stria terminalis and the medial preoptic area of the male golden hamster. *Brain Res., 590,* 18-28.

56. Sweidan, S., Edinger, H., & Siegel, A. (1991). D2 dopamine receptor-mediated mechanisms in the medial preoptic-anterior hypothalamus regulate affective defense behavior in the cat. *Brain Res., 549,* 127-137.

57. Tonkonogy, J. M. (1991). Violence and temporal lobe lesion: head CT and MRI data. *J Neuropsychiat. Clin. Neurosci., 3,* 189-196.

58. Turner, B. H. (1981). The cortical sequence and terminal distribution of sensory related afferents to the amygdaloid complex of the rat and monkey. In Y. Ben-Ari (Ed.), *The Amygdaloid Complex* (pp. 51-62). North Holland: Elsevier.

59. Vaernet, K. (1983). Temporal lobotomy in children and young adults. *Advances in Epileptology: XVth Epilep. Internat. Symp.,* 255-261.

60. Watson, R. E., Troiano, R., Poulakos, J. J., Weiner, S., Block, C. H., & Siegel, A. A. (1983). [^{14}C]2-Deoxyglucose analysis of the functional neural pathways of the limbic forebrain in the rat. I. The amygdala. *Brain Res. Rev., 5,* 1-44.

61. Zagrodzka, J. & Fonberg, E. (1977). Amygdalar area involved in predatory behavior in cats. *Acta Neurobiol. Exp., 37,* 131-135.

CHAPTER 4

ALCOHOL'S EFFECTS ON PHYSIOLOGY AND "AGGRESSION": WHAT IS THE NATURE OF THE LINK?

PAUL F. BRAIN

Tis not the eating, nor 'tis not the drinking that is to be blamed, but the excess.
Table Talk 54, John Selden 1584-1654

INTRODUCTION

Many cultures have expressed concern about the impact of excessive alcohol ingestion on human violence. I have argued elsewhere, however, (Brain, 1986a;b) that the popular 'simple' view that alcohol ingestion causes hostile behavior and, hence leads to violent crime, is based on a number of over-simplifications. Although alcohol consumption is statistically *correlated* with diverse expressions of 'hostility', the public's perception is that man's oldest drug either stimulates 'aggression mechanisms' or disinhibits (removes a block from) such processes (presumed to be generally checked by higher, cognitive functions).

PAUL F. BRAIN • School of Biological Sciences, University College of Swansea, Singleton Park, Swansea SA2 8PP, Wales, U.K.

Aggression: Biological, Developmental, and Social Perspectives, edited by Seymour Feshbach and Jolanta Zagrodzka. Plenum Press, New York, 1997.

My basic contention is that the question 'Does alcohol ingestion increase violent crime?' is only *apparently* simple. Complications which make interpretation difficult are evident at a variety of levels. The first set of complicating factors surround measures of alcohol consumption. They include the fact that little account is generally taken of alcohol consumption in non-aggressive/non-criminal portions of the population. Alcohol consumption is notoriously evident in city centers on a Saturday night and it would be remarkable if any human activity at this time were *not* associated with alcohol ingestion. Further, the time course of alcohol in the blood in relation to behavioral change is generally obscure (even in animal models of such phenomena). In addition, the chronic alcoholic shows a metabolic pattern of post-alcohol changes different to that of the occasional drinker, alcohol is metabolized *in vivo* into a variety of substances (of varied behavior potency?), beverages contain complex congeners which may have differing behavioral influences, diet influences the rate of alcohol absorption from the digestive tract and there is an *expectancy* effect of drinking which can be as strong as the action of alcohol *per se*.

Of direct relevance to the present account is the recognition that there are several complications concerning alcohol's postulated 'mechanism' of action on the physiology assumed to underpin behavioral change. Alcohol is an extremely non-specific drug whose effects are not limited to a specific receptor site(s) (cf. morphine), it changes the lipid environment of neurons and it seems to alter virtually every index of neurophysiological action in particular components of the nervous system (as these changes vary from component to component, there is no easy way to integrate them). The acute and chronic effects of alcohol exposure may also differ, as individuals habituate to the effects of this relatively ubiquitous drug. Further, alcohol ingestion has profound effects on the endocrine system (hormonal disturbances can account for some behavioral changes) and the drug, to some degree, influences its own dynamics of exposure by modifying the efficiencies of the liver and the kidneys.

A further obvious group of complicating factors of great relevance to this topic, concern the diversity of the concept of 'aggression'. I have explored these considerations in animals and humans in detail elsewhere (Brain, 1990a). Briefly, 'aggression' clearly refers to a heterogeneous group of activities in which considerations of actual or potential harm, intentionality (deliberateness) aversiveness to the 'victim' and arousal may be used to validate the application of this epithet. 'Violence' is simply a synonym for 'aggression' in which an extra degree of excessiveness is attributed by the individuals judging the response. Different authorities seem extremely variable in their willingness to include different items (e.g. crimes against property, sexual offenses and dangerous driving) under the heading of 'violence'. Different cultures and different historical times may also dictate whether an action is regarded as 'violent' or not. Further, precisely the same motor action (or verbal response) may be judged criminal or legitimate depending on the circumstances and the authority/individual making the evaluation. Perhaps one should add that the kinds of 'aggression' emphasized by social psychologists and anthropologists often appear qualitatively different from those studied by biologists (see Brain, 1984). In addition, it appears likely that alcohol, the metabolites generated from the drug and/or the social context of drinking can change 'motivation', the production of social signals, the perception of a situation and processing by sensory/higher neural elements in individuals. Obviously, as social aggression involves at least two individuals, the precise impact of alcohol on the *social interaction* (and our interpretation of this) can be quite complex.

A further layer of complexity relates to the human data base in which our perception of the alcohol/violence association is rooted. Certainly, in both the UK and the USA plea-bargaining (where individuals plead guilty to lesser crimes to avoid a trial) can distort any attempted correlation. Alcohol ingestion can also increase the likelihood of a person being a victim of violence ('the battered alcoholic syndrome') as well as reducing a court's view of a witnesses' credibility. Further, 'aggressors' have been known to misreport alcohol ingestion offering a legally non-valid (but sometimes effective) 'excuse' for their actions. Alcohol consumption *and* violence may be popular concomitant activities of certain groups (e.g. *some* cases of 'football hooliganism' in the UK). Mere possession of alcohol containers (i.e. bottles and cans) may be regarded in some legal circumstances, as equivalent to possession of offensive weapons. Some alcoholics may involve themselves in 'crime' to support an expensive habit and alcoholism can force persons into social strata where violent crime is more probable. Alcohol-related 'bungling' of crimes may increase the probability of capture (increasing the apparent association between ingestion of the substance and behavior) whereas efficient criminal organizations are said to frown upon the use of drugs or alcohol by their operatives prior to making a 'hit' (making such individuals *less* likely to be represented in the statistics). These interpretational difficulties should *not* be used to suggest that alcohol has no important consequences on public disorder but they do emphasize the unreliability of our available data base. Some of the factors will increase the apparent association between alcohol ingestion and hostility whereas others do the opposite.

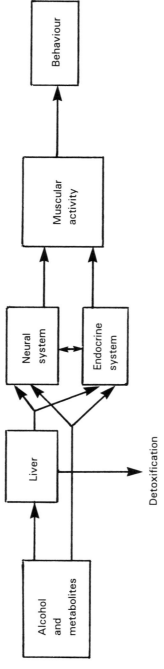

FIGURE 1. Effects of alcohol on the subprocesses which might connect physiology with behaviour. *N.B.* Alcohol and its metabolites may also exert direct actions on muscular activity etc.

TABLE 1. Papers on the Effects of Alcohol on Liver Functioning in Animals From "Alcohol and Alcoholism" 1986-1990

Author(s)	Year	Species	Basic conclusion
Tiernan & Ward	1986	rat	Ethanol reduces protein synthesis.
Tuma et al.	1990	various	Ethanol (via acetaldehyde?) disorders protein trafficking.
Mazzanti et al.	1987	rats	Chronic ethanol increases iron absorption—plays a role in liver disease.
Cunnigham et al.	1990	various	Chronic ethanol produces generalized depression of mitochondrial energy metabolism.

NEW DATA

I (and most other behavioral specialists) am convinced that alcohol does not exert a simple pharmacological action on 'aggression'. A recent review of papers on animals and humans in the journal *Alcohol and Alcoholism* (1986-1990) seems to broadly confirm and extend my reservations.

The impact of alcohol and its metabolites on physiology and, ultimately, behavior are best summarized in Figure 1 (see page 6). Alcohol and its metabolites clearly have profound influences on liver function in animals (Table 1) and humans (Table 2). Recent data suggest that ethanol has marked effects on protein metabolism and energy generation by this organ. This metabolic disturbance can clearly lead to conditions such as fatty liver disease and alcoholic hepatitis in humans which, not only impair health directly, but influence susceptibility to infective diseases. There is evidence that detrimental changes in liver function occur even in heavy drinking non-alcoholics. Obviously, impairing the liver's metabolic role will have powerful effects on the rate of removal of alcohol from the system and the balance of ethanol-derived metabolites.

Alcohol has profound influences on many aspects of neural functioning in animals (see Table 3) and humans (see Table 4). Such effects can be mediated directly by alcohol or via liver metabolites. In rodents, alcohol increases the fluidity of the neuronal membrane, changing the transport of ions across this structure and produces major changes in a variety of neurotransmitters in a range of neural structures. More subtly, it alters regional localization of metal ions within neural structures and

TABLE 2. Papers on the Effects of Alcohol on Liver Functioning in Humans
From "Alcohol and Alcoholism" 1986-1990

Author(s)	Year	Location	Sample	Age range (years)	Basic conclusion
Ryle	1986	—	—	—	Fatty liver disease associated with chronic ethanol ingestion.
Sherlock	1990	—	—	—	Alcoholic hepatitis caused by ethanol misuse.
Chick et al.	1987	Scotland	576	—	Gamma glutamyl transferase and mean liver cell volume increased in heavy drinkers. Also increases in serum ferritin.
Plant	1990	—	—	—	Alcohol related liver disease damages the immune system.

changes thiamine transport in the brain. Acetaldehyde may produce brain damage by forming abducts and cytotoxic free radicals which harm living tissue. All these actions seem likely to have major influences on the activities of the central nervous system. The human data confirms that even acute exposure to ethanol changes neural activity whereas long-term exposure (as in alcoholics) induces brain shrinkage, other anatomical deficits, electrophysiological changes and fortunately rare debilitating conditions such as the Wernicke-Korsakoff syndrome. The neural system not only influences muscular activity but may modulate certain kinds of endocrine change. The brain is obviously the prime organ of behavior.

Changes in endocrine factors can influence activities of the central nervous system and modulate muscular activity (thus ultimately influencing behavior). There is good recent evidence in animals (Table 5) and humans (Table 6) that alcohol and alcohol metabolites can change a broad range of indices of hormonal production. In animals, it is now thought that ethanol influences the second messenger process of hormonal action as well as exerting reliable actions on thyroid and testicular activity. Data from humans reveals that alcohol ingestion can modify insulin regulation of energy production, sex steroid production (notably the elevation of oestrogens and feminization of some *male* alcoholics) as well as disturbances in the renin-angiotensin and adrenocortical systems. Some of these actions occur acutely whereas as others are responses to

TABLE 3. Papers on the Effects of Alcohol on Neural Functioning in Animals From "Alcohol and Alcoholism" 1986-1990

Author(s)	Year	Species	Basic conclusion
Leonard	1986	various	Alcohol increases the fluidity of the neuronal membrane by reducing the unsaturated: saturated fat ratio. Results in modified transport of Ca^{++}, other electrolytes and neurotransmitters across the cell surface.
Rehman	1986	rats	Alcohol alters $(Na^+ K^+)$ ATPase which, in turn, changes regional localization of zinc, copper and lead in the brain.
Kuriyama & Ohkuma	1990	rats/mice	Chronic alcohol treatment influences metabolism and receptor binding of a range of neurotransmitters.
Poldrugo	1987	rats	Acute ethanol decreases endogenous gamma hydroxybutyric acid in the striatum which can influence dopaminergic neurons.
Morinan	1987	rats	Chronic ethanol decreases serotonin turnover in the striatum.
Anokhina et al.	1988	rats	Alcohol preferring animals higher levels of blood dopamine than avoiding strains.
Patrini et al.	1988	rats	Both acutely and chronically ethanol increases thiamine transport in the brain when the vitamin is at high concentration.
Pratt et al.	1990	various	Acetaldehyde implicated in alcoholic brain damage via adduct (with proteins) formation and via formation of cytotoxic free radicals?
Hashimoto et al.	1989	mice	Acetaldehyde significantly decreases norepinephrine in cerebral cortex and brainstem and dopamine in brainstem-associated with motor effects and coma.

long-term exposure. There is evidence that acute and chronic hormonal responses to exposure can be very different. The feminizing effect of *chronic* alcoholism, suggests that the claimed link between testosterone production and hostility, should also be examined with care (see Brain, 1990b). Although alcohol cannot influence hostility by *stimulating* testicular hormone production, the simultaneous ingestion of alcohols and

TABLE 4. Papers on the Effects of Alcohol on Neural Functioning in Humans From "Alcohol and Alcoholism" 1986-1990

Author(s)	Year	Location	Sample	Age range (years)	Basic conclusion
Harper & Kril	1990	—	—	—	Alcohol has wide-ranging effects on the nervous system. Some actions interfere with physiological and neurochemical functions but ultimately structural damage occurs. Brain shrinkage (usually involving loss of white matter) notable in alcoholics but also some evidence in moderate (30-80 g/day) drinkers.
MacDonell et al.	1987	—	—	—	Brain autopsy, computerized tomography scans and nuclear magnetic resonance data demonstrates anatomical deficits in detoxified alcoholics.
Bishai & Bozzetti	1986	—	—	—	Alcohol can produce Wernicke-Korsakoff syndrome—caused at least in part by a deficient bioavailability of thiamin.
Begleitter & Porjesz	1990	—	—	—	Electrophysiological changes in alcoholic patients.
Anokhina et al.	1988	USSR	115	25-52	Increased dopamine in the blood and evidence of functional disorders in neurochemical processes regulating catecholaminergic neuromediation in alcoholics.
Bannister et al.	1988	Leeds	8	25-37	Acute alcohol ingestion raises plasma GABA levels in healthy male volunteers.

androgens (hard drinking body builders?) may be a particularly potent combination.

Both the neural and endocrine consequences of ethanol exposure can exert actions on the heart/muscle (effectors largely producing be-

TABLE 5. Papers on the Effects of Alcohol on Endocrine Functioning in Animals From "Alcohol and Alcoholism" 1986-1990

Author(s)	Year	Species	Basic conclusion
Hoek & Rubin	1990	various	Ethanol influences the second messenger process via actions on membrane-associated signal transduction mechanisms.
Mannisto et al.	1987	rat	Ethanol intake decreases TSH levels but little effect on prolactin or GH.
Widenius	1987	rat	Very low ethanol (but not acetaldehyde) concentrations reduce testosterone production by testicular material *in vitro*.
Akane et al.	1988	rat	Ethanol inhibits testicular steroidogenesis by suppressing at least 2 steps in the metabolic chain.

havioral actions and changing 'vigor'). Recent data from animals (Table 7) and humans (Table 8) suggests that ethanol produces deficits in muscle tissue by changing protein synthesis and generating atrophy and myopathy. Some of these changes could have behavioral or mood-influencing consequences. The broad action of ethanol seems, however, to impair muscular activity, hardly generating a 'super-male' condition characterized by 'dominance'.

The massive literature concerning attempts to relate alcohol ingestion to changes in 'aggression' in animals and man is reviewed in chapters in Brain (1986a), Brain et al (1993), and by Klaus Miczek and his colleagues (1990). I do *not* propose to dwell on the complexities of this easily available but high variable data. Newer findings on the effects of alcohol on behavior in animals (Table 9) and on behavior *and* physical trauma in humans (Table 10) *are* provided for consideration. Data with animals suggests that a whole range of separate behavioral phenomena are rooted in the specific but widespread effects of ethanol on discrete neuronal mechanisms. These are by no means limited to effects on 'aggression'. Further, there is support for the view that alcohol ingestion is causally related to residual impairment of cognitive-perceptual functioning. In humans recent British data confirm that alcohol ingestion is strongly associated with trauma, perpetration of violence *and* being a victim of violence. The recent reviews have generally shared my conclusion that the precise proportion of interpersonal violence *caused* by alcohol *cannot* be identified from available data. However, studies on humans strongly suggest an association between protracted alcohol in-

TABLE 6. Papers on the Effects of Alcohol on Endocrine Functioning in Humans
From "Alcohol and Alcoholism" 1986-1990

Author(s)	Year	Location	Sample	Age range (years)	Basic conclusion
Shah	1988	USA	4 males 1 females	25-45	Alcohol produces a higher steady state of infused glucose and insulin with lower glucose metabolism than controls. Alcohol may depress tissue sensitivity to insulin.
Connelly et al.	1987	Bristol U.K.	12 males 12 females	22-53 20-44	Mild hypoglycemia and glucose intolerance can occur in regular heavy (> 50 units/week) but, otherwise normal, drinkers c.f. light (< 7 units/week) drinkers.
Myking et al.	1987	Norway	20 Alcoholics 20 Controls	28-65 29-67	Chronic alcoholics have significantly *elevated* estrogens and sex steroid binding globulin but *reduced* estrone sulfate and apparent free testosterone c.f. controls. Some patients hypogonadism and/or feminization.
Mander et al.	1988	Scotland	2 males 3 females	30-52	Alcoholic patients admitted for detoxification—elevated levels of anti-diuretic hormone, renin and supine aldosterone 24-48 hrs after abstinence. Supine aldosterone still elevated after one week.
Mander et al.	1989	Scotland	14 males 5 females	34-66	Alcoholics drinking on day of admission—raised levels of renin, aldosterone and cortisol. Falls in renin and cortisol over 1st 4 days of abstinence.

TABLE 7. Papers on the Effects of Alcohol on Heart/Muscle Functioning in Animals
From "Alcohol and Alcoholism" 1986-1990

Author(s)	Year	Species	Basic conclusion
Adickes & Mollner	1986	rat	Early exposure to ethanol produces deficits in muscle tissue, especially in the heart.
Tiernan & Ward	1986	rat	Ethanol reduces protein synthesis in the whole body and in individual tissues including muscle and the heart.
Preedy & Peters	1990	rat	Skeletal muscle myopathy by ethanol exposure.

TABLE 8. Papers on the Effects of Alcohol on Heart/Muscle Functioning in Humans
From "Alcohol and Alcoholism" 1986-1990

Author(s)	Year	Location	Sample	Age range (years)	Basic conclusion
Kelbaek et al.	1988	Denmark	7 males	21-30	In healthy volunteers, heart rate and cardiac output increased 1-8 hrs after alcohol ingestion. Reduced total peripheral resistance?
Mills et al.	1986	London U.K.	15 males 4 females	30-63 40-71	Chronic alcoholics independently show muscle atrophy and deficits in peripheral nerve conduction.
Preedy & Peters	1990	—	—	—	Skeletal muscle myopathy (especially in fast twitch fibers) caused by prolonged ethanol misuse.
Dancy & Maxwell	1986	—	—	—	Alcohol positively (if rarely) associated with dilated cardiomyopathy.

gestion and residual impairment of cognitive-perceptual functioning. The drug also greatly influences the results of memory tests in alcoholics.

It seems likely that at least a proportion of the violent acts that have been associated with alcohol ingestion, are consequences of this drug's effects on neural processing and hence on the individual's ability to pro-

TABLE 9. Papers on the Effects of Alcohol on Behavior in Animals
From "Alcohol and Alcoholism" 1986-1990

Author(s)	Year	Basic conclusion
Parsons & Stevens	1986	Support for the view that protracted alcohol ingestion causally related to residual impairment of cognitive-perceptual functioning.
Kiianmaa	1990	Separate behavioral phenomena caused by specific effects of ethanol on discrete neuronal mechanisms.

duce *appropriate* responses or to respond to the signals of others in what is perceived as an *appropriate* manner. Alcohol is also likely via such a mechanism to impair our judgement of the behavior of others and individuals suspected of alcohol ingestion are *regarded* differently from 'sober' humans. It can be argued that these changes essentially interfere with social 'dialogue' by increasing the probability of misinterpretation. There is some evidence that alcohol will produce comparable changes in laboratory mice (Brain et al, 1993). The fact that alcohol consumption often occurs under relatively crowded circumstances in bars etc. may compound such problems (this is *not* to advocate solitary drinking).

It also seems to me, a scientist whose major research effort has concerned infra-human animals, that a problem of many animal 'models' of alcohol and violence (e.g. fighting in male mice and rats) is that the behavior studied is clearly adaptive and organized in those subjects whereas many of the human activities that provide a focus in alcohol studies are clearly non-adaptive and/or the result of disorganization. Even the animal models of 'aggression' generate different results when one attempts to assess the impact of alcohol (Brain et al, 1993). Alcohol at moderate to high doses generally *reduces* fighting and threat in animals (due to its broadly sedative actions). Cases where low doses of ethanol apparently augment attack in rats and mice may represent a failure of the drug to interfere with behavioral changes consequent upon prior experience (i.e., 'learning') rather than being the stimulatory portion of a biphasic action. Perhaps the defensive, 'fear'-related portions of agonistic behavior provides more obvious parallels for some alcohol-related changes in humans? Defensiveness is clearly increased in alcohol-treated mice. Such animal data has at least led us to recognize that alcohol cannot have a simple effect on 'hostility' and that one has to consider the broad spectrum of effects of any drug on behavior. It is notable that 'ethological' studies (Blanchard and Blanchard, 1987) on the

TABLE 10. Papers on the Effects of Alcohol on Behavior and Physical
Trauma in Humans
From "Alcohol and Alcoholism" 1986-1990

Author(s)	Year	Location	Sample	Age range (years)	Basic conclusion
Redfern et al.	1988	Liverpool U.K.	765	—	22.4% of trauma patients requiring admission had consumed alcohol prior to accident. High incidence of spinal and ankle fractures especially in young/middle-aged males.
Norton & Morgan	1989	—	—	—	Individuals consuming alcohol "several times more likely to perpetrate violence, or to be victims of violence, than individuals who do not consume alcohol." Proportion of interpersonal violence caused by alcohol *cannot* be identified from available data.
Parsons & Stevens	1986	—	—	—	Suggestion of an association between protracted alcohol ingestion and residual impairment of cognitive-perceptual functioning but *not* absolutely established.
Levy & Losowsky	1987	—	—	—	Abnormalities of visual evoked potentials apparent in drinkers even when psychometric test normal.
MacDonell et al.	1987	Scotland U.K. Dublin Eire	—	20-59	Two automated neuro-psychological test (Cogfun and the perceptual maze test) confirm that detoxified alcoholics show impaired abilities to abstract and conceptualize and in visual-spatial and simple sensory-motor performance.
Glenn et al.	1988	U.S.A.	76 males 67 females	21-62	The more withdrawals (24 hrs abstinence followed by ethanol consumption), the poorer the memory test performance in alcoholics. A stronger effect in females?

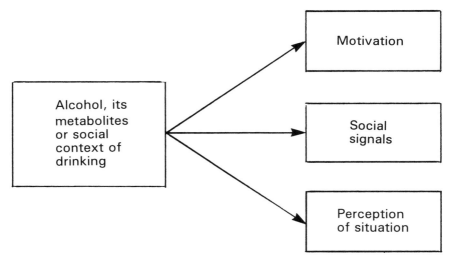

FIGURE 2. Synopsis of the effects of alcohol on behavior (from Brain, P. F. (1986b) multidisciplinary examinations of the 'causes' of crime. The case of the link between alcohol and violence *Alcohol and Alcoholism* 21: 237-240).

impact of alcohol on the behavior of colonies of rats to intruders of varied sex and social status show little impact of the drug on any type of intruder (animals that are vigorously attacked by untreated subjects). Alcohol apparently, however, makes residents of colonies more likely to attack members of their own group (especially females). One could argue that such a drug action is evidence that treated rats also fail to produce *appropriate* responses.

I have argued (Brain, 1986b) that any drug can exert (directly or indirectly) effects on social interactions by influencing at least three subprocesses (see Figure 2). Alcohol is no exception and can have an impact on social disorder by altering:

a) 'motivational' processes (changing internal factors which increase or reduce the *probability* of producing particular behavior in a defined situation);
b) the perception of social cues from the environment and from other individuals;
c) the production of 'social cues' that are passed between individuals.

CONCLUSION

Naturally, one has to consider the possibility that in a public situation, *all* these changes occur in several interacting individuals as well as dealing with the fact that people will make varied evaluations of the 'appropriateness' of the viewed behavior. Although we have tended to assume that alcohol ingestion creates problems via changing motivation 'a', relatively little consideration has to be directed to the impact of the drug on the production of and detection of social signals (which are harder to investigate). One might also add that alcohol (via its effects on the brain) can obviously change how an individual evaluates the varied data received and computes 'appropriate' responses. I hope, however, it is obvious from my account that alcohol has an extremely complex influence on human social behavior, suggesting that, at least some examples of its effects on public disorder, are expressed by impairing effective social dialogue rather than by influencing 'aggression circuits'. Abolishing alcohol will not abolish 'hostility'. We should, however, recognize that excessive ingestion of alcohol can make normal social interactions exceedingly difficult. It is this aspect of alcohol's actions that should receive more attention. It would be unremarkable if some effects of other, more specific, drugs also had actions via these routes.

REFERENCES

Blanchard, R. J. & Blanchard, D. C. (1987). The relationship between ethanol and aggression; studies using ethological models. In B. Olivier, J. Mos & P. F. Brain (Eds.), *Ethopharmacology of Agonistic Behavior in Animals and Humans*, pp. 145-161. Martinus Nijhoff, Dordrecht.

Brain, P. F. (1984). Biological explanations of human aggression and the resulting therapies offered by such approaches: A critical evaluation. In R. J. Blanchard & D. C. Blanchard (Eds.), *Advances in the Study of Aggression, Volume 1*, pp. 63-102. Academic Press: New York.

Brain, P. F. (1986a). *Alcohol and Aggression*, Croom-Helm, Beckenham, Kent.

Brain, P. F. (1986b). Multidisciplinary examinations of the 'causes' of crime: The case of the link between alcohol and violence. *Alcohol and Alcoholism, 21*, 237-240.

Brain, P. F. (1990a). *Mindless Violence? The Nature and Biology of Aggression*, University College of Swansea, Swansea, U.K.

Brain, P. F. (1990b). Hormonal aspects of aggression. Paper presented at *Symposium on the Understanding and Control of Violent Behavior* (Destin, Florida. April 1-4).

Brain, P. F., Miras, R. L. & Berry, M. S. (1993). Diversity of animal models of aggression: Their impact on the putative alcohol/aggression link. *Journal of Studies on Alcohol.* Supplement 11: 140-145.

Miczek, K. A., DeBold, J. F., Haney, M., Tidey, J., Vivian, J. & Weerts, E. M. (1990). Alcohol, drugs of abuse and violence. Paper presented at *Symposium on the Understanding and Control of Violent Behavior* (Destin, Florida April 1-4).

PART II

DEVELOPMENTAL INFLUENCES ON AGGRESSION

CHAPTER 5

LEARNING AGGRESSION FROM MODELS: FROM A SOCIAL LEARNING TOWARD A COGNITIVE THEORY OF MODELING

KAJ BJÖRKQVIST

INTRODUCTION

It is a well-established fact that the level of aggressiveness of children tends to correlate with that of their parents. For instance, Huesmann et al. (1984) found clearly significant correlations, in their longitudinal study stretching over two generations. Although a hereditary factor cannot be strictly ruled out, such findings suggest that if one wishes to understand the origins and patterns of human aggression, it is of utmost importance to devote more research to the issue of how aggressive behavioral patterns are established and transmitted within the home. The question of how mothers and fathers serve as models thus becomes a vital focal point.

KAJ BJÖRKQVIST • Department of Psychology, Abo Akademi University, 65100 Vasa, Finland.

Aggression: Biological, Developmental, and Social Perspectives, edited by Seymour Feshbach and Jolanta Zagrodzka. Plenum Press, New York, 1997.

The present study investigates the modeling effect of fathers and mothers on the aggressive patterns of, on one hand, their sons, and, on the other hand, their daughters. As a background for the study, the author takes the opportunity to discuss the social learning theory of modeling, and its shortcomings.

THE SHORTCOMINGS OF TRADITIONAL SOCIAL LEARNING THEORY

Miller and Dollard (1941) were the first to present a fully fledged theory explaining why and how learning from models occurs. In their classic work *Social Learning and Imitation*, the authors attempted to link modeling to the general framework of behaviorist theory, the dominant school of thought at that period of time. According to them, modeling is the same as *vicarious conditioning*: an individual imitates a model only if the model is successful in reaching his/her goals with the behavior in question (i.e. positive vicarious reinforcement).

This proposition was perfectly in line with the general thinking of the behaviorist movement: all learning processes were regarded as caused by reinforcement due to reward and punishment, and, accordingly, modeling was seen as vicarious conditioning.

The most influential theoretician on modeling is undoubtedly Bandura. In 1963, he and his colleagues described how children mimicked the aggressive behavior of film models (Bandura, Ross and Ross, 1963a, 1963b). Bandura presents his theory in full in *Aggression: A Social Learning Analysis* (Bandura, 1973). It is noteworthy that while vicarious reinforcement is discussed in considerable detail (*ibid.*, pp. 202-207), the degree of identification between imitator (learner) and model is not mentioned at all: The subject index lists the Freudian notion of "identification with the aggressor" (i.e. a specific defense mechanism), a different field of interest altogether (the truth of which he wisely disagrees with; Bandura, 1973, pp. 86-89). Although identification is mentioned briefly in another context (*ibid.*, p. 67), it is obvious that Bandura did not consider it to be a factor of great importance in the modeling process. This is puzzling, since Bandura and Huston (1961) in fact made a study on the effect of identification as a mediator in the process of incidental learning. His theory, stressing vicarious reinforcement, is clearly an extension of the Miller-Dollard (1941) theory, and well-anchored in the behaviorist "reward-and-punishment" paradigm.

The present author does not suggest that the principle of vicarious conditioning is incorrect, only that it is insufficient: that one particular principle alone is not enough to explain imitation of models, and it has been overemphasized in the theory of modeling hitherto. As the Bandura and Huston (1961) study reveals, Bandura certainly must have realized that other principles besides whether the model is successful or not also play a role: for some reason or another, he chose to neglect the implications of this fact in his theoretical discussion, focusing on vicarious reinforcement instead, in an attempt to limit the principles of modeling to one only. Social learning theory should be extended to encompass other principles.

In Björkqvist and Österman (1992), the authors indicate that some of their results on parental influence on children's aggressiveness *cannot be explained in terms of vicarious conditioning only*. In real life, goals are not necessarily achieved by aggressive means, and, if the vicarious reinforcement hypothesis is correct, modeling ought not to occur in such cases, i.e. when the model does not achieve goals by his or her aggressiveness.

Fraczek (1989) coined the term *habitual aggression* to describe hostile actions that do not arise from frustration, and which are unconnected with the purpose of attaining specific goals or rewards. As pointed out by him, individuals may be habitually aggressive although their aggressiveness actually is a hindrance to rather than promoting goal achievement. If a child is exposed only to aggressive models, how can that child ever learn nonaggressive conflict resolution strategies? That is, the *amount of exposure* to a certain model situation may be more crucial than whether the model is successful or not.

Huesmann and Eron (1988) suggest that what children actually learn from models are *cognitive scripts*, which become strengthened by rehearsal in different forms: repeated observation of live models, viewing of violent films, and mental rehearsal in the children's fantasy.

FOUR CENTRAL MODELING FACTORS

The present author suggests that at least four factors are important as far as imitation of models is concerned (the given order should not be understood to imply order of importance):

1. the degree of similarity between the model situation and the actual situation,
2. identification with the model in question,
3. whether the model is successful or not (vicarious reinforcement), and
4. the amount of exposure to the model situation in question.

The reader may notice a similarity between factors 3 and 4 and the *Law of Effect* and the *Law of Experience*, as described already by the associationist Thorndike (1898), in his early work on animal learning and intelligence. Evidence for the importance of the degree of *similarity* between model and actual situation was found already in studies carried out during the 60's on the "cue" effect, by Berkowitz and his colleagues (e.g. Berkowitz and Geen, 1966, 1967; Berkowitz and LePage, 1967). The impact of each factor is likely to vary from case to case and from one situation to another, and their relative importance should offer splendid possibilities for elegant designs in laboratory experiments, for the mind bent on such enterprises.

The following discussion focuses on the importance of only one of these four factors, namely identification. If an individual does not identify with a model, she or he is not likely to incorporate the behavioral patterns of the model into her or his own repertoire, even if the amount of exposure is quite extensive (provided that the imitator has been exposed to alternative scripts, offering a choice). In Björkqvist and Österman (1992), it was found that when the emotional relationship between physically aggressive fathers and their sons was very negative, the level of aggressiveness (measured with the inventory by Buss and Durkee, 1957) of the sons was *lower* than that of boys who had a good emotional relationship with physically aggressive fathers. Thus, it would seem that identification served as a mediating variable.

The assignment of importance to identification in the modeling process is not new per se; e.g., Huesmann and Eron (1988) found identification with TV models to be an important predictor of aggressiveness, and suggested that if children like and identify with aggressive models, they rehearse "aggressive scripts" in their own minds, thereby strengthening the tendency to behave in a similar manner. Identification with models could be interpreted in behaviorist terms as a kind of secondary reinforcement: if the observer has an affectionate bond to the model, this will predispose the person to imitate the behavior of the model for the satisfaction this will provide. This is possible, perhaps even likely (although difficult to prove), and it may certainly be part of the truth. However, it cannot explain habitual aggression, when the observer imitates negative behavioral patterns of a model whom he or she does not even like. If the amount of exposure is overwhelming, the observer has not been able to integrate alternative scripts.

In critical, stressful situations, when an individual is highly activated in physiological terms, he or she is likely to react on a "gut" feeling, relying on the first behavioral script coming to mind. This may well be an aggressive script—which the individual normally would not use— adapted from a violent film or any other model situation, provided that a firm enough association to this particular script has been created. In order to understand why a particular script is being chosen, the impact of the four factors mentioned has to be weighted against each other.

Whether an innate aspect of modeling, a drive to imitate, exists or not is difficult to prove. However, the purpose of this discussion is to analyze *how* modeling occurs, rather than *why*.

In the following, the term *cognitive modeling* will be used as a denotation of the hypothesis put forward here. As a theory of learning, this view is linked to the framework of cognitive psychology, rather than to the behaviorist tradition, as Bandura's social learning theory in fact is. It is somewhat closer to the pre-behaviorist, associationist tradition of Thorndike: observational learning takes place when associations are being strengthened. Accordingly, everything that strengthens associations—similarity, amount of exposure, and identification, *as well as* reward and punishment—is likely to affect imitation. Thorndike's original view attempted to explain only animal learning, and in mechanistic terms, while the modern associationist view on human learning is a kind of cognitive theory: associations are mentally formed and affected by attributions made by the observer. As far as modeling is concerned, the observer learns scripts of behavior (Schank and Abelson, 1977) and applies them in situations where he or she attributes them to be appropriate.

THE PRESENT STUDY

The purpose of the study presented below was to investigate the extent to which adolescents of both sexes imitate their parents' patterns of behavior when they are angry, both at home and with their peers. The study was conducted within the general theoretical framework presented above. It was not designated, however, to be a test of the cognitive modeling hypothesis as such.

In a previous study (Björkqvist and Österman, 1992), parental influence on aggressiveness was investigated with a sample of adolescents as subjects. It was found that parental influence could be explained by two mechanisms: (1) an emotionally frustrating home atmosphere, in accordance with the frustration-aggression hypothesis (Dollard *et al.*, 1939, Miller, 1941), and (2) modeling. The results indicated that identification was an important factor in the modeling process, which paved way for the cognitive modeling hypothesis mentioned above.

In order to avoid possible age specific artifacts, four age groups of adolescents (11, 13, 15, and 17 years of age) were used as subjects in the present study. They were presented with the *Anger Scale* (Björkqvist and Österman, 1992), which was constructed for the specific purpose of investigating the modeling process in aggressive behavior. There are three versions of the Anger Scale: the Mother, Father, and Self Versions.

In the Mother Version, subjects are asked, "What does your mother do when she gets angry?" The children are presented with aggressive and nonaggressive alternatives, and they make estimations of the extent to which their mothers behave in the manner suggested by the scale items. They assess the behavioral patterns of their fathers when angry, as well as of themselves, in a similar fashion. It is thus possible to examine the situations and extent to which the subjects use the same methods as their parents.

The study was explorative, comparing the modeling effect of mothers with that of fathers, on adolescents of both sexes, and in two types of environment: at home, and with peers. The help of Karin Österman and my students Carina Hagqvist and Anette Hagström in the collection of data is gratefully acknowledged.

METHOD

SUBJECTS

The original sample consisted of 404 randomly sampled adolescents from Kokkola, Finland. In order to limit the subjects to those with both their mother and their father living with them, single-parent families were excluded, thereby reducing the sample to 369 subjects. Their distribution according to age group and sex is presented in Table 1. Fifty-five percent of the subjects of the oldest age group (about 17 years of age) were junior high school students, and 45% attended vocational schools. This distribution is quite representative for adolescents of this particular town.

TABLE 1. The Distribution According to Age and Sex in the Four Age Groups

Age group	Mean age (sd)	N of Girls	N of Boys
I	11.5 (0.50)	31	50
II	13.5 (0.50)	66	43
III	15.4 (0.52)	40	57
IV	17.6 (0.63)	40	42
Total	14.6 (2.22)	177	192

THE ANGER SCALE

The Anger Scale was adapted from Björkqvist and Österman (1992). Subjects assess what they and their parents do when they are angry, on a five-point scale, ranging from 0 (never) to 4 (very often). There is a Mother Version, a Father Version, and a Self Version of the test. In the Self Version, the subjects were requested to evaluate how they themselves behave when they are angry, in two different situations: at home and with their peers. The items of the Mother Version were as follows: (1) "She shouts at the person she is angry with", (2) "she does not want to see the person", (3) "she explains why she is angry", (4) "she threatens the person", (5) "she hits the person", (6) "she pulls the person's hair", (7) "she teases the person", (8) "she treats the other person as if (s)he didn't exist".

The Father and the Self Versions consisted of items describing exactly the same types of behavior, but phrased as answers to the questions, "what does your father do when he gets angry?", and "what do you do when you get angry?" ("at home?"—"with your friends?").

It is important to note that the items were aimed at mapping varied, not similar, types of behavior, and therefore included non-aggressive as well as aggressive behaviors. Thus, measurement of internal consistency (Cronbach's a) of the instrument would be meaningless.

RESULTS

The data were analyzed by means of item-wise multiple regressions, in which parental behaviors (e.g., "mother hits", "father hits") served as predictors (independent) variables, and the subjects' own behavior ("I hit") as predicted (dependent) variables. In this way, it was possible to analyze not only whether parental behavior predicted (i.e., served as a model for) the subjects' own behavior, but also which parent—mother or father—was imitated more, according to subjects' evaluations. The results are presented in Tables 2-5. Since differences between the different age groups did not appear to a greater extent, the results of all four cohorts are combined.

Table 2 presents the extent to which mothers' and fathers' behavior when angry predicts the behavior of adolescent girls when they get angry at home. The table indicates that modeling occurs, and girls appear to imitate their mothers and their fathers to an equal extent in the home environment. This is true for both aggressive and nonaggressive behaviors (e.g., "I explain why I'm angry"). While some types of behavior ("I shout at the person I'm angry with", and "I do not want to see the person") are

TABLE 2. Item-wise Multiple Regressions, Predicted Variable: Girls' Behavior When Angry at Home

Predicted Predictors	R	R^2	B	(SeB)	b	t	p <
"I shout at the person I'm angry with"	.47	.22					
Mother shouts			.20	(.08)	.20	2.64	.01
Father shouts			.30	(.07)	.33	4.16	.001
"I don't want to see the person I'm angry with"	.46	.21					
Mother doesn't want to see			.23	(.11)	.16	2.03	.05
Father doesn't want to see			.58	(.13)	.36	4.60	.001
"I explain why I'm angry"	.51	.26					
Mother explains			.28	(.08)	.28	3.57	.001
Father explains			.25	(.07)	.29	3.70	.001
"I threaten the person I'm angry with"	.42	.18					
Mother threatens			.42	(.08)	.43	5.54	.001
Father threatens			-.03	(.08)	-.03	-.34	n.s.
"I hit the person I'm angry with"	.26	.07					
Mother hits			.23	(.16)	.13	1.41	n.s.
Father hits			.27	(.15)	.16	1.78	.10
"I pull the person's hair"	.38	.14					
Mother pulls the hair			.26	(.11)	.22	2.47	.05
Father pulls the hair			.24	(.11)	.20	2.24	.05
"I tease the person I'm angry with"	.36	.13					
Mother teases			.28	(.10)	.26	2.72	.01
Father teases			.14	(.10)	.13	1.36	n.s.
"I treat the other person as if (s)he didn't exist"	.46	.22					
Mother treats as if . . .			.38	(.10)	.28	3.76	.001
Father treats as if . . .			.33	(.09)	.27	3.61	.001

predicted somewhat better from the father's behavior, others ("I threaten" and "I tease") are predicted better from the mother's behavior.

Table 3 presents the extent to which the behavior of adolescent boys, when angry at home, is predicted by the behavior of their parents. The picture is very different from the one presented in Table 2. Four items ("I do not want to see the person", "I hit", "I tease", and "I treat the person as if (s)he does not exist") are predicted better from the father's behavior, and two items ("I shout at the person", and "I explain why

TABLE 3. Item-wise Multiple Regressions, Predicted Variable: Boys' Behavior When Angry at Home

Predicted Predictors	R	R²	B	(SeB)	b	t	p <
"I shout at the person I'm angry with"	.49	.24					
Mother shouts			.26	(.08)	.25	3.32	.001
Father shouts			.32	(.08)	.32	4.18	.001
"I don't want to see the person I'm angry with"	.33	.11					
Mother doesn't want to see			.13	(.08)	.12	1.53	n.s.
Father doesn't want to see			.36	(.11)	.26	3.38	.001
"I explain why I'm angry"	.52	.28					
Mother explains			.28	(.08)	.28	3.54	.001
Father explains			.30	(.08)	.31	3.93	.001
"I threaten the person I'm angry with"	.34	.11					
Mother threatens			.20	(.09)	.20	2.31	.05
Father threatens			.20	(.09)	.18	2.17	.05
"I hit the person I'm angry with"	.33	.11					
Mother hits			.11	(.11)	.08	.98	n.s.
Father hits			.49	(.13)	.29	3.71	.001
"I pull the person's hair"	.22	.05					
Mother pulls the hair			.27	(.11)	.21	2.40	.05
Father pulls the hair			.02	(.12)	.02	.17	n.s.
"I tease the person I'm angry with"	.38	.15					
Mother teases			.20	(.10)	.15	2.04	.05
Father teases			.39	(.10)	.30	4.02	.001
"I treat the other person as if (s)he didn't exist"	.44	.19					
Mother treats as if ...			.22	(.10)	.17	2.17	.05
Father treats as if ...			.49	(.12)	.32	4.10	.001

I'm angry") are predicted equally well from the behavior of both parents. Only one item ("I pull the person's hair") is predicted better from the behavior of the mother. It appears, therefore, that adolescent boys, when angry at home, imitate their fathers more than they imitate their mothers.

Table 4 presents the extent to which adolescent girls' behavior, when angry with their peers, is predicted by the behavior of their parents. The result is astonishing: The fathers' behavior does not contribute to the prediction of the girls' behavior at all. Mothers, on the other hand, seem

TABLE 4. Item-wise Multiple Regressions, Predicted Variable: Girls' Behavior When Angry at Their Peers

Predicted Predictors	R	R²	B	(SeB)	b	t	p <
"I shout at the person I'm angry with"	.23	.05					
Mother shouts			.15	(.08)	.18	2.02	.05
Father shouts			.06	(.07)	.08	.91	n.s.
"I don't want to see the person I'm angry with"	.22	.05					
Mother doesn't want to see			.21	(.08)	.22	2.47	.05
Father doesn't want to see			.00	(.10)	.00	.05	n.s.
"I explain why I'm angry"	.40	.16					
Mother explains			.28	(.08)	.30	3.50	.001
Father explains			.12	(.07)	.14	1.69	.10
"I threaten the person I'm angry with"	.42	.18					
Mother threatens			.26	(.05)	.38	4.86	.001
Father threatens			.06	(.05)	.09	1.11	n.s.
"I hit the person I'm angry with"	.26	.07					
Mother hits			.33	(.10)	.30	3.25	.001
Father hits			-.10	(.10)	-.09	-.99	n.s.
"I pull the person's hair"	.23	.05					
Mother pulls the hair			.21	(.07)	.27	2.96	.01
Father pulls the hair			-.07	(.07)	-.09	-.94	n.s.
"I tease the person I'm angry with"	.20	.04					
Mother teases			.12	(.10)	.12	1.71	n.s.
Father teases			.11	(.10)	.11	1.08	n.s.
"I treat the other person as if (s)he didn't exist"	.24	.06					
Mother treats as if ...			.25	(.11)	.18	2.21	.05
Father treats as if ...			.12	(.10)	.09	1.13	n.s.

to have a strong modeling effect, as revealed by significant regression coefficients on seven of the nine items.

Table 5, which presents the behavior of adolescent boys when angry with their peers, reveals a very similar picture. Mothers appeared to be imitated on six of the nine items, while only one type of behavior, a nonaggressive item ("I explain why I'm angry") is predicted equally well by the behavior of the fathers.

TABLE 5. Item-wise Multiple Regressions, Predicted Variable: Boys' Behavior When Angry at Their Peers

Predicted Predictors	R	R^2	B	(SeB)	b	t	p <
"I shout at the person I'm angry with"	.31	.10					
Mother shouts			.24	(.08)	.25	3.06	.01
Father shouts			.08	(.08)	.09	1.10	n.s.
"I don't want to see the person I'm angry with"	.42	17					
Mother doesn't want to see			.41	(.07)	.42	5.53	.001
Father doesn't want to see			.04	(.09)	.03	.05	n.s.
"I explain why I'm angry"	.46	.21					
Mother explains			.25	(.08)	.26	3.14	.01
Father explains			.25	(.08)	.26	3.18	.01
"I threaten the person I'm angry with"	.31	.10					
Mother threatens			.21	(.08)	.23	2.66	.01
Father threatens			.12	(.08)	.12	1.36	n.s.
"I hit the person I'm angry with"	.25	.06					
Mother hits			.40	(.12)	.25	3.18	.01
Father hits			−.03	(.14)	−.02	−.21	n.s.
"I pull the person's hair"	.22	.05					
Mother pulls the hair			.30	(.12)	.21	2.44	.05
Father pulls the hair			.01	(.12)	.00	.05	n.s.
"I tease the person I'm angry with"	.17	.03					
Mother teases			.17	(.10)	.13	1.65	n.s.
Father teases			.10	(.10)	.08	.94	n.s.
"I treat the other person as if (s)he didn't exist"	.20	.04					
Mother treats as if ...			.14	(.11)	.11	1.28	n.s.
Father treats as if ...			.17	(.12)	.12	1.40	n.s.

DISCUSSION

To summarize the results: first, regardless of sex, adolescents tend to imitate mothers more when angry with their peers, while the impact of the fathers is enhanced when they are angry at home. Second, it is evident that the modeling effect of the same-sex parent is relatively stronger than the effect of the parent of the other sex, indicating identification with the same-sex parent. Mothers do, however, have an overall greater impact than fathers. A result of the amount of exposure?

Adolescent boys tend to imitate the aggressive behavior of their fathers more than that of their mothers at home, while they imitate their mothers to a greater extent when angry with their peers. Adolescent girls, on the other hand, imitate their·fathers and their mothers equally much when angry at home, while with their peers, they imitate their mothers more than·boys do.

The reason why both girls and (especially) boys imitate their mothers more than their fathers when angry with their peers is not clear. The result is so consistent, however, that it is difficult to conceive of it as an artifact. Is the aggressive behavior of fathers regarded by the children as more appropriate in the home environment than with peers?

A limitation of the study is the fact that the aggressive behavior of the adolescents—both at home and with their peers—was measured by self-estimation, while estimations of the parents' behavior was made by the children. Since aggressive behavior is usually condemned by social norms, peer estimation techniques are considered more reliable instruments for the measurement of aggression (cf., e.g., Lefkowitz et al., 1977; Olweus, 1980; Huesmann and Eron, 1986; Huesmann et al., 1987; Lagerspetz et al., 1988). If it were easier for adolescents to admit being aggressive at home than to admit being aggressive with their peers, the results may have been distorted by an attitudinal difference: the self reports of their behavior at home could be trusted, but not their reports about aggressive behavior directed towards friends. It appears unlikely, however, that the findings of this study are attributable to such an attitudinal difference, the existence of which is uncertain in the first place. It would not, in any case, explain why significant predictions are obtained more from mothers' than from fathers' aggressive patterns, in the case of conflicts with peers. Further research is needed to illuminate these questions.

Another limitation is that the present study was conducted with Finnish adolescents as subjects. Wide variation with respect to aggressive styles is known to exist in different cultures, especially in regard to sex (Björkqvist, 1994; Björkqvist and Niemelä, 1992; Burbank, 1987; Österman et al., 1994). In Finland, the results were consistent in four age groups of adolescents. Replications in other countries would reveal the extent to which these findings are cross-culturally valid.

REFERENCES

Bandura, A. (1973). *Aggression: A Social Learning Analysis.* Englewood Cliffs, NJ: Prentice-Hall.

Bandura, A., & Huston, A. C. (1961). Identification as a process of incidental learning. *Journal of Abnormal and Social Psychology, 63,* 311-318.

Bandura, A., Ross, D., & Ross, S. A. (1963). Transmission of aggression through imitation of aggressive models. *Journal of Abnormal and Social Psychology, 63,* 575-582.

Bandura, A., Ross, D., & Ross, S. A. (1963b). Vicarious reinforcement and imitative learning. *Journal of Abnormal and Social Psychology, 67,* 601-607.

Berkowitz, L., & Geen, R. G. (1966). Film violence and the cue properties of available targets. *Journal of Personality and Social Psychology, 3,* 525-530.

Berkowitz, L., & Geen, R. G. (1967). Stimulus qualities of the target of aggression: A further study. *Journal of Personality and Social Psychology, 5,* 364-368.

Berkowitz, L., & LePage, A. (1967). Weapons as aggression-eliciting stimuli. *Journal of Personality and Social Psychology, 7,* 202-207.

Björkqvist, K. (1994). Sex differences in physical, verbal, and indirect aggression: A review of recent research. *Sex Roles, 30,* 177-184.

Björkqvist, K., & Niemelä, P. (Eds.)(1992). *Of Mice and Women: Aspects of Female Aggression.* San Diego, CA: Academic Press.

Björkqvist, K., & Österman, K. (1992). Parental influence on children's self-estimated aggressiveness. *Aggressive Behavior, 18,* 411-423.

Burbank, V. K. (1987). Female aggression in cross-cultural perspective. *Behavior Science Research, 21,* 70-100.

Buss, A., & Durkee, A. (1957). An inventory for assessing different kinds of hostility. *Journal of Consulting Psychology, 21,* 343-349.

Dollard, J., Doob, L. W., Miller, N. E., Mowrer, O. H., & Sears, R. R. (1939). *Frustration and Aggression.* New Haven, CN: Yale University Press.

Fraczek, A. (1989). Categories of aggression. Communication at The Polish-Finnish Symposium on Aggression in Jablona, Poland, 16-18 Nov.

Huesmann, L. R., & Eron, L. D. (Eds.) (1986). *Television and the Aggressive Child: A Cross-National Comparison.* Hillsdale, NJ: Lawrence Erlbaum.

Huesmann, L. R., Eron, L. D., Lefkowitz, M. M., & Walder, L. O. (1984). Stability of aggression over time and generations. *Developmental Psychology , 20,* 722-736.

Lagerspetz, K. M. J., Björkqvist, K., & Peltonen, T. (1988). Is indirect aggression typical of females? Gender differences in aggressiveness in 11- to 12-year-old children. *Aggressive Behavior, 14,* 403-414.

Lefkowitz, M. M., Eron, L. D., Walder, L. O., & Huesmann, L. R. (1977). *Growing Up to be Violent. A Longitudinal Study of the Development of Aggression.* New York, NY: Pergamon.

Miller, N. E. (1941). The frustration-aggression hypothesis. *Psychological Review, 48,* 337-342.

Miller, N. E., & Dollard, J. (1941). *Social Learning and Imitation.* New Haven, CN: Yale.

Olweus, D. (1980). Familial and temperamental determinants of aggressive behavior in adolescent boys: A causal analysis. *Developmental Psychology, 16,* 644-660.

Österman, K., Björkqvist, K., Lagerspetz, K. M. J., Kaukiainen, A., Huesmann, L. R., & Fraczek, A. (1994). Peer and self-estimated aggression and victimization in 8-year-old children from five ethnic groups. *Aggressive Behavior, 20,* 41-428.

Schank, R., & Abelson, R. (1977). *Scripts, Plans, Goals and Understanding: An Inquiry into Human Knowledge.* Hillsdale, NJ: Lawrence Erlbaum.

Thorndike, E. L. (1898). Animal intelligence. *Psychological Monographs, 1*(8).

CHAPTER 6

ATTITUDES TOWARD VIOLENCE AND THE DIRECTION OF THE DEVELOPMENT OF A CHILD'S AGGRESSION

Lucyna Kirwil

INTRODUCTION

According to a system theory (Bell & Harper, 1977), socialization in the family is the process by which the range of permitted behavior manifested by parents and by a child is maintained. As part of the process, each party (i.e., the parents and the child) allows the other, behavior of a certain range of intensity, frequency, and situational appropriateness. If the range in question is exceeded, the party determining this takes action aimed at ensuring that the other party acts in a way that falls within the defined range. For the parents, the range is defined by an uppermost behavioral limit (in terms of intensity and/or frequency) that they are in a position to tolerate from the child.

Lucyna Kirwil • Institute of Social Prevention and Resocialization, University of Warsaw, 20 Podchorazych St., 03420 Warsaw, Poland.

Aggression: Biological, Developmental, and Social Perspectives, edited by Seymour Feshbach and Jolanta Zagrodzka. Plenum Press, New York, 1997.

As Grusec and Kuczynski (1980) say, the behaviors tolerated by parents in a particular field include aggressive behavior among various manifestations of disobedience. If the upper limit of permissiveness is exceeded, the parents will begin to exert an influence on the child in order that the intensity of the child's behavior be reduced. In contrast, parents may seek to intensify the behavior of a child who passes below the lower limit of what is permitted, for example by behaving in a manner that they consider insufficiently aggressive.

Thus, in accordance with the claims of the aforementioned theory, parents have a defined range of permissiveness towards aggression in their children which may be assumed to be linked to the parents' own attitude to the use of violence. If the aggressive behavior of the child lies outside the parental range of permissiveness towards aggression, then the parents seek to match the child's behavior to the standards maintained by applying a range of socializational measures, namely: punishments or rewards, and the provision of formulae for behavior or else information on the norms bearing on the aggressive behavior.

In turn, through his or her behaviors and properties, a child defines the range of behaviors (socializational measures) of his or her parents. It emerges, for example, that the parents of aggressive children are more likely to tolerate aggression from their children than are the parents of non-aggressive children (Olweus, 1980; Maccoby & Martin, 1983). The process by which a balance is obtained between the range of parental permissiveness and the behavior of the child requires considerable *socializational flexibility*—i.e., flexible reactions from parents to the behavior of the child and to other changes arising in the family.

The results of several studies (Bell & Harper, 1977; Parke, 1978; Patterson, 1982) on the socializational correlates of the development of a child's behavior, allow it to be assumed that socializational flexibility is a function of features of an external system in relation to the parent-child system—i.e., that of *the family as a whole*—and of *the parent-child system* itself, as well as of features of the system in the family associated with the use of violence, which will be referred to in what follows as *the violence system*.

It may be thus assumed that greater socializational flexibility is conditioned by such properties characterizing the functioning of a whole family as: a higher level of education among parents, higher (but not extreme) cohesion, non-rigid organization of family life and positive communication, as well as such properties of the parent-child system as: the expectation of self-guidance from the child, the discerning assessment of the child's behavior, the use of egalitarian, supportive, and confronting techniques in upbringing, and the cognitive coping with the problems of bringing up a child. Finally, socializational flexibility should be linked to such properties of the violence system in families as the application by parents of the so-called "persuasive disciplinary techniques" (Bandura & Walters, 1959), as opposed to the technique of scolding and hitting (cf. Patterson, 1982) characterized by rigidity of reaction, as well as to the complexity of the norms (as opposed to univocality of norms including absolute prohibitions), which are conveyed to the child in relation to aggressive behavior.

According to the aforementioned system theory of development (Bell & Harper, 1977), socializational measures are only undertaken by parents when the behavior of the child does not accord with the permitted range, i.e., in the case of aggression in situations when the parents do not approve of the use of violence and the child displays aggressive behavior, or else at a time when the use of violence is approved of, but the child behaves in a non-aggressive way. Both of these combinations represent points of entry for the construction of a model for the socialization of a child's aggression in the family, which accords with the assumptions of the system theory of behavioral development presented in Table 1 in the two columns on the left.

TABLE 1. A Model of the Relationship between the Violence Approval, a Child's Level of Aggressiveness and Socializational Flexibility in the Family Environment, and Direction of Development in Child's Behavior

Attitudes towards violence in the child's family	Aggressiveness of the child	Socializational flexibility of the family	Effect on the behavior-direction of development of child's aggression
Violence is not approved of	High	Low	Path 1: HIGH AGGRESSION
		High	Path 2: AGGRESSION DECLINES
Violence is approved of	Low	Low	Path 3: LOW AGGRESSION
		High	Path 4: AGGRESSION INCREASES (DEVELOPS)

According to the model presented, the effect—in the form of the direction of development of a child's aggression—is related to whether or not violence is approved of in the family environment, to the initial level of aggressiveness of the child, and to whether or not the family environment is characterized by socializational flexibility. It may be expected that:

1. If the parents do not approve of violence, children displaying earlier high aggression still manifest it where socializational flexibility is lacking (Path 1 in the model), or manifest lower aggression in conditions where socializational flexibility is present (Path 2 in the model);
2. If the parents approve of violence, children displaying earlier low aggression remain low in aggressive behavior where socializational flexibility is lacking (Path 3), but become highly aggressive if such conditions are present (Path 4).

The theoretical hypotheses formulated are concerned with change versus stability in level of aggression displayed by the child in relation to the determinants of socializational flexibility in both cases of non-concordance. Not taken into account here are such combinations of concordance between the behavior of the child and attitudes of the parents as: approval of violence and initial aggression in a child, or disapproval of violence and non-aggression in a child. These can be easily explained in terms of the theory of social learning (Bandura, 1977; Bronfenbrenner, 1970).

Of particular interest are the situations posed by families where the parents approve of violence and the children are initially unaggressive and where the parents disapprove of violence and the children are initially aggressive. Positive verification of the formulated theoretical hypotheses would allow for at least a partial explanation of why some children of aggressive parents remain non-aggressive, while some children of non-aggressive parents become aggressive. This problem is of significance in the process of resocializing aggressive children, and particular interest may be attached to the grasping of differences in a social context which arise between children of growing aggressiveness and those of disappearing (or declining) aggressiveness. In order to account for the developmental changes in a child's level of aggression where there is non-concordant relationship between parental attitudes and the child's initial aggression, we find the construct of socializational flexibility to be meaningful and helpful.

According to the theory described at the outset, children of increasing aggressiveness are derived from initially non-aggressive children in an environment in which violence is approved of, and in which there is a high level of socializational flexibility. In turn, children of declining aggressiveness are derived from those initially displaying the trait in an environment in which violence is not approved of, and in which socializational flexibility is either lacking or limited.

The aim of the research undertaken was to establish the constellation of different socializational factors which determined socializational flexibility in four groups of children selected in accordance with the criterion of the approval or disapproval of violence in the family environment, as well as the four combinations made up of the degree of aggressiveness displayed by children at the outset of the work and after a two-and-a-half year interval.

The combinations of children's aggressiveness degree—initially and after 2.5 years—allowed for the identification of those maintaining a sustained level of aggressiveness, those of declining aggressiveness, those remaining non-aggressive and those becoming increasingly aggressive.

METHOD

Subjects and Groups Studied

Four-hundred fifty-two children (252 boys and 200 girls) were studied at the outset and a second study was carried out with them after 2.5 years had passed. The age range of the children in the first study was 8-12 years. Measurement among the studied children's parents (300 mothers and 292 fathers) was carried out once.

The criteria for the selection of groups were the level of violence approval in the studied child's family and the levels of aggressiveness of the child during the first measurement and the second measurement.

The level of violence approval in the family of the tested child was established on the basis of measurement with violence approval scale described in an earlier work (Kirwil, 1988). The whole sample of parents was divided into two sub-samples using a median-split of the score on that scale.

Both measurements of *the intensity of the child's aggressiveness* were carried out with the version of the peer-nomination technique used previously by Huesmann & Eron (1986), as well as Fraczek (1986). The instrument was reliable: coefficient alpha was equal to .88 in the first measurement and .90 in the second one. Account was taken of the two measurements of the intensity of interpersonal aggressiveness of the children, and the following four groups were selected:

1. sustainedly aggressive (AA)—index from both measurements above the arithmetic mean;
2. decreasingly aggressive (AN)—index from the first measurement above zero and that from the second equal to zero, or index from the second measurement in comparison to the first measurement smaller by at least one standard deviation;
3. sustainedly non-aggressive (NN)—index from both measurements equal to zero;
4. increasingly aggressive (NA)—index from the first measurement equal to zero 0, index from the second one above zero.

Groups AA and AN did not differed significantly on level of aggression in the first measurement, however group AA was slightly higher in the raw score.

To consider only the non-concordant situations referred to above, the first and second groups retained those children whose families had indices of violence approval lower than the median, while the third and fourth groups were left with those children whose families had indexes for the approval of violence that were higher than the median.

The number of children in the groups so-selected was very variable:

1. in the group AA: 13 with data from mothers, 12 with data from fathers;
2. in the group AN: 50 with data from mothers, 42 with data from fathers;
3. in the group NN: 45 with data from mothers, 34 with data from fathers;
4. in the group NA: 24 with data from mothers and 16 with data from fathers.

Representation of sexes in the four groups of children was proportional, with higher number of boys than girls.

VARIABLES

In the accepted paradigm of the research, the variable providing the explanation was given by combining the pattern of change in the level of a child's aggressiveness with the level of approval of violence in the child's family environment (operationalized as affiliation to one or other of the four groups mentioned above). The variables explained were the different ones describing the theoretical variable of socializational flexibility. Three groups of subvariables were distinguished within these ranges: variables characterizing the functioning of the child's whole family system, variables of the parents-child system, and variables characterizing the violence system in the family.

Approval of Violence in a Child's Family

The level of violence approval in a child's family was defined as the degree of the mother's and father's consent to a wide range of violent acts in various situations. Violence approval was measured by means of the Social Attitudes Questionnaire of Moral Approval of Aggressive Acts (Lagerspetz & Westman, 1980), adapted into Polish by Fraczek et al. (1985). The questionnaire is constructed as a list of rating scales for eight categories of violent acts (for instance, hitting somebody, killing somebody, torturing somebody, shouting at somebody). Each category of violent act was accompanied by the list of situations, circumstances, or reasons that may serve as a justification for the violent act. Six justifications were used: self-defense, defense of others, emotional excitement, punishment, defense of personal property, solving problems in communication. Each parent separately was asked to rate to what extent each act is justified under each type of justification. The answers were rated on 3-point scales, ranging from absolutely unjustified through sometimes justified to fully justified, scoring respectively 0, 1, 2. Index of violence approval in the child's family was based on the total sum for fathers and mothers divided by the number of items and two (number of parents).

Those parents whose index of violence approval was lower than 1 were qualified as disapproving violence, and those whose index was equal or above 1 were qualified as approving violence (median split).

Variables Characterizing the Functioning of the Child's Whole Family System

The degree of family cohesion was defined as the experiencing by members of the family of emotional bonds and behavioral union (Moos & Moos, 1981; Kirwil, 1993).

The degree of organization of the family was understood as the strictness of the rules for co-existence in the family and of the way in which compliance with these principles is monitored (cf. Moos & Moos, 1981; Kirwil, 1993).

The degree of positiveness of communication in the family was explained in terms of the openness and ease of understanding between family members (Olson, D. H., McCubbin, H. I., Barnes, H., Larsen, A., & Muxen, M., 1983);

Employed in the measurement of these variables was a family climate scale drawn up on the basis of the items selected from *FES* by Moos & Moos (1981), as well as from the Parents-Adolescent Communication Scale of Olson et al. (1983). The scores on each subscale ranged from 0 to 3. The reliability of the subscales of the scale constructed reflected coefficient alphas from .61 to .82.

Variables Characterizing the Parent-Child System

The measured variables were: the parents' preferences of parental values, type of upbringing, discernment in the evaluation of a child's behavior and type of strategy of coping with problems created by the child.

The degree of parents' preference of parental values: maturity, conformity, and autonomy of the child's behavior, understood in relation to the concept of Kohn (1976) and measured on a scale of 13 values with a modified responding scale (Kirwil, 1991). Factor analysis of the responses of parents indicated that—for the studied sample—*maturity* was defined by the child's ability to co-exist in accordance with society's norms, self-guidance and emotional control. *Conformity* meant child was living in accordance with the principles of good manners and social sex-roles, obedience and diligence. *Autonomy* meant the independence of a child from his/her parents. The reliability of the scales measuring these variables—separately in mothers and fathers—ranged from .75 to .88.

The type of upbringing was described by the type of parent-child interaction in upbringing evident in the style of communication, type of reaction to child's behavior and type of demands, which parent directs to the child in the process of upbringing. Three modes of upbringing were established as an outcome of factor analyses: *egalitarian-confronting, unstable-punitive,* and *with undefined requirements and avoidance of confrontation.* The egalitarian-confronting mode of upbringing considers the rights of a child to be equal and which permits discussion of matters giving rise to conflicts. The unstable-punitive mode of upbringing has been characterized by instability of parent's reactions and a tendency to punish a child. The mode of upbringing with undefined requirements and the avoidance of confrontation is characterized by conflicting requirements and a lack of discussion of matters giving rise to conflicts. Used in measurement was a technique devised by Walper and Silbereisen (1986). The reliability of the 2-3 items scales varied from .44 to .69.

Parent's discernment in the evaluation of a child's behavior was understood as the taking-into-consideration of various dimensions of evaluation, namely, the results of the child's behavior, societal norms and the child's level of self-control. Measurements were made by asking parents to respond—on a 4-degree scale of the true-false type—to a question asking if they took account of the different aspects given for a child's behavior when it came to evaluating whether or not a child was behaving in a permitted way. A higher summed index for all the aspects was indicative of a higher degree of discernment. The instrument was constructed on the basis of the questionnaire employed by Hinsch, Schneider, & Pfinsten (1983).

The strategy of coping with the problems caused by a child involved four types: *cognitive restructuring of a problem, discussion of a problem in the family, power assertion towards the child,* and *advice seeking.* Used in measurement was the scale drawn up by £apiñski (1988). The reliability of the subscales measuring the use of the different strategies varied from .50 to .75.

Variables Characterizing the Violence System in the Family

The parent's tendency to use *particular disciplinary techniques* to socialize child's aggression and the specific *norms for aggression manifestation conveyed to the child* were considered as of greatest importance among the set of variables characterizing the violence system in a child's family.

The list of *disciplinary techniques* to socialize consisted of *bans on behaviors,* the *reinforcement of alternative behavior, shame induction,* the provision of *information about the feelings of a victim, scolding, corporal punishment, TV watching prohibition,* the provision of *information about the possibilities of counter-reaction on the part of the victim,* the *ignoring of the child's behavior,* simple *request for obedience,* and *praise.* Measurements were made by asking each of the parents to define how true it was that they would react in each of the given ways. A 4-degree scale was applied in the case of four specific manifestations of aggression by the child. An overall index was calculated for all the situations. The reliability of the measure so-generated was found to vary between .66 and .84.

The *norms for aggression manifestation conveyed by parents to the child* were established with the following assumptions and measurements. The *level of complexity of the norm for aggression* which should regulate aggression manifestations was considered to be related to the level of responsibility for own behavior. The level of complexity is reflected in the description of the norms for aggression. It was assumed that a norm banning aggression without exception was not complex since different circumstances determine the degree to which society is willing to permit the use of aggression (Ferguson & Rule, 1980; Fraczek, 1985). Norms taking into account the conditions under which the behaviors mentioned might arise were termed complex. Ultimately, 7 norms were formulated in relation to the possibilities for causing pain and aggression (cf. Ferguson & Rule, 1980). The first of these prohibited such behavior without exception, while the remainder defined the various conditions under which the behaviors in question might occur. The norms were determined in accordance with the degrees of responsibility for behavior enumerated by Heider (1958). The parents had to select one norm which should direct their child. It was qualified then as complex or not.

RESULTS

The analysis of results focused on whether and in relation to which variables there were differences between the following groups of children:

1. sustainedly aggressive children (group AA) and children with decreasing aggressiveness revealed in the second measurement (group AN);
2. sustainedly non-aggressive children (group NN) and those with increasing aggressiveness revealed in the fourth measurement (group NA).

F tests (one-way) and t tests were used to establish level of statistical significance of the differences between the compared groups. Analysis of non-parametric data on norms conveyed to the child made use of techniques based on the chi-square test.

COMPARISONS OF VIOLENCE APPROVAL IN A CHILD'S FAMILY

The mean index of violence approval in each of the tested groups is shown in Table 2. As can be seen from Table 2, there were no significant differences between AA and AN groups, as well as between NN and NA groups in the index of their parents' approval of violence, while there were the intended differences between the first pair of groups and the second one. At the same time the values of the indexes were higher for the sustainedly aggressive children and children with increasing aggression in comparison to the other group in the pair—these differences, however, were not statistically significant. The parents

TABLE 2. Mean Index of Violence Approval in Child's Family in the Four Groups of Children (Variances Have Been Omitted in Order to Increase the Clarity of the Presentation of the Results)

Variable	Group AA (1)	Group AN (2)	Group NN (3)	Group NA (4)	Groups different at the level p < .05
Violence approval in a child's family	.69	.47	1.26	1.57	1, 2 < 3, 4

Note: Group AA—sustainedly aggressive children, group AN—children of declining aggressiveness, group NN—sustainedly non-aggressive children, group NA—children of increasing aggressiveness.

of groups AA and AN represented rather a disapproval of violence, while the parents of groups NN and NA show rather an approval of violence.

COMPARISONS OF THE WHOLE FAMILY SYSTEM

Data characterizing the family system of each of the studied groups—as obtained from mothers and fathers—are presented in Table 3. Significant differences in the level of parents' education were obtained between sustainedly non-aggressive children (group NN) and children with increasing aggressiveness (group NA). Significance of difference in the functioning of the family was reached only between sustainedly aggressive children (group AA) and those from other groups (AN, NN and NA).

Differences between Sustainedly Aggressive Children and Those of Declining Aggressiveness

The significantly lower father's education found in sustainedly aggressive children as compared to those with declining aggression suggests the existence of circumstances for lower socializational flexibility in the former.

Other significant differences between the groups were confined to data obtained from mothers. In comparison to the mothers of children of declining aggressiveness, those of sustainedly aggressive children were more likely to assess the cohesion, organization, and communication in their families as low. A similar trend was also suggested by the results obtained from fathers, but in this case the differences did not achieve statistical significance.

TABLE 3. Mean Measures for Characteristics of the Family System in the Four Groups of Children (Variances Have Been Omitted in Order to Increase the Clarity of the Presentation of the Results)

Variable	Group AA (1)	Group AN (2)	Group NN (3)	Group NA (4)	Groups different at the level p < .05
Level of education (years of schooling)					
Father	8.4	12.2	12.3	11.7	1 < 2, 3, 4; 3 > 4
Mother	12.5	12.9	13.6	10.7	3 > 4
Functioning of the family in mother's perception					
Cohesion	1.52	2.22	2.12	2.06	1 < 2, 3, 4
Organization	1.25	1.64	1.55	1.71	1 < 2, 4
Communication	1.22	1.94	1.84	1.68	1 < 2, 3, 4
Functioning of the family in father's perception					
Cohesion	1.81	2.01	2.04	1.93	—
Organization	1.48	1.64	1.53	1.58	—
Communication	1.58	1.83	1.88	1.71	—

Note: Group AA—sustainedly aggressive children, group AN—children of declining aggressiveness, group NN—sustainedly non-aggressive children, group NA—children of increasing aggressiveness.

The sustainedly aggressive children as opposed to the children with declining aggressiveness originate from less cohesive and less organized families with poor communication. These characteristics together with the lower educational level of fathers suggest a typing of the family as chaotic rather than flexible.

High (but not extreme) cohesion and communication in the families of children with declining aggressiveness suggest existence of conditions for socializational flexibility. Keeping in mind that both groups under discussion do not differ significantly on the parents' disapproval of violence, it might be expected that declining of a child's aggression takes place in the families with higher cohesion and organization, and better communication.

Differences between Sustainedly Non-aggressive Children and Those Increasingly Aggressive

Sustainedly non-aggressive group and the increasingly aggressive group of children were not significantly different on their parents' approving of violence. As can be seen from Table 3, statistically significant differences between these groups were confined to the difference in the level of education of both parents, with parents of increasingly-aggressive children having been less educated. Despite that difference, the level of education of both parents of children with increasing aggressiveness is not very low. To the extent that level of education may be related to the flexibility in socialization, these parents may also react in a flexible way when socializing their child.

No difference was noted for any characteristics of family functioning.

PARENT-CHILD SYSTEM

Data characterizing the groups in relation to the variables of the parent-child system are presented in several tables separately discussed for three groups of variables: parental values, mode of upbringing child and evaluation of child's behavior, and coping strategies.

Parental Values

The parental values preferences in each of the four groups of the children's parents are shown in Table 4. The pattern of the obtained differences shows that the most distinct group on parental values is the group AA which is different in some respects from group AN (both selected as the children of parents disapproving of violence) and NA. At

TABLE 4. Mean Measures (Factor Scores) of Preferences for the Parental Values (Element of the Parents-Child System) in Four Groups of Children

Parental values	Group AA (1)	Group AN (2)	Group NN (3)	Group NA (4)	Groups different at the level p < .05
Mother:					
Maturity	.30	.28	−.02	−.29	2 > 4
Conformity	−.72	.18	−.21	.24	1 < 2, 4
Autonomy	.04	.02	.04	−.28	—
Father:					
Maturity	−.63	.26	−.04	−.05	1 < 2
Conformity	−.36	−.01	−.37	.17	—
Autonomy	0.49	−.05	−.01	−.63	1 > 4

Note: Group AA—sustainedly aggressive children, group AN—children of declining aggressiveness, group NN—sustainedly non-aggressive children, group NA—children of increasing aggressiveness.

the same time there are no significant differences between the two groups of children who had been selected as the children of parents approving of violence (NN and NA).

Occurrence of significant differences has to be noted for the group NA, having parents approving of violence. They are different on crucial values from both groups of children whose parents disapprove of it.

First, the mothers of children with increasing aggression in comparison to the mothers of children with declining aggression prefer significantly less maturity. Thus, for the children with increasing aggression their parents' approval of violence is accompanied by low maturity demand.

At the same time the group with increasing aggression is different from the group of sustainedly aggressive children not only on the level of their parents' approval of violence. This group has parents who prefer more conformity (mother) and less autonomy (father) in their children's behavior.

Differences between Sustainedly Aggressive Children and Those of Declining Aggressiveness. The compared groups differ in parental values in that the mothers of children of declining aggressiveness expected that their children would be more conformist. In turn, the fathers of that group of children were more likely to expect that their sons and daughters would show intellectual, social and emotional maturity.

Mothers of sustainedly aggressive children want them to be nonconformist and at the same time mature, while their fathers stress autonomy instead of maturity. Such pattern of parental values indicates incongruent educational expectations directed by the parents to these children.

Expectations of both parents of children with declining aggression differ from expectations of parents of sustainedly aggressive children in that the former both most want their children to be mature (both mother and father of children with declining aggression indicated maturity as the most preferred value), which suggests congruence in educational demands.

Congruence between parents might be a recognizable factor indicating socializational flexibility. The condition for congruence is that each parent considers the educational attitudes of the other one, which suggests that he or she is sensitive to and flexible in regard to a child's behavior and to another parent's reaction to it.

Differences between Sustainedly Non-aggressive Children and Children of Increasing Aggressiveness. As it was mentioned above, there were no significant differences between sustainedly non-aggressive children and children with increasing aggressiveness. However, the numbers in Table 4 suggest that parents' expectations are in different directions. Parents of the sustainedly non-aggressive group want their children first of all to be nonconformist, which can be seen in the lowest (and negative) indexes obtained by both parents' in their preferences for conformity. Mothers and fathers of children with increasing aggression want them to be rather conforming. Additionally, fathers first preference for these children is that they behave in a non-autonomous way.

Parents of sustainedly non-aggressive children want, first of all, their children to be non-conforming, since the lowest (and negative) indexes were obtained for the parents' preferences for conformity. Thus the pattern of the preferred values for non-aggressive children suggests an existence of a between-parents congruence in expectations directed to the child.

In contrast to the support obtained for the experimental hypothesis in comparisons of the groups with parents disapproving of violence, the results obtained by the comparisons of the groups with parents approving of violence suggest that between-parents congruence and socializational flexibility is more probable in sustainedly non-aggressive children than in children with increasing aggression. This interpretation is contrary to the hypothesis. However it should be noted that the low between-parents congruence described might reflect a high instability in parents-child system and, in this sense, to a certain extent it might be indicative of excessively high flexibility in a family, i.e., chaos.

Mode of Upbringing of Child and Evaluation of Child's Behavior

As is shown in Table 5, there is only one significant difference between each of the two pairs of comparison under discussion when indexes of mean intensity of particular types of upbringing a child and evaluation of his or her behavior were compared. Between-group differences appeared in comparisons among the four groups.

The pattern of results obtained does not reflect systematic and significant differences in comparisons made between both groups with parents disapproving violence (groups AA and AN) as well as in comparisons between both groups with parents approving it (groups NN and NA). The most evident result is indicative of distinctiveness of the group AA, i.e., sustainedly aggressive children. In comparison to the parents of the group with increasing aggression, both parents of the sustainedly aggressive children raise their children with undefined require-

TABLE 5. Mean Measures (Factor Scores) for Modes of Upbringing and Evaluation of Child's Behavior by Parents

Variable	Group AA (1)	Group AN (2)	Group NN (3)	Group NA (4)	Groups different at the level < .05
Mode of mother's upbringing:					
Egalitarian & confronting	−.29	.25	.13	−.13	—
Unstable-punitive	.25	−.30	.14	.30	—
With undefined requirements avoidance of confrontation	.78	.11	.05	−.47	1 > 4
Mode of father's upbringing:					
Egalitarian & confronting	−.60	.10	−.03	.61	1 < 4
Unstable-punitive	.37	−.11	.19	.16	—
With undefined requirements & avoidance of confrontation	.71	−.24	.08	−.38	1 > 4
Evaluation of child's behavior by mother, with regard to:					
Results of behavior	−.30	−.29	.26	.02	1 < 3
Societal norms	−.40	.06	.22	−.17	—
Self-control*	1.43	1.69	2.21	1.75	1, 2, 4 < 3
Evaluation of child's behavior by father, with regard to:					
Results of behavior	.59	−.17	.16	.22	1 > 2
Societal norms	−.06	−.03	.17	.09	—
Self-control*	1.89	1.83	2.06	2.23	—

*raw score (sum for the scale)
Note: Group AA—sustainedly aggressive children, group AN—children of declining aggressiveness, group NN—sustainedly non-aggressive children, group NA—children of increasing aggressiveness.

ments and avoidance of confrontation. At the same time fathers of these children show less egalitarian and confronting attitudes.

These differences indicate that the upbringing system of sustainedly aggressive children in comparison to that system in children with increasing aggression is both more unclear and more authoritarian.

The group under discussion differs also from the group of sustainedly non-aggressive children in the evaluation of a child's behavior by mother. Mothers of this group rely less for evaluation of the child on the consequences of behavior and on self-control, while mothers of the sustainedly non-aggressive children place a higher importance on self-control than do mothers in any of the other three groups.

With regard to the comparisons bearing on the experimental hypotheses, there are few significant differences. Since the direction of the findings are of interest, we will review these, recognizing the constraint in interpretation imposed by the absence of statistical significance.

Differences between Sustainedly Aggressive Children and Those of Declining Aggressiveness. Typical of sustainedly aggressive children are undefined requirements and lack of confrontation in upbringing by both parents and concentration of the father on results of behavior when child is evaluated as well as instability, punitiveness and, in general, lack of discernment in evaluation of child's behavior on the mother's part.

Typical of children with declining aggression are egalitarian and confronting, low unstable-punitive mothers as well as fathers with more defined requirements, who do not focus on results of behavior when the child is evaluated.

The described pattern of results, which is not significant, is in accordance with expectations and suggest greater socialization flexibility in parents of children with declining aggression.

Differences between Sustainedly Non-aggressive Children and Children of Increasing Aggressiveness. Typical of sustainedly non-aggressive children are mothers and fathers moderate in type of upbringing of the child and discerning in the evaluation of the child's behavior, i.e., using varying criterias of evaluation.

Typical of children with increasing aggressiveness are mothers who tend to use unstable-punitive socialization practices and who are not discerning in evaluating the child. However, the fathers tend to be egalitarian and confronting and use the result of a child's behavior and lack of self-control in a child rather than societal norms as the basis of behavior evaluation of the child.

Comparing these groups, it appears that children of increasing aggressiveness experience unstable, internally conflicting system of interactions with their parents. That system seems to be extremely flexible, i.e., chaotic.

Parental Coping Strategies

The analyses of methods used by parents in coping with the problems of raising the child suggest that the parents of each group favor specific strategies. Table 6 presents these findings. Almost all between-groups differences obtained for coping strategies reached the statistical trend level only. However, the direction of the differences reflect greater

TABLE 6. Mean Measures (Factor Scores) of Strategies of Coping with the Problems of Raising the Child (Element of the Parents-child System) in Four Groups of Children

Copying strategy	Group AA (1)	Group AN (2)	Group NN (3)	Group NA (4)	Groups significantly different
Mother:					
Cognitive restructuring	−.74	.40	.15	−.43	1 < 2*
Problem discussion	.47	−.20	.02	.08	1 < 2+
Power assertion	.29	−.17	.12	.01	—
Advice seeking	.23	.11	.02	.00	—
Father:					
Cognitive restructuring	.28	.04	.11	−.10	—
Problem discussion	.04	.07	−.16	−.60	—
Power assertion	−.36	.22	−.37	.17	2 > 1, 3+
Advice seeking	−.58	.00	.24	−.59	3 > 1, 4+

+p < .10; *p < .05
Note: Group AA—sustainedly aggressive children, group AN—children of declining aggressiveness, group NN—sustainedly non-aggressive children, group NA—children of increasing aggressiveness.

consistency with expectation in the case of comparisons between AA and AN groups than the groups NN and NA comparisons.

Differences between Sustainedly Aggressive Children and Those of Declining Aggressiveness. A further difference lay in the manner of coping with the problems of raising a child: mothers of children of declining aggressiveness made greater use of cognitive restructuring. The lower use by them of the discussion of problems in the family reached the .10 level of significance only.

Mothers of sustainedly aggressive children seem to cope using other techniques such as power assertion and advice seeking. The usage of cognitive restructuring by the mothers of children of declining aggressiveness can be considered as a flexible socialization strategy, even when the mothers do not use other coping strategies.

In turn, the fathers of sustainedly aggressive children tend to avoid power assertion and advice seeking. It can be seen also from the direction of between-groups differences that they tend to use more cognitive restructuring and less advice seeking, than fathers of children with decreasing aggressiveness who are more likely to exhibit to the child their authority through power assertion. Such findings would indicate the group of sustainedly aggressive children as having a more flexible family setting, with regard to paternal behavior, if they were significant.

Differences between Sustainedly Non-aggressive Children and Children of Increasing Aggressiveness. The only difference between these groups which may be discussed as suggestive was found in advice-seeking by fathers. The fathers of sustainedly non-aggressive children paid rather more attention to the advice of other people when coping with their child-rearing problems, while the fathers of children with increasing aggressiveness avoided this coping strategy.

The findings which merit notice, but are still not significant, are that the most typical strategy of mothers of children with increasing aggressiveness seems to be a lesser use of cognitive restructuring and the most typical strategy of fathers seems to be a lesser use of the verbal strategies: problem discussion and advice seeking.

Also of interest is the suggestive finding that children in the sustainedly non-aggressive group have fathers who tend to avoid power assertion, while children of increasing aggression have fathers who prefer to cope by usage of power assertion.

These differences, while not significant, are indicative of higher flexibility in sustainedly non-aggressive children, an outcome inconsistent with that hypothesized.

VIOLENCE SYSTEM

Violence system variables consisted of parental usage of disciplinary techniques directed towards child's aggression and norms for aggression manifestation conveyed to child.

Disciplinary Techniques

Table 7 presents the variables of the violence subsystem as they concern reactions to the aggressive behavior of a child. There were no significant differences between the AA and AN groups, which suggests that in the groups in which the parents disapprove of violence, the disciplinary techniques usage is similar.

Several significant or almost significant differences were observed in the comparison of both groups of children selected as having parents approving violence: NN and NA.

NA appeared the most distinctive among the fourth groups examined. The parents of the children from that group showed the most intensive usage of several disciplinary techniques and, for that reason, differed from some groups significantly. Mothers of these children inform more often about feelings when aggression takes place than mothers of sustainedly aggressive children. They use significantly more often

TABLE 7. Mean Measures for Characteristics of the System of the Parents'
Reactions to the Aggressive Behavior of a Child (Element of the Parents-
Child System) in the Four Groups of Children

Parent's reactions	Group AA (2)	Group AN (3)	Group NN (1)	Group NA (4)	Groups significantly different
Mother					
Bans on the behavior	10.71	10.79	11.05	10.74	—
Reinforcement of alternative behavior	10.71	10.04	10.34	10.38	—
Shame induction	7.14	10.24	10.46	5.39	—
Information on the feelings of a victim	8.14	9.81	9.67	10.00	1 < 2, 3+; 1 < 4*
Scolding	9.43	7.74	7.86	9.12	3 < 4+; 2 < 4*
Corporal punishment	4.83	3.75	3.74	4.46	—
TV watching prohibition	7.14	5.89	5.60	5.39	—
Information on victim's counter-reaction possibility	6.00	6.82	5.55	6.87	2 > 3+
Ignoring	5.14	6.15	4.25	6.45	3 < 2, 4*
Simple request for obedience	10.71	10.33	10.60	10.13	—
Praise	1.71	1.56	1.68	2.08	2 < 4+
Father					
Bans on the behavior	9.67	10.03	10.29	11.08	4 > 1, 2+
Reinforcement of alternative behavior	9.68	9.46	9.68	9.08	—
Shame induction	8.89	9.51	9.65	10.46	1 < 4*
Information on the feelings of a victim	8.11	5.05	8.70	9.53	—
Scolding	7.88	7.65	7.96	7.69	—
Corporal punishment	4.25	3.71	4.29	3.15	—
TV watching prohibition	5.00	5.72	6.50	4.58	3 > 4+
Information on victim's counter-reaction possibility	6.67	6.02	5.48	5.45	—
Ignoring	5.12	5.05	4.80	7.69	4 > 3, 2*
Simple request for obedience	9.78	9.61	9.54	9.75	—
Praise	1.88	2.03	2.86	1.75	—

+p < 0.10; * p < 0.05

Note: Group AA—sustainedly aggressive children, group AN—children of declining aggressiveness, group NN—sustainedly non-aggressive children, group NA—children of increasing aggressiveness.

scolding and tend to use more praising than mothers of children with decreasing aggression.

On the other hand, fathers of children with increasing aggression use shame induction significantly more often and tend to prohibit aggressive behavior more often than fathers of sustainedly aggressive children. In comparison to the fathers of children with decreasing aggression they significantly more often ignore their child's aggressive behavior.

Differences between Sustainedly-aggressive Children and Children of Declining Aggression. While the differences did not attain statistical significance, mothers of children of decreasing aggressiveness tend to provide more feedback than mothers of sustainedly aggressive children in regard to the feelings experienced by victims of aggression. When the ranks of frequency of particular techniques usage are concerned, it should be noted that they also tended more often to induce shame in a child after his/her aggressive behaviors (rank 3 on the frequency list of preferred techniques) than mothers of sustainedly aggressive children (rank 7 on that list).

While these findings are suggestive with regard to the expectation of greater flexibility in the family system of children with decreasing aggression, given the large number of comparisons, they provide only modest support.

Differences between Sustainedly Non-aggressive Children and Those of Increasing Aggressiveness. A series of significant differences and trends were noted when these two groups were compared for the ways in which parents reacted to the child's aggression. Mothers of increasingly aggressive children had a more marked tendency to ignore aggression (a significant difference) or to scold (trend). Also, the fathers of these same children were more likely to ignore manifestations of aggression (a significant difference) and less likely than those of sustainedly non-aggressive children to impose a ban on the watching of TV (a trend only).

When comparing ranks for frequency of usage of particular techniques, it is noteworthy that mothers of increasingly aggressive children tend not to use shame induction technique (rank 9 in comparison to rank 2 among mothers of sustainedly non-aggressive children).

Summing up the described differences between the two groups of children with parents approving of violence, the parents of children with increasing aggression seem to be more tolerant of and variable with regard to their children's aggression than parents of sustainedly non-aggressive children.

Norms for Aggression Conveyed to a Child

No significant difference was found for the type of norms conveyed by parents to their children. However, the trends of the differences in the complexity and flexibility of the norms conveyed are of interest.

Differences between Sustainedly-aggressive Children and Children of De-clining Aggression. Since the groups were different in size, proportions instead of frequencies are used to indicate the type of norms concerning aggression conveyed by the parents to the child.

Analysis of the types of norm relating to aggression, (not-complex vs. complex norms with the assumption that complex ones are typical of higher socializational flexibility) revealed that .80 of mothers of sus-tainedly-aggressive children conveyed non-complex norms, with .20 mothers conveying the complex norms. In turn, for the group of children of declining aggressiveness .69 mothers conveyed to their children the non-complex norms and .31 mothers conveyed the complex norms. The difference between the groups is not statistically significant (chi-square = 2.410, df = 1, n.s.).

The respective proportions established for fathers were: .71 (convey-ing the non-complex norms) to .29 (conveying the complex norms) for the group of sustainedly-aggressive children, and .50 (conveying the non-complex) and .50 (conveying the complex norms) for the group of children of decreasing aggressiveness (chi-square = 1.88, df = 1, n.s.).

There appears to be a trend toward greater socialization flexibility in the parents of children with declining aggression.

Differences between Sustainedly Non-aggressive Children and Those of In-creasing Aggressiveness. The compared groups were very similar in the ratio of mothers conveying the non-complex and complex norms to their children (the numbers were .64 to .36 in the sustainedly non-aggressive group and .71 to .29 in the group of increasing aggressiveness; chi-square = 2.142, df = 1, n.s.). A similar situation applied to the norms conveyed by fathers, with proportions of: .59 for fathers conveying the non-complex norms and of .41 for fathers conveying the complex norms in the sustainedly non-aggressive group, .50 fathers conveying the non-complex norms to .50 fathers conveying the complex norms in the increasingly-aggressive group (chi-square = .275, df = 1, n.s.).

SUMMARY AND CONCLUSIONS

The aim of the research carried out was to establish if children from families with similar attitudes to violence, but different patterns of change in the level of manifested aggressiveness, were characterized by different constellations of socializational variables which could be inter-preted as indicating the presence or absence of socializational flexibility in a family environment

The results obtained provide some confirmation of the a priori expectations regarding the directions of differences between groups of sustainedly aggressive and decreasingly aggressive children. However, many of the findings are at the trend level only. The summation below is based on both the significant findings and the trends, since many differences were in accord with expectations.

The family systems of sustainedly aggressive children whose parents disapproved of violence were found to be characterized by poor communication, weak organization, and limited cohesion, conditions unpropitious for an environment of socializational flexibility but suitable for the emergence of the chaos of impacts stressed by Patterson (1982) when comparing aggressive and non-aggressive children.

The value systems of the mothers of sustainedly aggressive children do not assume conformity in the behavior of a child, while the value systems of fathers lack any expectation that a child's behavior should be mature. Interactions with the child feature undefined requirements and an avoidance of confrontation over contentious questions. The father does not display power assertion when problems with the upbringing of a child arise, while the mother is inclined to discuss the problem within the family circle. According to the suggestions of Olson et al. (1983) and Patterson (1982), these properties of the family system may be considered conditions unfavorable to socializational flexibility. The relatively limited tendency for mothers to provide a child with information on the emotional consequences of his or her aggression in his or her victims (i.e., feelings) combined with the relatively high tendency for scolding and corporal punishment further suggests limited flexibility in the system by which mothers react to displays of aggression from children in the group under discussion (cf. Bandura & Walters, 1959; Patterson, 1982).

The contrasting characteristics obtained for the groups of children of declining aggressiveness (who were selected to the study only when their parents disapprove of violence) do lend themselves to interpretation as being symptomatic of socializational flexibility in the family environment. The families of the children in question are cohesive (but also organized), have good communication, have mothers and fathers expecting conformity from children, and have fathers expecting maturity of behavior. Mothers also provide their children with information on the emotional effects of aggressive behavior on the victims of that aggression. In addition, the results concerning the interactions with the child—although not differing significantly—do suggest a tendency for parents to confront the child with opinions and confirm the organization of relations on the basis of parity. Such a socializational context is closer to the assumption of flexibility than the context described for the group of sustainedly aggressive children.

It would appear that in the families in which violence has been disapproved of, decreasing aggression is more likely where a child grows up in conditions of greater socializational flexibility, while sustained aggression is more likely if the upbringing occurs where this flexibility is lacking and where—in the case of the present study at least—it is replaced by a chaotic family environment.

The second of the formulated expectations concerned the differences between children from families approving of violence. It had been expected that the sustainedly aggressive children from such families would be those from environments characterized by a lack of socializational flexibility, while the increasingly aggressive ones would be those from environments with its presence. These expectations were not confirmed by the obtained results.

In describing their child's behavior, the mothers of increasingly aggressive children approving of violence attached little weight to behavioral self-control. The fathers, in turn, had a tendency to consult others when the child caused problems. Almost significant differences were noted in the systems by which the aggression shown by the child was reacted to: mothers of increasingly aggressive children were more likely to scold than those of sustainedly non-aggressive children, while fathers were more likely to forbid the watching of TV. Significant differences were obtained for ignoring aggression: both parents were more likely to ignore the aggression displayed by their child. From the point of view adopted here (cf. Olson et al., 1983), such socializational conditions in which there are fewer bans and more ignoring of behavior, should be considered more flexible than those in the comparison group of sustainedly non-aggressive children, but on the other hand may be indicative of as more chaotic ones.

It is worth noting that the aforementioned differences were associated with differences in the level of education of parents, which is lower in the group of children showing increased aggressiveness. Thus the distribution of the findings obtained may be related to differences in the level of parental education which were noted between the groups compared.

To sum up on the basis of the results obtained, it may be said that where parents do not approve of violence, the condition for the socialization of aggression—understood as the reduction of aggressiveness—is socializational flexibility in the family environment of the child, while the condition for the sustaining of aggression is socializational chaos in the family environment.

On the other hand, there is a lack of an adequate basis upon which to claim that the development of aggression (i.e., an increase in aggressiveness) is conditioned by the socializational flexibility of the family environment in conditions where violence is approved of. This is because the significant flexibility of the kind referred to was only noted in the violence subsystem in this case. Continued research with a more careful choice of groups will be required to obtain a wider confirmation of the hypotheses formulated on the basis of the system theory of the development of aggression.

In subsequent research, the results would probably be clearer and more consistent where the procedure of selection according to the parents' approval of violence allowed the use of more extreme but homogeneous groups on that variable. In this study the groups were selected on the median split basis, which may have contributed to a high level of heterogeneity in other examined variables as well.

There is one more important reason which could be responsible for the varied confirmation of the hypotheses—the combination of approving of violence by the parents and the increasing of aggression in children when they were not previously aggressive does not happen very often. It might be that these parents underestimated their level of violence disapproval and that they were also the parents who approved of violence. For that reason, a better tool for the measurement of aggression approval in family setting should be employed.

Nevertheless, the obtained results suggest the usefulness of the theoretical construct of socializational flexibility for explaining why children of the parents of disapproving violence remain aggressive and why children of parents approving of violence become aggressive.

ACKNOWLEDGMENTS: The great part of the presented research was supported by grant for problem CPBP 08.03.III.4 (from the Institute of Social Prevention and Resocialization, University of Warsaw), directed by Professor Adam Fraczek. Correspondence concerning this chapter should be addressed to Lucyna Kirwil, Institute of Social Prevention and Resocialization, University of Warsaw, 00-721 Warsaw, ul. Podchorazych 20, Poland.

REFERENCES

Bandura, A. (1977). *Social learning theory*. Englewood Cliffs, NJ: Prentice-Hall.
Bandura, A., & Walters, R. H. (1959). *Adolescent aggression*. New York: The Ronald Press Company.

Bronfenbrenner, U. (1970). Czynniki spoleczne w rozwoju osobowosci. (Social factors in personality development). *Psychologia Wychowawcza, 1,* 1-17.

Bell, R. O., & Harper, L. V. (1977). *Child effects on adults.* Hillsdale, NJ: Erlbaum.

Ferguson, T., & Rule, B. G. (1980). Effect of inferential set, outcome severity, and basis of responsibility on children's evaluations of aggressive act. *Developmental Psychology, 16,* 141-146.

Fraczek, A. (1985). Moral approval of aggressive acts: A Polish-Finnish comparative study. *Journal of Cross-Cultural Psychology, 16,* 41-54.

Fraczek, A. (1986). Socio-cultural environment, television viewing, and the development of aggression among children in Poland. In L. R. Huemann, & L. D. Eron (Eds.), *Television and the aggressive child: A cross-national comparison* (pp. 119-159). Hillsdale, NJ: Erlbaum.

Grusec, J. E., & Kuczynski, L. (1980). Direction of effect on socialization: A comparison of parent's vs. the child's behavior as determinants of disciplinary techniques. *Developmental Psychology, 16,* 1-9.

Heider, F. (1958). *The psychology of interpersonal relations.* New York: Wiley.

Hinsch, R., Schneider, M., & Pfinsten, U. (1983). *Parental attribution on children's aggressive behavior.* The paper presented at the Second European Conference of ISRA, Zeist, The Netherlands.

Huesmann, L. R., & Eron, L. D. (1986). *Television and the aggressive child: A cross-national comparison.* Hillsdale, NJ: Erlbaum.

Kirwil, L. (1986). *Charakterystyka zmiennych w kwestionariuszu dla rodziców (A characterization of variables in questionnaires for parents),* (Tech. Rep. CPBR.11.8, TULIPAN 1986). Warsaw: Institute of Psychology, Polish Academy of Sciences.

Kirwil, L. (1988). Children's aggressiveness in a context of parental justification of violence. In L. Pulkkinen & J. M. Ramirez (Eds.). *Aggression in children* (pp. 88-102). Seville: Publicationes de la Universidad de Seville.

Kirwil, L. (1991). Wartosci rodzicielskie matek i ojców a zachowania spoeczne dzieci (The parental values of mothers and fathers and the social behavior of children). *Kwartalnik Pedagogiczny, 4,* 98-109

Kirwil, L. (1993). Zmiany klimatu w rodzinie z dorastajacym dzieckiem (Changes in the climate of a family with adolescent children). In Z. Smoleñska (Ed.), *Badania nad rozwojem w okresie dorastania* (pp. 139-163). Warsaw: Wydawnictwo Instytutu Psychologii PAN.

Kirwil, L., & Kwiatkowska, A. (1985). *Test aprobaty moralnej agresji—wyniki badañ walidacyjnych (A test of the moral approval of aggression—results of validating research).* (Tech. Rep. MR.III.18, 1985). Warsaw: Institute of Psychology, Polish Academy of Sciences.

Kohn, M. L. (1976). Social class and parental values: Another confirmation of the relationship. *American Sociological Review, 41,* 538-545.

Lagerspetz, K., & Westman, M. (1980). Moral approval of aggressive acts: A preliminary investigation. *Aggressive Behavior, 6,* 119-130.

£apiñski, B. (1988). Stres rodziców zwiazany z socjalizacja dziecka w wieku dorastania— jego determinanty i dzialania zaradcze (Parental stress associated with the socialization of an adolescent—its determinants and copying strategies), *Psychologia Wychowawcza, 4,* 390-405.

Maccoby, E. E., & Martin, J. A. (1983). Socialization in the context of the family: Parent-child interaction. In P.H. Mussen (Ed.), *Handbook of child psychology, No. 4, Socialization, personality and social development* (pp. 1-101). New York: J. Wiley and Sons.

Moos, R. H., & Moos, B. S. (1981). *Family Environment Scale Manual.* Palo Alto: Consulting Psychologists Press.

Olson, D. H., McCubbin, H. I., Barnes, H., Larsen, A., & Muxen, M. (1983). *Families: What makes them work?* Beverly Hills: Sage Publications.

Olweus, D. (1980). Familial determinants of aggressive behavior in adolescent boys: A causal analysis. *Developmental Psychology, 16,* 644-660.

Parke, R. D. (1978). Children's home environments. In I. Altman & J. F. Wohlwill (Eds.), *Children and the environment* (pp. 139-163). New York: Plenum Press.

Patterson, G. R. (1982). *A social learning approach: Vol. 3: Coersive family process.* Eugene, OR: Castalia Publishing Company.

Walper, S., & Silbereisen, R. K. (1986). *Individuelle und familiare Konsequenzen oekonomisher Einbussen.* Unpublished manuscript. Berlin TU-Drop Jugenforschung, Berlin.

CHAPTER 7

EMOTIONAL INSTABILITY, PHYSICAL AND VERBAL AGGRESSION, AND PROSOCIAL BEHAVIOR AS PRECURSORS OF SCHOLASTIC ACHIEVEMENT AND SOCIAL ADJUSTMENT

G. V. CAPRARA, C. BARBARANELLI, M. INCATASCIATO, C. PASTORELLI, AND A. RABASCA

INTRODUCTION

Over the past twenty years we have conducted a number of studies to better understand the role social abilities play in child development. A first generation of studies was aimed at proving the psychometric and ecological validity of three measures respectively related to Emotional Instability (EI), Physical and Verbal Aggression (PVA) and Prosocial Behavior (PB), using a multimethod-multiinformant strategy.

G. V. CAPRARA, C. BARBARANELLI, M. INCATASCIATO, C. PASTORELLI, AND A. RABASCA • Department of Psychology, University of Rome, Via dei Marsi 78, 00185 Rome, Italy.

Aggression: Biological, Developmental, and Social Perspectives, edited by Seymour Feshbach and Jolanta Zagrodzka. Plenum Press, New York, 1997.

Convergent and discriminant validity of the three measures was supported by multitrait-multimethod analysis (Barbaranelli, Caprara & Pastorelli, submitted for publication). Construct validity was supported by significant and positive correlations of EI and PVA with the total behavior score from the Teacher Report Form of the Child Behavior Checklist (TRF/CBC) (Achenbach & Eldebrock, 1983, 1986) as well as by significant, positive correlations of PB with adaptive characteristics as measured by the TRF/CBC. Ecological validity was supported by significant and positive correlations of EI and PVA with peer rejection as well as by significant and positive correlations of PB with popularity. The same pattern of correlations among measures and between criteria and measures was replicated in children's self reports, teacher ratings and peer nominations (Caprara & Pastorelli, 1993).

Furthermore, the three measures originally edited in Italian, have been validated in English under the supervision of Concetta Pastorelli during her stay at the Western Psychiatric Institute and Clinic in Pittsburgh, in Spanish under the supervision of Maria Vittoria del Barrio of the Universidad Nacional de Education a Distancia of Madrid, in Polish under the supervision of Adam Fraczek of the Polish Academy of Sciences, in Hungarian under the supervision of Susanna Kulcsar of the Eotvos Lorand University of Budapest and in Czechoslovakian under the supervision of Ivo Czermak of the Czech Academy of Sciences. A second generation of studies was then started, with longitudinal research aimed at identifying the best predictors of children's scholastic achievement and social adjustment. The following study reports preliminary findings concerning the predictive power of the three measures and the three informants with regard to scholastic achievement and sociometric status after a four-year interval.

METHODS

SUBJECTS

The participants in this study were middle-class students attending public schools in a residential community located near Rome and their teachers. The target subjects included 299 children (161 males and 138 females), first assessed when they were in second and third grade (Time 1), ranging in age from seven to nine, then reassessed when they were in sixth and seventh grade, ranging in age from 11 to 14 (Time 2). Self reports, teacher ratings and peer nominations measuring the variables of theoretical interest were collected, in the schools, by two female experimenters over a period of several days.

VARIABLES

Emotional Instability (EI), Physical and Verbal aggression (PVA) and Prosocial Behavior (PB) were the predictor variables of interest. Emotional instability is defined as the tendency to show a lack of adequate self control in social situations because of an incapacity to refrain from impulsiveness and emotionality. Physical and Verbal Aggression is defined as the tendency to express behaviors aimed at hurting others physically and verbally. Prosocial Behavior is defined as the tendency to express sharing, trust, kindness, cooperativeness and friendliness. The predicted variables of interest were school achievement revealed by final grades and sociometric status in popularity and rejection.

PROCEDURE

The following measures were collected: Time 1

a. EI, PVA and PB children self reports (answer format: 1 = never; 2 = sometimes; 3 = often) (Table 1).
b. EI, PVA and PB teacher ratings. A modified version of the scales, developed for children, was used for the teacher. In this version, each item was reformulated using the third person. The response format was the same (1 = never; 2 = sometimes; 3 = often).
c. EI, PVA and PB peer evaluations based on nominations of the three children who have shown the most behaviors related to the three constructs. Peer nomination measures were developed on the basis of those items which proved to have higher loadings in the factorial structure of EI, PVA and PB. These were (EI) disturb others, (PB) give help, and (PVA) fight a lot.

The following measures were collected: Time 2

a. scholastic achievement revealed by final grades
b. popularity and rejection by having peers select the three classmates they would like to play and study with and the three classmates they would neither want to play with nor study with.

Three sets of stepwise multiple regression analyses were performed with school achievement, popularity, and rejection as criteria variables for sixth and seventh grade and EI, PVA, and PB self report, teacher

TABLE 1. Emotional Instability, Physical and Verbal Aggression and
Prosocial Behavior Scales

Emotional Instability	Physical and Verbal Aggression	Prosocial Behavior
—I am impatient	—I get into fights	—I try to make sad people happier
—I make trouble for others	—I kick and hit or punch	—I spend time with my friends
—I shout	—I get even when I am mad	—I try to help others
—I interrupt others while they are talking	—I threaten others (I tell them I am going to do something bad	—I share things I like with my friends
—I play loud games	—I hurt others	—I am gentle
—I bother others	—I bite others to hurt them	—I let others use my toys
—I have bad moods	—I argue with other children	—I like to play with others
—I am impolite	—I tell lies	—I trust others
—I don't respect others	—I say bad things about other kids	—I hug my friends
—I cry	—I like to fist fight	—I help others with their homework
—It's hard for me to stay still	—I push and trip others	
—At school I talk to my friends when I shouldn't	—I am envious (when someone has something I like, I want it)	
—I get mad	—I tease other kids	
—I play dangerous games	—I use bad words (I swear)	
—I play with matches and fire	—I insult other kids or call them names	

ratings, and peer nominations as predictor variables for second and third grade (Table 2).

In females, PB and EI peer nominations were found to be the most important predictors of scholastic achievement, accounting for 23% of variance. PB peer nominations and self report were found to be the most important predictors of popularity, accounting for 15% of variance. EI as rated by teachers and PB peer nominations were found to be the most important predictors of rejection, accounting for 25% of variance.

In males, PB peer nominations were found to be the most important predictors of scholastic achievement and popularity, accounting respectively for 23% and for 11% of variance. EI and PB peer nominations were found to be the most important predictors of rejection, accounting for 26% of variance. Overall, PB peer nominations in second and third grade for both males and females were the most important predictors of scholastic achievement, popularity and rejection four years later.

The relative importance of the examined predictors at Time 1 versus criteria at Time 2 was further investigated by structural equation modelling, using the EQS program (Bentler, 1989). The combined male and female sample was considered for this analysis. A model was tested in which PB, PVA and EI were defined as latent variables, measured by self report, teacher ratings and peer nominations. These three latent variables were posited as predictors of latent popularity, rejection and Academic Achievement (Figure 1).

The model fit the observed data fairly well, showing a chi square of 56.78 (p < .051), and goodness of fit indexes of practical relevance (such as Bentler's CFI and Bentler and Bonnet's NFI and NNFI) much above .90. Prosocial Behavior was the best predictor of all three criteria, showing significant beta coefficients (respectively .61 on Academic Achievement, −.58 on Rejection, .55 on Popularity). Aggression was important in predicting Rejection by peer group (beta = .39); it showed a moderate influence on Academic Achievement (beta = −.14), and was not significantly related to later Prosocial Behavior. Emotional Instability did not show significant beta coefficients with the three criteria considered in this study; this trait can be considered as irrelevant in predicting later rejection, popularity and academic achievement.

DISCUSSION AND CONCLUSION

To summarize and further discuss the above findings, the relevance of peers as informants and of prosocial behavior as determinants of social adjustment should be underlined. These findings confirm the scarce

TABLE 2. Multiple Regression Analysis. Predictor Variables: Prosocial Behavior (S, T, P)*; Physical-Verbal Aggression (S, T, P)*; Hyperactivity (S, T, P)* for 2nd and 3rd Grade. Criteria Variables: Academic Achievement; Popularity; Peer Rejection for 6th and 7th Grade

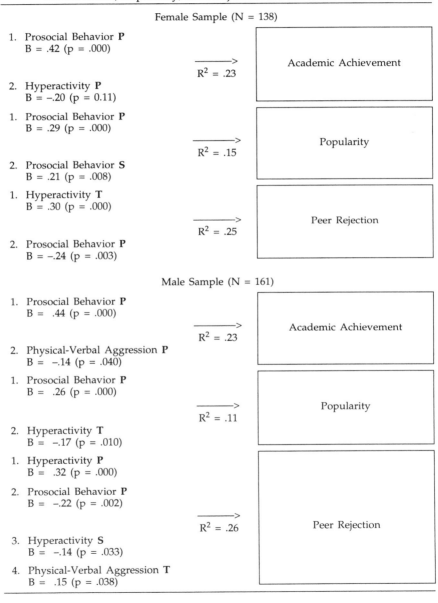

Female Sample (N = 138)

1. Prosocial Behavior **P**
   B = .42 (p = .000)

   ————> R² = .23   Academic Achievement

2. Hyperactivity **P**
   B = −.20 (p = 0.11)

1. Prosocial Behavior **P**
   B = .29 (p = .000)

   ————> R² = .15   Popularity

2. Prosocial Behavior **S**
   B = .21 (p = .008)

1. Hyperactivity **T**
   B = .30 (p = .000)

   ————> R² = .25   Peer Rejection

2. Prosocial Behavior **P**
   B = −.24 (p = .003)

Male Sample (N = 161)

1. Prosocial Behavior **P**
   B = .44 (p = .000)

   ————> R² = .23   Academic Achievement

2. Physical-Verbal Aggression **P**
   B = −.14 (p = .040)

1. Prosocial Behavior **P**
   B = .26 (p = .000)

   ————> R² = .11   Popularity

2. Hyperactivity **T**
   B = −.17 (p = .010)

1. Hyperactivity **P**
   B = .32 (p = .000)

2. Prosocial Behavior **P**
   B = −.22 (p = .002)

   ————> R² = .26   Peer Rejection

3. Hyperactivity **S**
   B = −.14 (p = .033)

4. Physical-Verbal Aggression **T**
   B = .15 (p = .038)

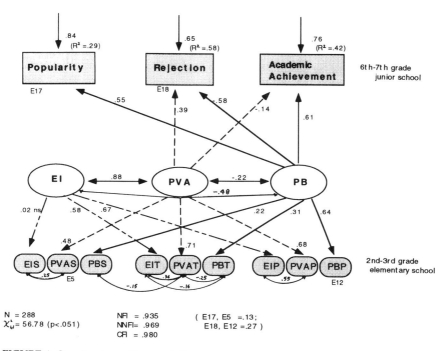

FIGURE 1. Structural equation model's graphical representation, using emotional instability, prosocial behavior and physical and verbal aggression as predictors of latent popularity, rejection and academic achievement. Variables = EI, emotional instability; PB, prosocial behavior; PVA, physical and verbal aggression. Evaluators = S, self report; T, teacher rating; P, peer nominations.

relevance of children's early self-reports in predicting favorable or unfavorable outcomes; they put the consideration traditionally accorded to teacher ratings in a new perspective, and greatly emphasize the role peers may have as sources of information (Loeber, Green, Lahey & Southamer-Loeber, 1989). Why children are good informants on other children but not on themselves deserves greater attention.

As documented elsewhere, children are psychometrically reliable when they report on themselves, just like adults. Factorial structure and Cronbach's alpha of the three scales are comparable in values and acceptability in children and adults (see Caprara & Pastorelli, 1993). Unfortunately, children's self reports are scarcely correlated with teacher ratings, peer nominations and other reports. As a matter of fact, reporting on oneself is different from reporting on others since different perspectives and different processes are implied. In the position of self reporter one relies mostly on intentions and feelings, whereas in the position of observer one relies mostly on outcomes and attributions.

It is likely that over the years the two perspectives will come closer as a result of the improvement of convergency between self reports and others evaluations in a variety of domains; but whether the higher correlations are due to the effect of reputation on self perception, or to the effect of the latter on the former, or to both deserves attention and needs to be clarified.

While in our study, teacher ratings are less relevant than expected, peers nominations, on the contrary, are much more powerful predictors of both scholastic achievement and sociometric status (Coie, Belding & Underwood, 1987). It is likely that the capacity to interact effectively with peers influences not only their acceptance but also their scholastic achievement, and it is not surprising that peers, who benefit most from it, are also the ones who appreciate most its impact.

Among the three measures considered here, the effect of Emotional Instability on rejection is totally mediated by physical and verbal aggression just as only the part Emotional Instability which turns into aggression or is associated with it contributes to rejection. In fact, physical and verbal aggression in seven- to nine-year-olds, contributes significantly toward predicting rejection by peers four years later. This is not surprising given the well-documented effect of aggression on rejection (Dodge & Coie, 1987) and the stability of aggression in children (Olweus, 1984).

Nor is the moderate direct contribution of aggression to negative scholastic achievement surprising. Although aggression is a rare phenomenon in the scholastic setting where our research was conducted, even less serious expressions are not easily tolerated. What we found surprising was the powerful role of prosocial behavior. Although post hoc, many arguments support our findings: We did not expect such a pervasive influence of prosocial behavior at an early age on subsequent outcomes and on the concurrent determinants. Not only does early prosocial behavior predict popularity, success in school and less rejection more than any other considered variable, but it is likely that it significantly modulates the influence of aggression on rejection and scholastic performance. Not all aggressive children are rejected nor are they poor students (see Olweus, 1978 for documentation).

There is no doubt about the role prosocial behaviors such as sharing, caring and cooperating play in fostering social adjustment in a regular scholastic setting, such as the one we have been studying over the past ten years, which, in many respects, is prototypical of the scholastic setting found all over Italy and probably over Europe or the USA. There has been a lot of discussion about social intelligence and affective education, from different perspectives and not always referring to the same phenomena. However, there is no doubt that the capacity to share the basic rules of social interaction and to express affect are crucial in setting in motion important experiences for fostering social adjustment. On the other hand it is more than likely that earlier emotional vulnerability and social disabilities may increase over the years, via others' feedback, leading to rejection and failure (Caprara & Zimbardo, in press).

It is not surprising that aggression received more attention than any other phenomenon in predicting social maladjustment, given the immediate visibility of its undesirable consequences. However, we suspect that too often it has been underestimated that, in the very frequent cases in which aggression is a rare phenomenon, abilities such as the ones referred to under prosocial behavior are much more relevant to popularity and success. Whereas being able to be valuable for others is often a source of interpersonal influence and of positive affect, and these in turn significantly influence the child's sense of efficacy as well as his/her achievements. Furthermore, not only may prosocial behavior be a powerful antagonist of aggression, but lack of prosocial abilities may turn into scholastic failure and aggression when earlier emotional vulnerability and earlier negative interpersonal experiences, via rejection and stigmatization, lead to hostility, disengagement and social withdrawal.

ACKNOWLEDGMENTS: Findings reported in this chapter are from research projects supported by grants from the Fondazione Cristina Mazzotti and from the Jacobs Foundation.

REFERENCES

Achenbach, M. T., & Eldebrock, C. (1983). *Manual for the Child Behavior Checklist and Revised Child Behavior Profile*. Burlington, VT: University of Vermont Department of Psychiatry.

Achenbach, M. T., & Eldebrock, C. (1986). *Manual for the Teacher's Reports and Teacher Version of the Child Behavior Profile*. Burlington, Author, VM.

Barbaranelli, C., Caprara, G. V., & Pastorelli, C. Construct Validity of three indicators of early adjustment/maladjustment (submitted for publication).

Bentler, P. (1989). EQS: A Structural Equations Program. Los Angeles, CA: BMDP Statistical Software.

Campbell, D., & Fiske, D. W. (1959). Convergent and Discriminant Validation, *Psychological Bulletin*, 56, 81-105.

Caprara, G. V., & Pastorelli, C. (1993). Early Emotional Instability, Prosocial Behavior and Aggression: Some Methodological Aspects. *European Journal of Personality*, 7, 19-36.

Caprara, G. V., & Zimbardo, P. Aggregation and Amplification of marginal deviations in the social construction of personality and maladjustment. *European Journal of Personality*, in press.

Coie, J. D., Belding, M., & Underwood, M. (1987). Aggression and Peer Rejection in Childhood. In B. B. Lahey & A. Kazdin (Eds.), *Advances in Clinical Child Psychology, Vol. 2*, 125-158.

Dodge, K. A., & Coie, J. D. (1987). Social information processing factors in reactive and proactive aggression in children and peer groups. *Journal of Personality and Social Psychology, 53*, 1146-1158.

Loeber, R., Green, S., Lahey, B., & Stouthamer-Loeber, M. (1989). Optimal informants on childhood disruptive behaviors. *Development and Psychopathology, 1*, 317-333.

Olweus, D. (1978). *Aggression in schools*. Washington/London/New York: Hemisphere/Halstead/ Wiley.

Olweus, D. (1984). Stability in aggressive and withdrawn inhibited behavior patterns. In R. M. Kaplan, V. J. Konecni & R. W. Novaco (Eds.), *Aggression in children and youth* (pp. 89-104). The Hague: Martinus Nijhoff.

CHAPTER 8

A LONGITUDINAL STUDY OF THE RELATIONSHIP BETWEEN AGGRESSIVE AND DEPRESSIVE TENDENCIES IN ELEMENTARY SCHOOL AGE BOYS AND GIRLS

SEYMOUR FESHBACH, NORMA FESHBACH, AND YORAM JAFFE

Aggression is a form of behavior that is typically directed outward. Aggression is associated with the affect of anger but is defined in behavioral terms so that aggression may take place without the affective accompaniments of anger. The aggressive child is characterized as aggressive because he or she strikes other children, directs hostile comments towards others, destroys property—that is, inflicts injury on some external object or person. There are also circumstances in which children will direct angry behavior toward themselves and experience self-directed injury

SEYMOUR FESHBACH • Department of Psychology, University of California, 405 Hilgard, Los Angeles, California 90095-1563.   NORMA FESHBACH • Department of Education, University of California, 405 Hilgard, Los Angeles, California 90095-1521.   YORAM JAFFE • Department of Psychology, University of Southern California, University Park, Los Angeles, California 90089.

Aggression: Biological, Developmental, and Social Perspectives, edited by Seymour Feshbach and Jolanta Zagrodzka. Plenum Press, New York, 1997.

and pain. However, this form of aggression is much less common and, in general, aggression entails social behaviors that are directed toward individuals and objects in the external environment. Depression, in contrast, is a construct that refers to an inward, asocial form of response. The affect of sadness and related dysphoric feelings are implicated in depression. However, while depression may be more closely linked to dysphoric affect than aggression is to anger, depression can be defined in behavioral terms such as social isolation and withdrawal, motor retardation, pessimism and reduced initiative.

In this chapter, we will report on a study that addresses the dynamic connection between aggression and depression as response tendencies with clinical significance rather than as clinical symptoms or syndromes as such. For reasons to be indicated below, the focus of the study is on the relevance of gender and age to the relationship between aggressive and depressive tendencies. This relationship is addressed both cross-sectionally and longitudinally. From a theoretical standpoint, there is interest in the direction of the relationship—whether inverse or direct, as well as in the factors influencing the degree of the relationship.

From a clinical standpoint, aggression and depression are respectively assigned to externalizing and internalizing childhood disorders— two major clusters of children's behavioral symptomatology. Aggression is seen as a form of acting-out behavior, usually reflecting under-control while depression is viewed as a self-directed set of behaviors, usually reflecting over—control (Achenbach & Edelbrock, 1983). The labels "externalizing" and "internalizing" have a dynamic as well as clinical significance. Clinically, the principal diagnostic question is whether these labels denote discrete sets of behavioral symptoms that reliably cluster together and that can be reliably differentiated.

Factor analytic studies of children's symptoms typically yield two factors that correspond to these diagnostic categories (Lachar & Lacombe, 1983). Yet a substantial number of investigations reflect significant overlap between these two syndromes (Kazdin, 1989; Kazdin & Esveldt-Dawson, 1986; Pfeffer, Zuckerman, Plutchik & Mizruchi, 1987). There is some evidence of a sharper dichotomy between internalizing and externalizing symptoms with more severe as compared to milder forms of psychopathology (Campbell & Stuart, 1978). However, as previously suggested, overlap is not infrequently reported (Mattison, Bagnato & Strickler, 1987; Treiber & Mabe, 1987). In a review of studies bearing on developmental differences in childhood depression, Kazdin (1989) concludes that a number of children who meet the diagnostic criteria for depression also meet the diagnostic criteria for conduct disorders. Indeed, some investigators have found a positive relationship between externalizing and internalizing symptoms (Fischer, Rolf, Hasazi & Cummings, 1984).

More specific indices of aggression and depression, as assessed by the Revised Missouri Children's Behavior Checklist have also been shown to be positively correlated (Sines, 1986). Although there are longitudinal studies addressing differential antecedents in children of each of these clinically related behaviors (e.g., Rubin & Mills, 1988), relatively little is known about developmental changes in their relationship. A more significant gap exists in regard to the role of gender in this relationship. The lack of data bearing on gender differences is surprising since aggression, in particular, has been shown to be strongly linked to gender (Feshbach & Feshbach, 1971; Feshbach, 1970; Parke & Slaby, 1983). In addition, there is a wealth of data bearing on gender differences in adult depression (Nolen-Hoeksema, 1987). The consideration of gender differences raises the theoretical and dynamic question of why one might anticipate a relationship between these two phenotypically very different modes of response. The early Freudian formulation of the dynamics of this relationship led to predictions of an inverse correlation between aggression and depression, the latter presumably being a consequence of aggression directed toward the self rather than outwardly. However, the studies cited above coupled with studies in adults, reflecting a positive correlation between extrapunitive and intrapunitive tendencies, (Feshbach & Singer, 1959) indicate that a direct rather than inverse relationship is more likely to be found.

There are a number of reasons why aggression and depression should be positively correlated. Firstly, if aggressive tendencies are very strong, then all forms of aggression—including aggression directed outwardly and aggression directed toward the self, are likely to be elevated. More importantly, some of the same conditions of rejection, frustration and loss that foster angry feelings and aggressive behaviors also foster depressive reactions. Dispositions to aggression and to depression may co-exist in a child although, at any particular time, a child may react either aggressively or respond in a depressed manner.

In addition to commonality of some of the factors mediating aggression and depression, depression may have a direct effect on aggression. Berkowitz (1989) has proposed, and has provided supportive evidence, that noxious states are antecedents to aggression. Such noxious states include depression as well as frustration and pain. Thus the discomfort associated with a depressive state may lower the threshold for aggressive behavior. A child's aggressive behavior, in turn, may have social consequences that foster depression in that child. A child who persistently responds aggressively is not likely to be a popular child.

Rather, the aggressive behavior is likely to result in peer rejection, iso-lation, punishment and other consequences that would engender depres-sive reactions in a child.

The above considerations lead one to anticipate a positive correla-tion between aggressive and depressive tendencies. However, the strength of this relationship will vary with developmental history and social context. An important factor related both to developmental history and social context is the child's gender. With regard to possible gender differences in the relationship between aggressive and depressive ten-dencies, the first factor of relevance that may influence this relationship is the greater aggressiveness of boys as compared to girls. While this sex difference varies with age and measure, there is a preponderance of data indicating that boys are more aggressive than girls and that aggres-sion in boys is socially more acceptable and more normative than ag-gression in girls. We focus on aggression rather than depression since much less is known about gender differences in depressive tendencies in children.

The greater aggressiveness of boys as compared to girls provides a theoretical basis for anticipating gender differences in the relationship between aggression and depression. Aggression, in addition to being in-fluenced by some of the same painful antecedents that lead to depres-sion, is affected by factors such as reinforcement and modeling of aggressive behavior that are independent of the depressive response. The depressive response, of course, may be influenced by factors that are independent of aggression. With regard to gender differences in aggres-sion, in general, there are more aggressive models for boys than for girls to imitate. Also, aggression in boys is more culturally accepted and more likely to be reinforced than aggressive behavior in girls. These differ-ences in reinforcement history affect gender differences in aggression but do not influence depression. However, at older ages, there appears to be a greater tolerance for depression in girls than in boys, a factor which could also affect the correlation between depression and aggression in older girls.

To the extent that there are differences in the factors influencing aggression and depression, the correlation between them should be low-ered. Consequently, the relationship between aggression and depression should be more attenuated for boys as compared to that of girls. One should expect, then, a higher correlation between depression and ag-gression in girls rather than in boys. In addition, if there are fewer factors influencing aggression in girls than in boys, and depression is one of the factors influencing aggression (Berkowitz, 1989) for both boys and girls, depression should be a more significant element in girls' than in boys' aggressive tendencies. The results of the study reported on here bear on these hypotheses.

One might also anticipate developmental changes in the relationship between aggression and depression that vary with the gender of the child. In particular, as girls mature and enter pre-adolescence, depressive, withdrawal, self-devaluative and related depressive responses may be viewed as more gender appropriate than aggressive responses to painful experiences of rejection and disappointment. At the adult level, there is considerable evidence of gender differences in depression, with females manifesting greater depressive tendencies than males (Hammen & Padesky, 1977). These considerations suggest a developmental change for girls in the degree of relationship between aggression and depression. It may be that with increasing age, the strength of the relationship declines in girls. This possibility will also be addressed by the data.

METHODS

SUBJECTS

The study was carried out at the Corrine A. Seeds University Elementary School, a laboratory school administered by the School of Education and Information Sciences of the University of California, Los Angeles. The population is economically, ethnically, and culturally diverse and is explicitly matched to the proportion of children from different backgrounds in the community. At Time 1, measures of aggressive and depressive tendencies were obtained for a sample of 67, 8-9-year-olds, and an older sample of 76, 10-11-year-olds. Both the older and younger groups were about equally divided as to sex. Forty-four of the 8-9-year-olds were retested two years later (Time 2). A third sample of 40 additional 10-11-year-olds was also tested at Time 2. Combining this latter group with the longitudinal sample and the 10-11-year-olds tested at Time 1 provides a sample of 160 "older" (10-11-year-olds) children for cross-sectional analyses (See Table 1).

PROCEDURE

The self-report inventories were administered to the 10-11-year-old children in their classrooms and to the 8-9-year-olds in small groups of less than ten children. For all groups, each item on an inventory was read aloud, and research assistants were available for individual assistance.

TABLE 1. Cross-Sectional and Longitudinal Samples

Age 8-9	Age 10-11	
Group 1 (n = 67): Time 1	Group 1 (n = 44):	Tested at Time 1 and Time 2
	Group 2 (n = 76):	Tested at Time 1
	Group 3 (n = 40):	Tested at Time 2
	TOTAL 10-11-year-olds n = 160	

THE CHILDREN'S DEPRESSION INVENTORY (CDI)

The CDI was developed by Kovacs (1978a, 1978b, 1980/81) for assessment of the severity of depression in 8-13-year-olds through the child's own report. The current version consists of 27 multiple-choice items representing a sample of affective, cognitive, physiological, and behavioral symptoms of childhood depression such as sadness, anhedonia, and sleep and appetite disturbances. Each item assesses one symptom by presenting three choices (sentences), graded from 0 to 2 in the direction of increasing clinical severity. the child is instructed to chose the one sentence "that describes you best for the past two weeks," . . . "that describes your feelings and ideas." The total score is obtained by summing across all items and can thus range from 0 to 54.

Although the scale has limitations as an indicator of depression, an earlier version of the scale correlated .55 with clinicians' independent global ratings of the severity of depression in a sample of children. A coefficient alpha of .86 was obtained for the current version, and a test-retest reliability of .72 over a one month interval has been reported (Kovacs, 1986).

SELF-REPORT MEASURES OF AGGRESSION

The measure of aggressive tendencies (Agg.), based on Bendig's (1962) revision of the Buss Durkee Inventory consists of 22 items. This scale has been used in a number of studies (Feshbach & Feshbach, 1969, 1982; Feshbach & Singer, 1971) and has been shown to have reasonable reliability (split half and test-retest) when used with elementary school age children as well as with young adults. There is some evidence for the construct validity of these measures. However, self-reports of aggression tend to be more weakly related to other indices of aggression, such as teacher ratings, peer ratings, and behavior observations, than the latter are to each other.

MEASURES COMPLETED BY THE TEACHERS

For each child in the study, the classroom teacher completed a 17-item inventory, each item entailing a five-point rating scale. Seven of the items tap aggression (TR Agg.) and nine assess aspects of depressive affectivity (TR Dep.). The Aggression Rating Scale has been used in an Empathy Training Study (N. Feshbach, 1984; Feshbach & Feshbach, 1982) as well as earlier studies, and has been shown to have satisfactory reliability and to relate systematically to other measures of aggressive behavior. The following are examples of aggression items rated by the teacher: (5) How often does the child make verbal threats to other children? ("I'm going to hit you"; "I'm going to take this pen", etc.); (8) How often does the child physically attach other children? (Biting, pinching, pushing, kicking, etc.). The depressive affectivity rating items were largely adapted from the CDI, with a few based on items from the Lefkowitz and Tesiny (1980) Peer Nomination Inventory of Depression. The following are examples of items included in this rating scale: (2) How often does the child play alone?; (4) how often does the child complain that he/she doesn't feel well?; (12) How often does the child seem to be happy and cheerful?

RESULTS

GENDER DIFFERENCES IN AGGRESSIVE AND DEPRESSIVE TENDENCIES

Although the correlations between aggressive and depressive tendencies are of primary interest, sex differences on these measures are also of interest since they may be germane to the obtained correlations. No significant differences were obtained on either the teacher or child assessment of aggressive or depressive tendencies at age 8-9. At age 10-11, boys' aggression, as assessed by teachers, was significantly higher than girl's aggression ($p < .001$). Since the means for the three 10-11-year-old groups (the longitudinal sample, those assessed at time 1 and those assessed at time 2) were quite similar for each of the measures employed, the data for all of the 10-11-year-olds are included in the cross-sectional comparisons. The gender differences in self-ratings of aggressive tendencies were negligible as was the difference on the depression inventory. While teachers' ratings of boys' depressive tendencies were higher than that of girls, the mean difference was significant at only the .10 level.

TABLE 2. Mean Scores on Measures of Aggression and Depression as a Function of Gender and Age

	Age 8-9			Combined Sample 10-11 (N = 160)		
	M	F	t	M	F	t
	(N = 32)	(N = 35)		(N = 80)	(N = 80)	
Aggression (Child's Self-Report)	10.4	9.5	.72	11.2	10.9	.47
Aggression (Teacher Rating)	15.0	15.4	.35	13.7	11.1	3.86***
Depression (Child's Self-Report)	6.6	6.5	.10	6.5	6.6	.13
Depression (Teacher Rating)	19.0	17.0	.13	17.8	16.3	1.82

*** $p < .001$

The gender differences at age 10-11 in teacher ratings of aggression is in accord with expectation. However, it was also anticipated that boys would manifest greater aggression than girls at the younger age. It was argued that greater aggression in boys was a reflection of differences in the factors affecting aggression in boys and in girls. Although the degree of aggression manifested by 8-9-year-old boys and girls was found to be similar, as assessed by self-ratings and teacher ratings, there might well be a difference in the factors influencing aggression in boys and in girls. If boys' aggression was more influenced by reinforcement of aggression behavior and girls' aggression by experiences of pain and frustration, then on would still expect to find the predicted stronger relationship between aggression and depression in girls as compared to boys.

CORRELATIONS BETWEEN AGGRESSIVE AND DEPRESSIVE TENDENCIES

Findings bearing on the relationship between aggression and depression are presented in Figures 1a and 1b. These figures present respectively, for girls and boys, correlations based on the self-report measures. The boxes on the left side of each diagram represent measures obtained at Time 1 for the 8-9-year-olds. The boxes on the right side of each diagram represent the data obtained for the entire 10-11-year-old sample—that is, combining the 10-11-year-olds tested at Time 1 with those tested at Time 2. The horizontal and diagonal arrows connecting the measures obtained at Time 1 with those obtained at Time 2 convey

FEMALES

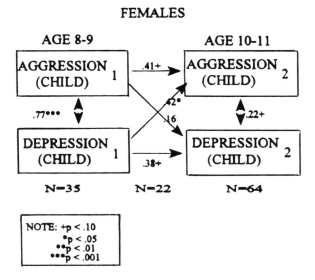

FIGURE 1a. Cross-sectional and longitudinal correlations of girl's self-ratings of aggressive and depressive tendencies.

the results for the longitudinal sample—that is, the subset of 8-9-year-olds who were also assessed at ages 10-11. The correlations between the boxes on the left and right sides of the diagram convey the cross-sectional relationships for the 8-9-year-olds and 10-11-year-olds, respectively. The arrows are intended to convey the time sequence in which the measures were administered and do not imply causation. From Figures 1a and 1b, it can be seen that for both girls and boys, aggressive and depressive tendencies, as assessed in the longitudinal sample, reflect similar stabilities over time, ranging from .36 to .41, significant at the .10 level. The correlations for the combined samples of boys and girls are .39 (p < .01) for aggression and .32 (p < .05) for depression.

In accordance with the hypothesized outcome, the correlation between aggression and depression at age 8-9 is much larger for girls (.77, p < .001) than for boys (.39, p < .05). Using a Z transformation, p-value of the difference between correlations is p < .10. The correlation between aggression and depression at age 10-11 for boys is about the same as at age 8-9 and, because of the larger N, is highly significant (p < .001). In contrast, the correlation of .22 for the older girls is much lower than that for the younger girls, and is lower than that obtained for boys, although not significantly so.

MALES

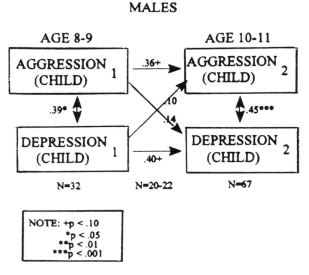

FIGURE 1b. Cross-sectional and longitudinal correlations of boy's self-ratings of aggressive and depressive tendencies.

TEACHER RATINGS OF AGGRESSIVE AND DEPRESSIVE TENDENCIES

Teacher ratings also provide a perspective on the relationship between aggressive and depressive tendencies, particularly since the teacher ratings correlate only modestly with the children's self-reports. As in the case of girls' self-ratings, teacher ratings of girls' aggressive and depressive tendencies are strongly correlated for the 8-9-year-olds. ($r = .68$) While the correlation is much lower for the older girls ($r = .38$), it is still highly significant. In contrast, for boys, the correlation between teacher ratings of aggressive and depressive tendencies are minimal and insignificant at both age levels. The difference obtained for the 8-9-year-olds between the correlation for girls of .68 and the correlation for boys of .10 is significant at the .01 level while the gender difference in these correlations for the older girls and boys falls short of insignificance.

Also of interest are the relationships between aggression and depression when one of these measures is based on the child's assessment and the other, on the teacher's assessment. When the child's self-ratings of aggression are correlated with the teacher's assessment of depressive tendencies, the correlations for both genders are non-significant. However, the inter-relationship between the child's self-rating of depressive tendencies and the teachers' ratings of aggression reflect a pattern similar to that found in the prior analyses of measures from the same source—particularly the children's self-ratings. Depressive and aggressive tendencies are again significantly correlated for the younger age group and are again higher for girls than for boys (.68 versus .39). For the 10-11-year-olds, neither correlation is significant.

The cross-sectional correlations between aggression and depression—those based on self ratings, those based on teacher ratings, those based on self-teacher ratings, strongly confirm the hypothesized gender difference in the relationship between aggression and depression for the younger age group. For the older age group, gender differences were inconsistent. At the same time, the correlations obtained between depression and aggression for the older age group were significant for the boys' and approached significance for the girls' self-ratings, and were significant for the teacher rating measures. Also, the correlations obtained for the older girls were substantially lower than those obtained for the younger girls.

Thus far, we have considered only the cross-sectional data. Although the cross-sectional data are the most germane with respect to the hypotheses of this study, the longitudinal data are also of interest. We have noted the stabilities over time for self-ratings of aggression and depression. The stability correlations obtained for teacher ratings were similar although slightly lower. It is of interest that girls' self-ratings of depressive tendencies at age 8-9 is predictive of girls' self ratings of aggression at age 10-11 ($r = .42$, $p < .05$) and is also predictive of teacher ratings of aggression ($r = .45$; $p < .05$). The only other significant longitudinal relationship was the correlation of .63 ($p < .01$) found between teacher ratings of boys' aggression at age 8-9 and boys' depression at age 10-11.

DISCUSSION

The relationship between aggressive and depressive tendencies in children appears to vary as a function of age, mode of measurement and, with the gender of the child. It was hypothesized that the correlation between aggression and depression would be stronger for girls than for boys. This hypothesis was substantiated for the 8-9-year-old age group but not for the 10-11-year-olds. For the younger girls, there is a much closer relationship between aggression and depression than that found for the younger boys. The relationship between aggression and depression for the older age children, is inconsistent with regard to the hypothesized gender difference. When the child's self-reports are used to assess both aggressive and depressive tendencies, the correlation for boys is actually higher than for girls. When teacher ratings are used to assess these variables, a significant correlation is obtained for girls but not boys. At the same time the relationship for the older girls is much smaller than that for the younger girls, the obtained difference approaching statistical significance.

The developmental decline in girls in the relationship between aggressive and depressive tendencies requires explanation. In this regard, it is noteworthy that depression in girls at age 10-11 is relatively weakly related to aggression at age 10-11. However, girls' self reports of depression at age 8-9 is substantially related to aggression at age 10-11 as well as at age 8-9. For girls then, depression at age 8-9 is a significant predictor of subsequent aggressiveness. For boys, more variable longitudinal relationships are reflected, depending upon the source of the measures. In view of the strong relationship between depressive tendencies in girls at age 8 with aggression at both ages 8-9 and 10-11, and the weak relationship of depression to aggression at age 10-11, it would seem reasonable to suggest that new factors may be influencing depression in the older girls that do not increase aggression, and that were less salient at the younger age period. One possibility is that social rejection assumes an increasing importance for girls as they approach preadolescence, and that girls are more socially oriented than boys. There is both theory and data to support these conjectures (Block, 1973).

It is probably also the case that older children are more likely than younger children to attribute the basis for rejection to their own behaviors and traits than to those of the individuals rejecting them. Self-attribution of blame is likely to foster depressive reactions while attribution of blame to others is likely to foster aggressive reactions (Weiner, 1985). The joint interaction between increased importance of social rejection and an increased tendency to self-blame when rejected could account for the pattern of relationships between aggression and depression obtained for girls.

An additional issue raised by the findings concerns the influence of measurement methods on the results, and especially on their interpretation. In particular, the negligible correlation between children's self-ratings (the CDI) and teacher ratings of depression raises a question as to the comparability and meaning of findings with these respective measures. For some analyses, self and teacher ratings of depression related similarly to measures of aggression while this was not the case for other analyses. The teacher appears to be capturing some component of the complex of affect and behaviors encompassed by the construct of depressive tendencies, but a different component than that which is most salient to the child. In order to understand the similarities and differences in the correlates of teacher and child assessments of depressive tendencies, research is needed to identify the specific bases for the child's self appraisals and the teacher's judgments.

From a theoretical standpoint, it is important to delineate more precisely the factors mediating the relationship between aggression and depression. We have proposed that aggression and depression would be positively correlated since they are each responses to experiences of pain and dysphoria. At the same time, aggression and depression may be differentially reinforced and differentially evoked by particular disturbing events, thereby reducing any correlation between them. And, as has been noted, differential attributions also may foster either an aggressive or a depressive reaction. Nevertheless, it is significant that none of the cross-sectional and longitudinal analyses that were carried out reflect an inverse relationship. The correlations between aggression and depression were either positive or negligible.

In addition to aggression and depression being correlated because they are linked to similar negative experiences, one must also consider possible dynamic connections between these two response patterns. The finding for girls of a positive relationship between depressive tendencies at age 8-9 and aggressive tendencies at age 10-11 is suggestive in this regard. Additional research is needed to account for this correlation which may reflect either a dynamic connection or response pattern stabilities over time. The one finding indicating a positive correlation in boys between aggression at age 8-9 and depression at age 10-11 is also suggestive. To account for the longitudinal relationships, one could invoke a psychoanalytic formulation regarding the direction of aggression in girls, first inward and then outward, and, in boys first outward and then inward. However, the evidence of positive relationships between aggression and depression argues against this type of formulation. Rather, in our view, one needs to look at the social consequences and stability of aggressive and depressive reactions over time and how these may vary with the gender of the child. In the case of girls, we have suggested that the correlation between depression at age 8-9 and aggression at age 10-11 is a function of the stability of aggressive tendencies during this time period and the strong initial correlation between aggression and depression. In the case of boys, where the correlation between aggression and depression at age 8-9 is low, their aggressiveness may result in experiences of social rejection and devaluation that foster depressive reactions as they enter pre-puberty.

Aggression and depression do not appear to be mutually exclusive personality dispositions. In many instances, clinical and social interventions concerned with reducing a child's aggressive behavior may also need to address depressive reactions. A better understanding of the dynamics mediating aggressive and depressive responses in children and their interaction should help in developing more effective intervention efforts.

REFERENCES

Feshbach, N.D. & Feshbach, S. (1969). The relationship between empathy and aggression in two age groups. *Developmental Psychology, 1,* 102-107.

Feshbach, N. D., & Feshbach, S. (1971). Children's aggression. *Young Children, 26*(6), 364-377.

Feshbach, N. D., ·& Feshbach, S. (1982). Empathy training the regulation of aggression: Potentialities and limitations. *Academic Psychology Bulletin, 4,* 399-413.

Feshbach, N. D. & Feshbach, S. (1987). Affective processes and academic achievement. *Child Development, 58,* 1335-1347.

Feshbach, S. (1970). Aggression. In P. H. Mussen (Ed.), *Carmichael's manual of child psychology.* New York: Wiley.

Feshbach, S., & Singer, R. D. (1971). *Television and aggression.* San Francisco: Jossey-Bass.

Fischer, M., Rolf, E., Hasazi, J., & Cummings, L. (1984). Follow-up of a pre-school epidemiological sample: Cross-age continuities and predictions of later adjustment with internalizing and externalizing dimensions of behavior, *Child Development, 55,* 137-150.

Hammen, C. L. & Padesky, C. A. (1977). Sex differences in the expression of depressive responses on the Beck Depression Inventory. *Journal of Abnormal Psychology, 86,* 609-614.

Kazdin, A. (1989). Depression in Children. In E. Mash and R. Barkley (Eds.), *Treatment of Childhood Behavior Disorders.* New York: Guilford.

Kazdin, A. & Esveldt-Dawson, K. (1986). The Interview for Antisocial Behavior: Psychometric characteristics and concurrent validity with child psychiatric inpatients, *Journal of Psychopathology and Behavioral Assessment, 8,* 289-303.

Kovacs, M. (1978a). *Children's Depression Inventory (CDI).* Unpublished manuscript, University of Pittsburgh.

Kovacs, M. (1978b). *The Children's Depression Inventory: A self-rated depression scale for school aged youngsters.* Unpublished manuscript, University of Pittsburgh, School of Medicine.

Kovacs, M. (1980/81). Rating scales to assess depression in school aged children. *Acta Paedopsychiatrica, 46,* 305-315.

Kovacs, M. (1986). A developmental perspective on methods and measurements in the assessment of depressive disorders: The clinical interview. In M. Rutter, C. E. Izard, & P. B. Read (Eds.), *Depression in young people: Developmental and clinical perspectives* (pp. 435-465). New York: Guilford.

Lachar, D., & LaCombe, J. (1983). Objective personality assessment: The Personality Inventory for Children and its applications in the school setting, *School Psychology Review, 12,* 399-406.

Lefkowitz, M. M., & Tesiny, E. P. (1980). Assessment of childhood depression. *Journal of Consulting and Clinical Psychology, 48,* 43-50.

Mattison, R., Bagnato, S., & Strickler, E. (1987). Diagnostic importance of combined parent and teacher ratings on the Revised Behavior Problem Checklist, *Journal of Abnormal Child Psychology, 15,* 617-628.

Nolen-Hoeksema, S. (1987). Sex Differences in Unipolar Depression: Evidence and Theory. *Psychological Bulletin, 101,* 259-282.

Parke, R. D., & Slaby (1983). The development of aggression. In P. H. Mussen (Gen. Ed.) & E. M. Hetherington (Vol. Ed.), *Handbook of Child Psychology, 4,* socialization, personality and social development (fourth Edition). New York: Wiley.

Pfeffer, C., Zuckerman, S., Plutchik, R., & Mizruchi, M. (1987). Assaultive behavior in normal school children, *Children Psychiatry and Human Development, 17,* 165-176.

Rubin, K. H., & Mills, R. S. L. (1988). The many faces of social isolation in childhood. *Journal of Consulting and Clinical Psychology, 56,* 916-924.

Sines, J. (1986). Normative data for the revised Missouri Children's Behavior Checklist Parent Forum, *Journal of Abnormal Psychology, 14,* 88-94.

Singer, R., & Feshbach, S. (1959). Some relationships between manifest anxiety, authoritarian tendencies, and modes of reaction to frustration. *Journal of Abnormal and Social Psychology, 59,* 404-408.

Treiber, F., & Mabe III, P. (1987). Child and parent perceptions of children's psychopathology in psychiatric outpatient children, *Journal of Abnormal Child Psychology, 15,* 115-124.

Weiner, B. (1985). An attributional theory of achievement motivation and emotion. *Psychological Review, 92,* 548-573.

PART III

SOCIAL INFLUENCES ON AGGRESSION

CHAPTER 9

POVERTY AND VIOLENCE

LEONARD D. ERON, NANCY GUERRA, AND L. ROWELL HUESMANN

What is the relation between poverty and violence? This is difficult to ascertain because violence is a multidetermined behavior and poverty is just one of the factors that help determine whether a person will respond with violence in a given situation. Many of these contributory factors are biological, many are psychological, social, economic and/or political. No one factor by itself can explain the cause of violence. It is only when there is a convergence of many of these factors that violence occurs. Poverty by itself does not explain much of the variance in violent behavior. However, each of the accompaniments of poverty probably contributes its own effect—homelessness, overcrowding, lack of opportunity, economic deprivation. And these then interact with the biological and psychological factors, e.g. low birth weight, neurological trauma, learning disorders, bad socialization practices of parents, etc.

One of the most obvious confounding factors in relating poverty to violence is race and vice versa, the relation of race to violence is confounded by poverty. We are all familiar with the grim statistics about

LEONARD D. ERON • Department of Psychology, University of Michigan, Ann Arbor, Michigan 48109-1109. NANCY GUERRA • Department of Psychology, University of Illinois, Chicago, Box 4348, Chicago, Illinois 60680. L. ROWELL HUESMANN • Research Center for Group Dynamics, Institute for Social Research, University of Michigan, Ann Arbor, Michigan 48106-1248.

Aggression: Biological, Developmental, and Social Perspectives, edited by Seymour Feshbach and Jolanta Zagrodzka. Plenum Press, New York, 1997.

139

the high rate of violent crime in the African-American community, especially among adolescent males. And we also know that African-Americans to a very disproportionate extent live in areas of poverty. It is a confounding factor that has been difficult to tear apart.

SOCIOLOGICAL EXPLANATIONS

Sociologists, in their efforts to separate the effects of race and poverty on rates of violence, have largely come to the conclusion that poverty, not race is the greatest predictor of violence. Racial differences in homicide rates are greatly reduced or disappear when the data are controlled by income. However, according to sociologists, the effect of poverty on violence is conditional on other variables, most notably mobility and change within the context of communities. Sampson (1993) has demonstrated that there is a significant interaction between mobility and low income which explains violence across many different neighborhoods in three different American cities. According to Sampson, mobility was positively associated with violent crime rates in poor neighborhoods, yet this association was not found in more affluent areas. Thus he concluded that communities that are characterized by rapid population turnover and high levels of poverty have significantly higher violent crime rates than mobile areas that are more affluent or poor areas that are stable.

The major factor implicated in this mobility is its association with the downward spiral which Wilson (1987) has described as a community becoming increasingly "underclass," with the middle class and professionals moving out. Therefore, according to sociologists, it is the constellation of factors in a community and not poverty or race alone which are critical in explaining violence, especially homicide. According to Wilson (1987) the economy of this country has dramatically shifted from a largely manufacturing economy to primary service industries. The manufacturing jobs have been shipped out of the Northeast and Midwest cities to Asia where wages are lower. Factories all over the United States have closed. This has resulted in the substantial decline of traditional jobs in cities for individuals with a high school education or less. As hundreds of thousands of factory jobs were demolished, many African-American men were left without a viable way to earn a living. The replacement jobs in the service industries generally require a higher level of skill and training than was available to them (Prothrow-Stith, 1991).

At the same time that this was occurring, many in the middle class were moving out of the inner cities leaving only the poorest of the poor. Hence, we see the emergence of the underclass. With the exit of many of the professionals who provided examples of the pathways to upward mobility for children; communities were destabilized, social networks were fractured, critical institutions closed, and organizing for political action was seriously diminished. This left the inner cities vulnerable to the epidemic of violence and drug trafficking which would soon follow.

This sociological account would seem to offer an explanation, grounded in the social and economic changes in communities, of why many of our urban centers became vulnerable to community violence. We can conclude from this brief review of social factors that the combination of poverty and lack of access to the economic pathways into the mainstream economy are the most significant predictors of youth involvement in violence.

PSYCHOLOGICAL EXPLANATIONS

However, just as poverty, by itself, cannot explain differential rates of violence to the satisfaction of sociologists, the social accompaniments of poverty cannot explain individual differences in the occurrence of violence to the satisfaction of psychologists. These macrosocial and macroeconomic variables, while of unquestionable importance, do not explain why some children living in these circumstances grow up to be violent and others do not. Clearly, not every African-American adolescent male living in poverty, in a single parent family, in a high crime, downwardly mobile neighborhood, closed off from many opportunities to advance educationally and occupationally, engages in violent behavior; only a minority of them do. The individual most likely to behave aggressively and violently is one who has been programmed to respond in this way through previous experience and learning. Somewhere in his or her background the individual who becomes violent and aggressive must have learned these ways to solve interpersonal problems, relieve frustration and acquire material possessions. These behaviors don't spring up spontaneously like Pallas Athena out of Zeus' head when the youngster reaches adolescence. In his or her past history the violence prone individual must have observed this behavior, seen it rewarded, might have personally engaged in it or at least fantasized about it and when the conditions are judged appropriate the individual responds with violent behavior.

The specific conditions which have been shown empirically to be most conducive to the learning and maintenance of aggression are those in which the child is reinforced for his or her own aggression (e.g. Patterson, 1986), is provided many opportunities to observe aggression (e.g. Bandura, 1973; Eron, Huesmann, Lefkowitz & Walder, 1972), is given few opportunities to develop positive affective social bonds with others (e.g. Hawkins & Weis, 1985), and is the object of aggression (e.g. Dodge, Bates, & Petit, 1990). While these conditions can exist in all social classes, they are more likely in the inner-city environment with its extreme economic and social deprivation (McLoyd, 1990).

Thus, rather than poverty per se, there also may be psychological factors associated with poverty for certain people at certain times that increase risk for aggression. These factors are correlated with poverty, but are not equivalents. Two factors that may be influential are stressful events and beliefs promoting aggression.

Individuals living in inner-city communities are exposed to a relentless succession of stressful events in the context of chronically stressful conditions. Stress exposure increases risk for a range of socio-emotional and behavioral problems (Compas, Howell, Phares, Williams, & Guinta, 1989; Pryor-Brown & Cowen, 1989; Rutter, 1990), and the effects of stress exposure are multiplicative rather than additive (Garmezy, 1987). Still, few studies of the stress-adjustment relation have focused on disadvantaged urban children who are exposed to multiple stressors, and even fewer studies have examined the effects of different types of stressors on aggressive behavior.

Growing up in disadvantaged urban settings may also encourage individual beliefs promoting aggression (Miller, 1958). Through observation and direct tuition, children may adopt normative beliefs approving of aggressive behavior as a means of gaining status, material rewards, or simply coping with fear of victimization (Guerra, Huesmann, & Hanish, 1994). Anderson (1990) reports that a "code of violence" often prevails among youth in impoverished urban areas whereby violence is seen as a legitimate and appropriate behavior. Normative beliefs approving of aggression have indeed been reported in samples of urban children (Huesmann, Guerra, Miller, & Zelli, 1992) although the relation between economic status and beliefs has not been evaluated.

In a large-scale prevention study in Chicago, the *Metropolitan Area Child Study*, it has been possible to examine the interrelations of some of these psychological factors with poverty to help account for the development of aggressive behavior in young children. Using two-waves of data collected from a large sample of children, the joint influence on aggression of (a) poverty; (b) stressful events (negative life events and exposure to violence); and (c) individual beliefs approving of aggression was investigated (Guerra, Eron, Huesmann, Tolan, & Van Acker, 1996).

Although the ecology of the inner-city environment is extremely complex and affects children at multiple levels, these factors have not been implicated in previous studies.

Within the context of this large-scale intervention study data were collected which it was expected would clarify the interaction of poverty with the extent of exposure to stressful life events, and the adoption of a set of values and beliefs supporting aggression. These data were collected from 1935 children who were present when data collection began and who remained at the same school until data collection was completed two years later. The ethnic distribution of the sample was 39% African-American, 42% Hispanic (primarily first-generation of Mexican descent), and 19% Non-Hispanic White. The sample was about evenly split between boys and girls (49% boys and 51% girls).

Aggression was determined using both teacher ratings on the *Child Behavior Checklist* (Achenbach, 1978) and peer nominations of aggression (Eron et al., 1972). The child's economic status was determined by eligibility for free lunch (none, partial, full), which is based on a family income that is slightly above the poverty level. Exposure to stress was measured by the 16-item *Stress Index* (Attar, Guerra, & Tolan, 1994) that included 6 items tapping stress due to exposure to neighborhood violence and 10 items measuring stressful life events. Beliefs about aggression were measured using the *Normative Beliefs About Aggression Scale* (NOBAGS), a 20-item scale tapping the acceptability of aggressive behavior (Huesmann et al., 1992).

LEVELS OF AGGRESSIVE BEHAVIOR

The aggression scores in this sample were quite high by national standards for children this age. The mean score for all boys and girls was .219 (SD = .178) on peer-nominated aggression. This indicates that, on average, children were nominated 21.9% of the times they could have been nominated on the aggression items. By contrast, in their study of a semi-rural, low- to middle-income population in 1960, Eron, Huesmann, Lefkowitz, and Walder (1972) found that, on average, children were nominated 11.9% of the time. The overall mean score on the CBC for all children was 6.56 (SD = 10.1), which falls at about the 70th percentile on national norms (Achenbach, 1991). Approximately 20% of the sample scored above 16, which would be about the 90th percentile on national norms.

The mean scores on peer-nominated aggression are plotted as a function of gender and grade in Figure 1. As expected, an analysis of variance revealed a significant gender by grade interaction, a main effect

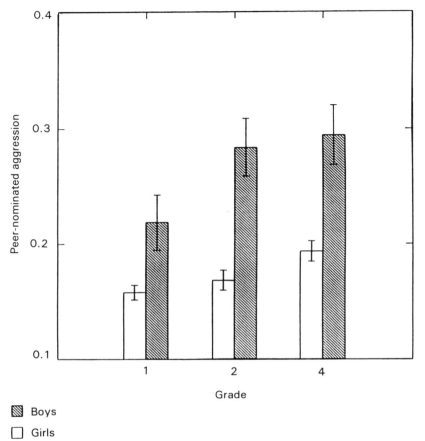

FIGURE 1. Mean peer-nominated aggression scores as a function of gender and grade.

for gender with boys more aggressive, and a main effect for grade with older children more aggressive. As Figure 1 reveals, this gender by grade interaction is caused primarily by boys increasing more in aggression from 1st to 2nd grade than girls. These effects for gender and grade were present within all three ethnic groups.

AGGRESSION, ECONOMIC STATUS, AND ETHNICITY

In Figure 2 peer nominated aggression is plotted for the three different levels of free lunch status and for the three ethnic groups. As

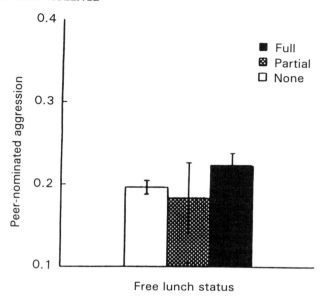

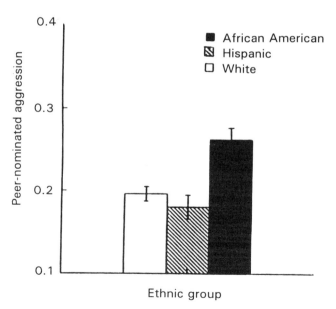

FIGURE 2. Mean peer-nominated aggression scores as a function of free-lunch status and ethnicity.

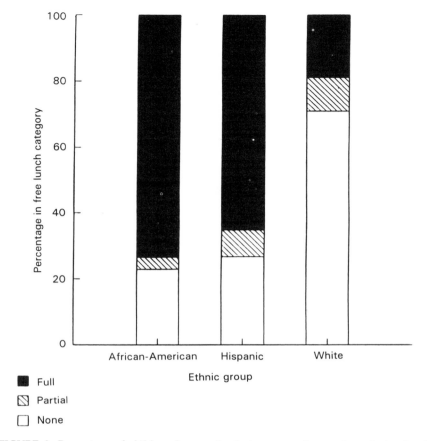

FIGURE 3. Percentage of children from each ethnic group who are in each free-lunch category.

expected, the poorest children display significantly more aggression. African-American children also display significantly more aggression than the other groups. However, as Figure 3 displays, free lunch status also varies significantly across ethnic groups, with African-American children having the highest proportion qualifying for free lunch. Taken together these figures illustrate a fundamental confounding in this population that makes it very difficult to separate the effects of poverty from other factors related to ethnicity. As a result we conducted subsequent analyses within ethnic groups as well as across groups.

SYNCHRONOUS RELATIONS AMONG AGGRESSION, ECONOMIC STATUS, STRESSFUL EVENTS, AND INDIVIDUAL BELIEFS

As shown in Table 1, aggression correlates weakly but significantly with free lunch status. This is consistent with the data presented above in Figure 2. In this same table data from the parent interview show that parents who have been employed more during the last year have less aggressive children, although the education level of the parents by itself does not predict aggression.

However, the strongest correlate of aggressive behavior is a child's normative beliefs about the appropriateness of aggression. These beliefs also correlate with free-lunch status. On the average, poorer children have beliefs that are more accepting of aggressive behavior, and children with more accepting beliefs behave more aggressively. Similarly, the two stress measures correlate very significantly with aggression, and relate significantly to free-lunch status. More impoverished children experience more neighborhood violence stress and more life events stress, and those children who experience more stress engage in more aggressive behavior.

When the correlations were computed for males and females separately there was little change. Similarly when the correlations of these variables are calculated separately for each ethnic group, as Table 2 indicates, the positive correlation between peer-nominated aggressive behavior and self-reported beliefs approving of aggression was highly significant in all three ethnic groups. The correlations between more aggressive behavior and exposure to life events stress and neighborhood violence stress also held up across ethnic groups. However, free lunch status only correlated with aggression for the non-Hispanic White children. There was substantial variation in economic status in the other two samples, but that variation did not relate to more or less aggressive behavior.

In order to estimate more accurately the separate contributions to aggressive behavior of the several correlates of poverty that we have measured, we calculated a series of multiple regressions. In Table 3 multiple regressions are presented (for all subjects and separately for males and females) relating children's aggressive behavior to free-lunch status, stressful events, and normative beliefs, with grade as a covariate. The first regression for each sample includes only the effects of grade and individual free-lunch status. This regression shows that for all children and for boys and girls separately, poorer children behave more

TABLE 1. Correlations between Aggressive Behavior, Economic Status, Stressful Events, and Individual Beliefs (N = 1,921)

	Economic Status				Stress		Beliefs	
	Peer-nom Aggress	Individ Free-lunch	Parent Employ	Parent Educat	Life Events	Neighbor Violence	Approval of Aggress	Hopelessness
Peer-nominated Aggression	1.00							
Free-lunch status	.07***	1.00						
Months employed in last year[a]	-.13**	-.24****	1.00					
Educational level[a]	.06	-.26****	.07	1.00				
Life Events Stress	.16****	.08***	-.07	-.04	1.00			
Neighborhood Violence Stress	.16****	.17****	-.06	-.10**	.37****	1.00		
Beliefs Approving of Aggression	.19****	.10****	-.08*	-.12***	.04	.05	1.00	

One-tailed: *p < .05; **p < .025; ***p < .01; ****p < .001
[a]n = 461 for these measures from parent interview data

TABLE 2. Correlations between Aggressive Behavior, Economic Status, Stressful Events, and Individual Beliefs by Ethnic Group (N = 1,921)

	White (n = 356)		Hispanic (n = 708)		African-American (n = 857)	
	Peer-nom Aggress	Individ Free-lunch	Peer-nom Aggress	Individ Free-lunch	Peer-nom Aggress	Individ Free-lunch
Peer-nominated Aggression	1.00		1.00		1.00	
Free-lunch status	.15***	1.00		1.00		1.00
Months employed in last year[a]	-.07	-.41****	-.05	-.08	-.08	-.36****
Educational level[a]	-.11	-.07	.08	-.17***	-.04	-.17
Life Events Stress	.11*	.10	.10**	.10*	.13***	.08
Neighborhood Violence Stress	.23****	.08	.08**	.05	.11**	.13***
Beliefs Approving of Aggression	.19****	.07	.20****	.09*	.15****	.04

One-tailed: *p < .05; **p < .025; ***p < .01; ****p < .001
[a]For these measures from the parent interview data, N = 123 for White, N = 226 for Hispanic, N = 109 for African-American.

TABLE 3. Standardized Regression Coefficients Predicting Peer-Nominated Aggression from Free-Lunch Status and Correlates of Economic Disadvantage (Complete data cases only)

| | Peer-nominated Aggression (91) First year | | | | | |
| | All Subjects (N = 966) | | Males (N = 499) | | Females (N = 467) | |
Predictor Variables	Regres 1	Regres 2	Regres 1	Regres 2	Regres 1	Regres 2
Grade	.14****	.12****	.12***	.08	.18****	.20****
Free-Lunch Status	.10**	.06	.07	.05	.14***	.08
Life Events Stress		.07*		.08		.11*
Neighborhood Violence Stress		.14****		.12**		.17***
Beliefs Approving of Aggression		.11***		.12		.01
R^2	.026****	.066****	.015***	.051****	.042****	.086****
df	963	5,960	496	5,493	464	7,418

One-tailed: *p < .05; **p < .025; ***p < .01; ****p < .001

aggressively independently of grade. The effects are not large but they are significant. The second regression for each sample shows what happens when stressful events and children's normative beliefs about aggression are added to the prediction. The most notable finding is that for the total sample, both life events stress and neighborhood violence stress are the best predictors of aggression, with aggressive normative beliefs also significant. Free-lunch status becomes non-significant as a predictor of aggression, suggesting that the relation between poverty and aggression must be partially due to associated stressful events and beliefs supporting aggression predicting aggressive behavior.

In Table 4 when the regressions are recomputed separately for the three ethnic subgroups, consistent with the correlations displayed earlier in Table 2, free-lunch status only has a significant relation to children's aggression in the non-Hispanic white subgroup. However, when all the variables are added into the equation, neighborhood violence stress had a significant effect on aggression in all subgroups. In addition, aggressive normative beliefs is a significant predictor for the white and Hispanic children, although not for the African-American children.

CONCLUSIONS

Both sociologists and psychologists have demonstrated that there is a relation between violence and poverty, but that poverty itself, defined as a lack of monetary resources, cannot explain why some individuals engage in violence and others do not. Researchers in each discipline have attempted to determine what it is about poverty that causes people to act in violent ways to vent frustration and to acquire possessions they want but cannot afford. Sociologists have demonstrated that the mobility associated with poverty is important in understanding its relation to violence.

Psychologists, in general, have not examined the mechanisms by which individual poverty affects an individual's propensity to behave violently. In this chapter, we have demonstrated that two correlates of poverty, level of stress experienced and normative beliefs about aggression, but not poverty itself, explains some variation in levels of aggressive behavior.

The missing part of the puzzle is how sociological factors such as mobility relate to individual variables such as stress and normative beliefs, and how together they relate to violent behavior. Sociological explanations highlight contextual factors that contribute to violence but still do not explain the precise processes by which these factors predict individual variation. In the same way, psychological explanations have

TABLE 4. Standardized Regression Coefficients Predicting Peer-Nominated Aggression from Free-Lunch Status and Correlates of Economic Disadvantage for Ethnic Subgroups (Complete data cases only)

| | Peer-nominated Aggression | | | | | |
| | White (N = 216) ETGRP = 4 | | Hispanic (N = 406) ETGRP = 5 | | African-American (N = 344) ETGRP = 1 | |
Predictor Variables	Regres 1	Regres 2	Regres 1	Regres 2	Regres 1	Regres 2
Grade	.10	.02	.08	.07	.22****	.22****
Free-Lunch Status	.16**	.13*	.02	.002	.07	.05
Life Events Stress	.06		.02			.07
Neighborhood Violence Stress		.17**		.13**		.09
Beliefs Approving of Aggression		.16**		.13**		.07
R^2	.026	.076	.002	.031	.045	.058
df	213	5,210	403	5,400	341	5,338

One-tailed: *$p < .05$; **$p < .025$; ***$p < .01$; ****$p < .001$

tended to focus on individual factors and individual pathology, without consideration of how these factors may be influenced by contextual events or circumstances. These separate strands of research must be woven together if we are to understand the complex mechanisms by which societal factors such as poverty influence violent behavior.

REFERENCES

Achenbach, T. M. (1978). The child behavior profile: I. Boys aged 6-11. *Journal of Consulting and Clinical Psychology, 46,* 478-488.

Achenbach, T. M. (1991). *Integrative guide for the 1991 CBCL/4-18, YSR, and TRF profiles.* Burlington, VT: University of Vermont Department of Psychiatry.

Anderson, E. J. (1990). *Streetwise: Race, class, and change in an urban community.* Chicago: University of Chicago Press.

Attar, B. K., Guerra, N. G., & Tolan, P. H. (in press). Neighborhood disadvantage, stressful life events, and adjustment in urban elementary school children. *Journal of Clinical Child Psychology.*

Bandura, A. (1973). *Aggression: A social learning analysis.* Englewood Cliffs, NJ: Prentice-Hall.

Compas, B. E., Howell, D. C., Phares, V., Williams, R. G., & Giunta, C. T. (1989). Risk factors for emotional/behavioral problems in young adolescents: A prospective analysis of adolescent and parental stress and symptoms. *Journal of Consulting and Clinical Psychology, 57,* 732-740.

Dodge, K. A., Bates, J. E., & Pettit, G. S., (1990). Mechanisms in the cycle of violence. *Science, 250,* 1678-1683.

Eron, L. D., Huesmann, L. R., Lefkowitz, M. M., & Walder, L. O. (1972). Does television violence cause aggression? *American Psychologist, 27,* 253-263.

Garmezy, N. (1987). Stress, competence and development: Continuities in the study of schizophrenic adults, children vulnerable to psychopathology, and the search for stress-resistant children. *American Journal of Orthopsychiatry, 57,* 159-174.

Guerra, N. G., Eron, L. D., Huesmann, L. R., Tolan, P., & Van Acker, R. (in press). A cognitive/ecological approach to the prevention and mitigation of violence and aggression in inner-city youth. In K. Bjorkquist (Ed.), *Cultural variation in conflict resolution.* Mahwah, NJ: Erlbaum.

Guerra, N. G., Huesmann, L. R., & Hanish, L. (1994). The role of normative beliefs in children's social behavior. N. Eisenberg (Ed.), *Review of Personality and Social Psychology, Development and Social Psychology: The Interface.* (pp.140-158) London: Sage.

Hawkins, J. D., & Weiss, J. F. (1985). The social development model: An integrated approach to delinquency prevention. *Journal of Primary Pediatrics, 6,* 73-97.

Huesmann, L. R., Guerra, N. G., Miller, L., & Zelli, A. (1992). The role of social norms in the development of aggression. In H.Zumckly & A Fraczek (Eds.), *Socialization and aggression* (pp.139-151). New York: Springer-Verlag.

Kotlowitz, A. (1991). *There are no children here.* New York: Doubleday.

McLoyd, V. C. (1990). The impact of economic hardship on Black families and children: Psychological distress, parenting, and socioemotional development. *Child Development, 61,* 311-346.

Miller, W. (1958). Lower class culture as a generating milieu of gang delinquency. *Journal of Social Issues, 14,* 5-19.

Patterson, G. R. (1986). Performance models for antisocial boys. *American Psychologist, 41,* 432-444.

Prothrow-Stith, D. (1991). *Deadly consequences.* New York: HarperCollins.

Pryor-Brown, L., & Cowen, E. C. (1989). Stressful life events, support and children's school adjustment. *Journal of Clinical Child Psychology, 18,* 214-220.

Ratter, M. (1990). Psychosocial resilience and protective mechanisms. In J. E. Rolf, C. S. Masten, D. Cicchetti, K. H. Neuchtenlein, & S. Weintraub (Eds.). *Risk and protective factors in the development of psychopathology* (pp. 181-214). Cambridge, England: Cambridge University Press.

Sampson, R. J. (1993). The community context of violent crime. In W. J. Wilson (Ed.) *Sociology and the public agency* (pp. 259-286). Newbury Park, CA: Sage.

Wilson, W. J. (1987). *The truly disadvantaged.* Chicago, IL: University of Chicago Press.

Chapter 10

CAN OUTFIT BE AGGRESSIVE? VALUES AND IMAGES OF PUNKS

Kirsti Lagerspetz, Ari Kaukiainen,
Päivi Myöhönen, and Kaj Björkqvist

When seeing young people in punk outfit in the streets, one is likely to wonder about certain issues. For instance, what precisely is the message that these people wish to convey through their conspicuous clothing and behaviour? Do they want to scare, irritate, attract attention, charm, express rebellion, criticize the society, or just emphasize their difference from other people? How do other people receive this "communication by outfit"? And are punks disposed to aggression and social behavior? These were some of the questions we wanted to get answers to in the present investigation.

Outfit has been used as a means of non-verbal communication, probably throughout the history of mankind. There are numerous examples of this usage: the military, the clergy, ethnic minorities like the gypsies, prostitutes, and youth subcultures. In some cases, the messages are easy to read and spell out. For instance, rank and branch of military

Kirsti Lagerspetz, Ari Kaukiainen, and Päivi Myöhönen • Department of Psychology, University of Turku, Arwidssoninkatu 1, SF–20 500, Turku, Finland. Kaj Björkqvist • Department of Psychology, Abo Akademi University, 65100 Vasa, Finland.

Aggression: Biological, Developmental, and Social Perspectives, edited by Seymour Feshbach and Jolanta Zagrodzka. Plenum Press, New York, 1997.

service can be known by the outfit of a lieutenant of almost any army. In other cases, the message is more ambiguous. And still, one may venture to say that always when a person appears in public, he or she conveys some messages to other people through his or her outfit, and other people are receiving the messages and answering to them by their own behavior. A movement whose members seem to send quite powerful messages of this type are the punks. But what are they saying?

Researchers of so called countercultures have pointed out that through their existence, these carry on a kind of aggressive dialogue with the main culture. Through the divergent appearance of its members, graffiti, pamphlets, music, and violence the movements seem to criticize, perhaps accuse, the main culture (Fornäs, Lindberg, & Sernhede 1984; Brake, 1985; Brinkman & Reinhard, 1989). According to Hebdige (1984), punks by their outfit make public the perverse elements of the main culture, like violence, sexuality, and fetishism, by emphasizing, yet mocking it.

When it is not possible for the members of a social group to attain the values held, to avoid the sanctions, and to obtain the gratifications offered by the main culture, the members create a system of their own with different ideals, rewards, and punishments (Willis, 1990). Adherence to these makes it possible for the members of the subgroup to gain respect, attain a positive self-identity, and feel that they compete successfully, at least within their own group.

Youth "subcultures" have been analyzed by many authors (e.g., Clarke, Hall, Jefferson & Roberts 1981, Wartenberg 1984, Fornäs, Lindberg & Sernhede, 1984, Stratton, 1985, Grabner 1985, Lamy & Lewin, 1985, Brake, 1985, Lehtonen, 1989, Fox 1987, and Widdicombe & Wooffitt, 1990). The subcultures have been seen by researchers as attempts at solutions to social and cultural problems prevailing in a society.

Stratton (1985) divides youth subcultures into commodity-oriented and spectacular ones. Commodity-oriented subcultures have a kind of program. They resist explicitly the social order, consumerism, the social class system, and middle class values. Spectacular youth cultures, on the other hand, are showing off their criticism through their own body; they express their message symbolically by dress, attitudes, music, and behavior. It seems that punk contains both types of members. According to some studies (Fox 1987; Widdicombe & Wooffitt 1990), within the punk movement there are two types of members: "real" and "hardcore" punks, that is, those who are committed to the ideology, and those who only use punk type outfit.

The punk movement has been described in Britain by Thompson (1979), in Germany by Becker, Eigenbrodt and May (1983), in Denmark by Bay (1984), in Sweden by Roe (1985), in Austria by Grabner (1985), in the United States by Fox (1987), in Italy by Bortino and Gilardi (1989), in Canada by Baron (1989), in the Soviet Union by Nemirovskij (1989), and in Scotland by Widdicombe and Wooffitt (1990).

The punk movement has a history of about twenty years. It started in Great Britain in 1976. Although we do not know about statistics of the frequencies of punks, the impression is that since the early 1980's, the frequency of punks has been declining (e.g. Fox, 1987, mentions this). Music is a central element in punk culture (Roe, 1985). The punk obtained musical influences mainly from the American "garage" bands, and British pub-rock.

Another typical feature of the punk movement, in addition to the music is, as already pointed out, the ostentatious clothing of the members. The outfit shows individual variation within the group, but it follows special unwritten rules which makes it easy for anybody to distinguish adherents to the punk movement from other people. In punk, dressing is the most powerful, although nonverbal, message (Hebdige, 1985).

The punk movement uses verbal dialogue, press, and written word only to a small extent. It is diffuse, unorganized, conflictual, scattered, and changing in its values, it does not have a coherent philosophy (Burr, 1984; Wartenberg, 1984; Hebdige, 1985), and it is not a political youth culture like the hippies were (Bortino & Gilardi 1989). This vagueness and informality allows for personal interpretations by the individual members as well as outsiders. It is a sign of appeal and strength on part of the youth movements that many of them have a tendency to spread to different countries all over the world.

The working class background of the members has been stressed in previous studies. For instance, in Great Britain punks at least previously came mostly from the working class (Lamy & Levin, 1985). However, presently members are recruited also from the middle class. In bigger cities, there are both working class and middle class groups of punks, which sometimes mix, but are mostly separate (Brake 1985). According to Fox (1987), in The United States "pretender" punks tend to have a middle class background, whereas "hardcore" punks come mostly from the working class. An emphasis on masculinity and aggression, and a high prevalence of drug abuse and deliquency have been described as typical of punks (Brake, 1985; Grabner, 1985; Gold, 1987).

There are studies in the literature on people's reactions to punks (e.g., Glick, DeMorest, & Hotze 1988), but published reports about their home background are scarce. These few studies (Burr 1984, Grabner 1985, Gold 1987) suggest that the primary family of the punks has often been shattered. According to Grabner (1985) the parents of punks in Vienna were commonly divorced. After the divorce, the mother was often incapable of taking care of the children, and the children were either transferred to children's homes or taken care of by the grandparents. Some of the mothers, however, kept their children. Eventually the situation became so stressful for many of these mothers that the atmosphere of the home was characterized by lack of care and of positive feelings. At the time when compulsory schooling ended, if not before, the limits of the family upbringing became visible. In the case of most punks, the transition from school to work or to further education was unsuccessful, leading to growing conflicts in the home. Accordingly, the young people moved out and did not want to keep contact with their home.

The main purpose of the present study was to investigate, how punks themselves conceptualize the messages which they convey to other people. In order to understand the background of these messages, we also tried to determine the kind of values, plans and fears the punks we interviewed had as compared to another group of young people. We were particularly interested in aggressive values and intentions. Furthermore, in order to understand more about why they held these values, i.e. wanted to be punks, we also interviewed them about their home background. We asked how they experienced their relations with the parents and the atmosphere in their home. In addition, we investigated how the punks' message is received by other people.

PARTICIPANTS

We studied punks living in the city of Turku (Finland). Eighteen punks were interviewed individually (nine females and nine males). These 18 will hereafter be referred to as the Punks. Their mean age was 19.0 years (variation range 15-23). They were approached, on the basis of their outer appearance, in the streets, cafés, and at punk concerts in the city. Some subjects were obtained through the Punks already included as subjects. Only one person asked declined to take part in the study.

The clothing had to be clearly punk style in order for a person to be included as a participant. The typical outfit was black in color. Leather jackets decorated with rivets, several earrings, rings, and other cheap jewelery, ragged clothes, with holes, and army surplus boots were common. The girls wore heavy make-up, especially around the eyes. The hair of both girls and boys was dyed, often black, sometimes red or some other color, styled and cut in a conspicuous way. For instance, a rather long hair was sprayed and combed to stand on end, or parts of the head was shaved while the hair was long in other places (one example is the "Iroquois" hairdo).

Besides the Punks, two control groups were included in the study. Control Group I was matched with the Punk group on age, sex, and the sociooeconomic status of their parents. They were interviewed individually, in the same way as the Punks. This group is referred to as the Controls.

The Controls consisted of 9 females and 9 males. Their mean age was 18.2 years (range 17-23 years). In order to obtain a matched control group, students in Turku upper secondary schools and trade schools were informed about the investigation, and offered to volunteer as subjects. From these volunteers, the control group was selected by matching with the Punks. For identification of the socioeconomic position we used the eight-point classification of the Statistical Centre of Finland (Tilastokeskus, 1983). Fourteen Punks and 16 Controls had a working class background, while 4 Punks and 2 controls had a lower middle class background. A typical feature of the punk subculture is that education and working are not popular among its members. Therefore, the groups could not be matched on basis of active studying or employment. Accordingly, only 5 Punks were holding a job, and four were studying, whereas 9 were unemployed. All Controls except one were either in the educational system (n = 12), or working (n = 5).

Control Group II, referred to as the Receivers, was included in order to supplement the study with information about how the message of punks is received. The Receivers were presented with two questionnaires. The first one concerned the message of the punk outfit, and the second one concerned beliefs about the values of punks. The Receivers were 34 college and open university students taking an introductory psychology class (25 females, 7 males, 2 unidentified). Their mean age was 24.6 years (range 19-42).

METHOD

INTERVIEWS

The interview was semi-structured consisting of two parts, one part with open-ended, and another with closed-ended questions. Items regarding future orientation and parental home were modified from Nurmi (1983), and with respect to work, a modified version of the classification by Argyle (1972) was used.

The answers to the open-ended questions were classified by three raters, who rated the answers independently. Inter-rater agreement was computed from half of the material, and it ranged for different areas from 66 to 100 per cent.

QUESTIONNAIRES

After the interviews the participants filled in the questionnaires. The message of the outfit was studied with 12 closed-ended questions. The answers to the scale items were given on a 3-point scale, where 0 represented "no agreement" and 2, "complete agreement." The items were derived partly from pre-interviews and partly from the literature. The items are shown in Table 1. The values were investigated with a questionnaire called "What is important in life?" (modified from Nurmi, 1983) consisting of 28 items. The items are presented in Table 2. The answers to the scale items were given on a 4-point scale, where 1 represented "no agreement" and 4, "complete agreement".

The questionnaires were presented to all three groups. The Punks indicated what they wanted to communicate to people with their outfit, and what they gave value to in life. Control Group I, the matched comparison group, answered what they wanted to communicate to people with their personal outfit, and what they evaluated in life. However, Control Group II, the Receivers (of the punk message), were asked to address what they believed that punks wanted to communicate to people with their outfit, and what they thought that punks give value to in life. Their answers were thought to give information about the impressions punks make on other people.

Since we considered that the scales might not fulfil the requirements of interval scales, and skewness due to the small group size might occur, group differences were tested by Mann-Whitney's U-test. Although the levels of significance are not always specifically mentioned in the text, we present only differences which were statistically significant, unless stated otherwise.

RESULTS

MESSAGE OF THE OUTFIT

Interview Results

In regard to their outfit, the Punks were asked if they wished to communicate something with the way they dressed (a) to people in general, and (b) to other punks. If so, they were then asked what they felt the message was. The Controls were asked whether they wanted to communicate something with the way they dressed to people in general and, again, what this message was.

The Punks wanted to convey a message to people in general (non-punks) more often (p < .01) than the Controls did. To other punks, they wanted to communicate less than to other people. However, even to other punks they wanted to communicate significantly more than the Controls wanted to other people.

Most of the Punks (72.2%) claimed, however, that they did not want to communicate anything at all to other punks. Twenty-two per cent of the messages to other punks could be categorized as support of shared ideals. However, to ordinary people, half of the Punks (55.6%) wanted to communicate their own personality, and 50.0% (the categories were not mutually exclusive) wanted to express punk ideals. Thirty-nine per cent wanted to communicate that differences between people should be accepted, and 22.2% wanted to irritate people.

The answers of the Controls to the open-ended questions were separated into three content categories. They said that they wanted either to "look clean and tidy" (33.3%), to "dress according to the occasion so that they felt comfortable" (33.3%), or they did "not want to communicate anything" (33.3%).

These results speak for the fact that the punk attire really is a means to send a message to the social environment, i.e., that the Punks had a more clear wish to communicate through their outfit than the Controls had. Furthermore, the message was directed more to people in general than to other punks.

Questionnaire Results

The messages of Punks and the Controls (Control Group I) wanted to send to other people by their outfit, and their differences are demonstrated in Figure 1.

The answers of both the Punks and of Control Group I correspond with the results from the interviews. Most of all, the Punks said that they wanted to evoke interest and emphasize their own individuality. High on the list of communication by outfit were also the wishes to look rebellious, to provoke or irritate, and to attract attention. The Punks excelled the Controls on all these issues.

The Controls wanted primarily and more than the Punks to look elegant and to charm and please. Neither Punks nor Controls wanted to scare or to look fierce.

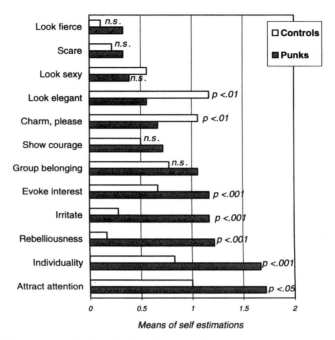

FIGURE 1. The message Punks and Controls claim they try to communicate by their outfit.
Means, Mann-Whitneys U-tests, and p-values.

Table 1 presents the means of the Punks' messages to other people,
coupled with the messages which the Receivers (Control Group II)
thought that punks were communicating. The items are arranged in the
order of importance of the Punks' messages. The rank order is indicated
by ordinal numbers from 1 to 12, for each group's answers.

The Receivers believed that, most of all, punks want to attract attention, and second, to emphasize that they belong to the punk movement.
The Punks did not admit to this: these items were only the fifth and sixth
on their list. Looking rebellious was an outfit message which Control
Group II had received correctly; it was the third on both the Punk list
and on the list of the Receivers. The second item on the Punk list, emphasizing the own individuality, which the Punks expressed also in the
interviews, was mentioned only as the fourth item by the Receivers.

Spearman's rank correlations (r_s) were calculated between the orders
of preference. The Punks' messages corresponded rather well to the Receivers' beliefs about them: the two ranking lists (in Table 1) correlated
significantly (r_s = .678, p < .015).

TABLE 1. Messages the Punks Claimed They Try to Communicate by Their Outfit, and the Receivers' Opinions about What Messages Punks Try to Convey. Rank Ordered Means of Evaluated Importance of Different Messages

| | Receivers | | | |
| | Punks | | Control group II | |
	Rank	Mean	Rank	Mean
Attract attention	1.	(1.72)	5.	(1.38)
Emphasize individuality	2.	(1.67)	4.	(1.64)
Look rebellious	3.	(1.22)	3.	(1.79)
Irritate	4.5	(1.17)	6.	(1.23)
Evoke interest	4.5	(1.17)	1.	(1.94)
Emphasize belongingness to Punk group	6.	(1.06)	2.	(1.79)
Show courage	7.	(0.72)	7.	(1.20)
Charm, please	8.	(0.67)	11.	(0.61)
Look elegant	9.	(0.56)	12.	(0.50)
Look sexy	10.	(0.39)	10.	(0.76)
Scare	11.5	(0.33)	8.	(0.96)
Look fierce	11.5	(0.33)	9.	(0.91)

On the other hand, the messages of the Punks and those of Control Group I did not correlate significantly (r_s = .266, n.s.). This indicates that punks and average youth wished to communicate different things through their outfit.

PEOPLE'S REACTIONS

In the interviews, the Punks reported that they had experienced negative comments or other negative feedback about their appearance, from both strangers and acquaintances, significantly ($p < .001$) more often than the Controls. There was no difference in positive comments received.

According to the Punks, their parents accepted the outer appearance significantly (p < .001) less than parents of the Controls did. The Punks had also experienced more often than Controls that one or both of their parents did not accept some of their child's friends because of their peculiar appearance.

The Punks were interviewed about the discrimination they thought that their outfit had caused them when looking for a job, going to restaurants, travelling, looking for housing, in shops, with the police, with other authorities, and with their parents. They were also asked about concrete difficulties in the above mentioned situations. These questions were answered only by the Punks.

Seventy eight per cent claimed having experienced difficulties in getting a job, and 67% in being allowed into restaurants. This discrimination they attributed to their punk outfits. Only 28% had experienced difficulties in finding lodging, and the same amount in being allowed on to the ferry to Sweden.

THE POLICE

Fifty six per cent of the Punks felt that they received unfair treatment by the police, 28% claimed that they always had to carry an identification card, 17% had been treated violently by the police, whereas 28% said that they never had any difficulties with authorities.

Both Punks and Controls were interviewed about conflicts they had experienced with the police. The Punks had experienced such conflict more often (p < .01). Twelve Punks and one Control had been arrested (p < .001). The Punks were of the opinion that they were locked up by the police more easily and for lesser reasons than other people. Ten Punks and two Controls reported that they had been caught stealing and pilfering. Both groups had been punished with fines equally often, but the reasons differed: the Punks had got their fines mostly for drinking alcohol or urinating in public places, and the Controls for motor offenses. Two Punks and 12 Controls had had no contact with the police. It is, of course, impossible to decide whether the Punks' more frequent conflicts with the police were a consequence of their conspicuous outfit, as the they themselves tended to think. Furthermore, these data are based on the participants own interviews, not on police records. However, it does not appear that the arrests of the Punks were for acts of violence.

VALUES

The Punk Values

To find out how committed the subjects were to being punk, we asked what kind of punks they thought they were, on a continuum from "hardcore" punk to just using punk-like clothing. No one said that clothing was the only way of identifying with the Punks. Half of the Punks subscribed to being "very highly" hardcore, whereas five considered themselves "rather much" so, and two said they were only "somewhat" hardcore Punks. All said they listened to what may be classified as punk music.

Most of the Punks felt that their movement was international. In practice this meant that some of the Punks kept contacts with punks living in other countries, read foreign punk periodicals, listened to foreign punk music, invited foreign punk bands to perform in Finland, and that Finnish punk bands tried to do gigs in other countries. Also, when travelling, the Punks had a feeling of solidarity with other punks, made friends easily with them, and could sometimes stay overnight in their places.

The Punks were asked to rank the issues that united them with other punks. The most important thing was considered to be the fact that they belong to the common punk movement, the next was musical taste, and the third was the outfit. Half of the Punks mentioned some other issue, for instance, way of life and behavior, activities, feeling of belongingness, and difference from other people.

We asked the Punks how much friends had influenced their choice to become a punk. No one admitted that friends or peers had affected their choice very much. About half of the Punks said that friends and peers had not had an effect on their choice at all. Interest in the punk movement, being and "becoming" a punk was generally seen as an individual choice.

Opposition against the Established Society

In order to test the hypothesis that punks are a "counterculture" criticizing the society, the Punks and Control Group I were asked to mention the four most important things in the society or the world to which they resisted, objected, or were opposed. If they could not think of four issues, they could mention a smaller number. All participants were opposed to something. The answers were sorted into content categories.

Both groups were most opposed to collective violence and violence exerted by the society, like war and torture. The second most important content category was disapproval of discrimination against sex, race, etc. This was mentioned equally often by both groups. The third most important category was opposition to social coercion, regulations and means of control. The Punks were more opposed to military service, to compulsory education, and against living according to fixed norms and standards. The next target of opposition was cruelty to animals, which also was opposed somewhat more by the Punks ($p < 0.05$).

The Punks objected to the principle of having to work more than the Controls did ($p < .001$); in fact, 22 Punks but only two Controls objected to work. Reasons mentioned were "ideological"; for instance, they objected to regular working times and wanted at least temporarily to spend periods of time without work. Unspecified reasons were such as "working is silly," or objections to monotonous, routine work.

The last content category was individual violence (for instance, violence in the streets). The groups did not differ in their frequency of mentioning this issue.

A Good World

The participants were asked what the world, in their opinion, should be like in order to be a good one. The Punks reported a total of 58 and the Controls 38 aspects characterizing a good world.

Both groups mentioned spontaneously almost the same characteristics as their first priorities. Peace was the most important aspect of a good world. Equality among people was mentioned second most often, somewhat more by the Punks ($p < .05$). The next aspects spontaneously mentioned by both groups were freedom of the individual, protection of nature, possibility of the individual to influence the society, and happiness and contentment of people.

Next the participants were asked to evaluate how important certain values and ideals, mentioned by the experimenters, were to them. Now differences between the groups became apparent. The order of importance of these issues is to a great extent also reflected in the answers to the questionnaire (see below).

Equality among people and equality between the sexes were more important to the Punks than to the Controls. Individual freedom was also considered more important by the Punks, they claimed that they were opposed to "wallowing in money", and that they approved more of work for protection of the environment, and protection of animals.

The Controls stressed the importance of success in professional life, longevity, a high standard of living, health, money, supporting oneself through work, and marriage or a steady relation with a partner of the opposite sex. They also supported more than the punks a good education, near and secure family relations, and having own children.

Most of the participants (totally 25) did not believe in the possibility that a "good world" would become a reality.

When asked, what the subjects had done in order to make the "good world" come true, the Punks claimed having been more active than the Controls did (p < .01). The Punks said that they had taken concrete action, for example, by objecting to armed service or by occupying empty houses. Both Punks and Controls claimed having tried to advance a "good world" through their general behavior toward other people.

What Is Important in Life? Questionnaire Results

All three groups filled in this questionnaire (cf. Table 2). The issues listed in Table 2 are arranged in the order of importance that the Punks felt was true for them.

When rank correlations of the preferences by the different groups were calculated, it turned out that the rank order of the Punks did not correlate significantly with the rank order of Control Group I (r_s = .233). However, the Receivers interpreted the message rather accurately. The rank order they thought would be supported by punks correlated significantly with the Punks' own evaluations (r_s = .754). At the same time, with respect to several issues, there are some notable differences between the rankings of the Punks and the Recievers.

The anwers of the Punks and of the Controls correspond mostly to the answers they gave in the interviews. Some features of the lists in Table 2 deserve special mention: individual freedom was mentioned as the most important issue by the Punks, and the Receivers had also grasped this. For the Controls, most important in life was health, ranked only thirteenth by the Punks. Ranked second by the Punks was equality among people. This the Receivers did not perceive: they thought that the second issue for the punks would be to show being different, which, in fact, was only the eleventh of the Punk preferences.

World peace was also more important for Punks than for Controls. Relations with other people were important for both Controls and Punks (although here too the Receivers significantly underestimated the

TABLE 2. What Is Important in Life? Ranks and Means (in Parentheses) of Punks' and Controls' Evaluations, and the Receivers' Beliefs about the Punks' Opinions

| | | | Receivers | | | |
| | Punks | | Control Group I | | Control Group II | |
	Rank	Mean	Rank	Mean	Rank	Mean
Individual freedom	1.	(4.00)	6.	(3.55)	1.	(3.91)
Equality among people	2.	(3.88)	20.	(3.16)	15.	(3.05)
Close and safe human relations	3.	(3.83)	2.5	(3.83)	16.	(3.47)
World peace	4.	(3.83)	16.	(3.11)	6.	(3.26)
Opportunity to make new friends	5.	(3.72)	10.	(3.33)	5.	(3.38)
Opposition to army and military service	6.	(3.61)	27.	(1.61)	9.	(3.20)
An eventfull life	7.	(3.55)	9.	(3.33)	3.	(3.58)
Possibilities to hobbies and self-fullfillment	8.	(3.55)	5.	(3.61)	10.	(3.17)
Equality between sexes	9.	(3.55)	18.5	(2.94)	13.5	(2.94)
Protection of nature	10.	(3.50)	21.	(2.61)	13.5	(2.94)
Showing that you are different	12.	(3.11)	22.	(2.05)	2.	(3.82)
Close and safe family relations	12.	(3.11)	2.5	(3.83)	17.	(2.82)
Health	12.	(3.11)	1.	(3.94)	16.	(2.85)
Being opposed to "wallowing in money"	15.	(2.88)	23.	(2.00)	8.	(3.20)
Not to live according to fixed norms and standards	16.	(2.72)	25.	(1.88)	7.	(3.23)
Acceptance and appreciation by others	17.5	(2.55)	18.5	(2.94)	27.	(2.08)
Success in work	17.5	(2.55)	7.	(3.50)	23.	(2.35)

(continued)

TABLE 2. (*continued*)

| | Receivers | | | | | |
| | Punks | | Control Group I | | Control Group II | |
	Rank	Mean	Rank	Mean	Rank	Mean
Education	19.	(2.33)	15.	(3.18)	24.	(2.26)
Protection of animals	21.	(2.27)	17.	(3.11)	12.	(3.00)
Opposition to compulsory education	21.	(2.27)	28.	(1.33)	19.	(2.76)
Money	21.	(2.27)	12.	(3.22)	25.	(2.26)
Children	24.	(2.25)	8.	(3.44)	20.	(2.64)
Supporting oneself by work	25.	(2.16)	4.	(3.77)	26.	(2.11)
Marriage or living together as a couple	26.	(2.12)	12.	(3.22)	21.	(2.52)
Long life	27.	(2.00)	12.	(3.22)	22.	(2.50)
Living without responsibilities	28.	(1.88)	24.	(1.94)	18.	(2.76)
High standard of living	29.	(1.72)	20.	(2.77)	28.	(1.94)
Religion	20.	(1.11)	26.	(1.83)	29.	(1.85)

importance of this value for Punks). The Controls were, however, more family oriented than the Punks.

Future Orientation

The subjects were asked questions about what they expected their future would be like. Both positive (hopes, goals, and plans) and negative (fears and threats) things were asked about.

Positive aspects related to family or marriage were more important to the Controls ($p < .05$).

More Controls than Punks planned to obtain a profession and hold a job. The most important reason for holding a job, according to both groups, was to earn money. The next frequent reason was the wish to do some interesting work. This was more important for Punks than for

Controls. Some of both the Punks and of the Controls wanted to work in order to have social relations with people. An additional reason for working, mentioned somewhat more often by Punks than by Controls, was passing time.

No Punks planned to have a college- or university-level education, but two Controls mentioned it as a possibility.

The Punks mentioned more negative future expectations, totaling 54 as contrasted to 31 mentioned by the Controls. The threat of war was the most important one. There was no difference between the groups in frequencies of mentioning war, but the Punks had taken action in order to oppose war and promote peace more frequently than the Controls ($p < .01$). For instance, they had refused to join the army.

The negative items that were mentioned next, and equally often by the groups, were death and illness, pollution of nature, and cruelty to animals. The groups did not differ in their estimation of how probable it was that these negative things would come true.

The participants were asked what they thought their lives would be like after ten years. The Controls could see more options in this respect, whereas almost half of the Punks were of the opinion that their lives after ten years will remain almost the same as they are now. Seven Punks also thought that their ideals and outer appearance will not change much during ten years, while the Controls expected more changes.

Parental Home

The living conditions of the groups were different: more Controls were living either with one or both of their parents, whereas more than half of the Punks ($n = 11$) had moved away from their parental home, five lived together with friends, and four cohabited with a partner of the opposite sex.

The participants were interviewed about how the atmosphere of the parental home was or had been. Since we did not see the parents, the interviews reflect only the experience of the participants.

Eight structured questions adopted from Nurmi (1983) were used. The Punks reported poorer relations with their mother ($p < .01$) and with their father ($p < .05$) than did the Controls. With their siblings, the Punks had somewhat poorer relations. The Punks considered that the atmosphere of their home had been less democratic ($p < .001$) and cooler ($p < .01$) than the Controls felt was true in their case. The Punks also considered the home atmosphere somewhat ($p < .05$) more tense, insecure, secretive, condemning, and restrained than the Controls. Conflicts with the parents about the future, work, profession, and life style were more common in the Punk group. This may, of course, as well be a result of the child's punk behavior as the cause of it. However, conflicts about studies and academic achievement were not different in frequency among the groups. The total scores of the items on the home atmosphere scale by Nurmi (1983) showed that the Controls felt that the atmosphere of their parental home was better than the Punks did (p < .01).

There was no overall difference between the groups in the parents' use of liquor, although the fathers of five Punks and of only one Control were large scale consumers of liquor, and the fathers of eight Punks and of three Controls used at least one bottle of distilled alcohol per week.

Alcohol and Drugs

The drugs were divided into four groups (according to Heinonen, 1980): cannabis (hashish and marijuana), thinner or glue, medicaments (e.g. tranquillizers), and other drugs (amphetamine, heroin, and opium). The difference between the groups was highly significant (p < .001) with respect to cannabis and medicaments, the Punks being the more frequent users. No participant said that they had used the substances classified as "other drugs." Punks reported using considerably more alcohol than did Controls (p < .001).

DISCUSSION

The Punks of this study experienced their own outfit as a message to other people. Although it has been maintained (Bortino & Gilardi, 1989) that punks deny any communication with outgroup members, the Punks interviewed in this study were able to name things they wanted to communicate to others.

Affinity with their own group has been mentioned (e.g. Clarke et al., 1981) as the main reason for the special outer appearance of punks. The present punks did not emphasize this aspect among the messages they communicated to people through their outfit. In the interviews, many of them claimed that identifying with the punks was not the most important reason to use punk-like clothing. More important was to express one's own individuality and to show that you are different from other people.

The Punks' first priority among values was individual freedom. On the other hand, commitment to a worldwide movement and the value of friends within it was also important for the Punks. How do individual freedom and individuality fit together with taking part in a movement?

As Willis has pointed out (1990, p. 16), all style and taste cultures (as he calls them) express a general trend to find and make an identity. The adolescent and early adult years are important from a cultural perspective, because in that period people begin to construct their identities through symbolic and other activities (ibid., p. 8). Being a member of the punk movement may offer an opportunity to differentiate oneself culturally and personally from people, especially from adults, in one's environment, without being alone in this search.

By their outfit, the Punks wanted to evoke interest. In the interviews, they said that they wanted to get people interested in the ideals of their movement, and force others to understand that people can be and are different. A vehicle for this was to stir and create sensation, especially in people other than punk.

It is obvious that the Punks used bodily symbolism as a means of opposition. Expressed in words, this opposition remained relatively commonplace to its contents. The Punks were opposed to values accepted by the mainstream society, they disdained using much money, and they opposed regulations and rules of the society. Anti-establishment values have also previously been found to be typical of punks (e.g. Fox, 1987). In this respect, the values of the present Punks corresponded to those held by members of a commodity oriented subulture, as defined by Stratton (1985).

Opposition against the society was also apparent in the Controls' answers, although to a lesser extent. Resistance of adults' values has, of course, always been typical of young people. For instance Rauste-von Wright (1982) found that Finnish adolescents thought that adults emphasized economic values and social success more than they themselves did.

In both the interviews and the questionnaire answers it emerged that the Punks were more idealistic than the Controls: they had more concern for peace, for equality among the sexes and among people, preservation of the environment, and protection of animals. These views were underlined by the result that more Punks than Controls claimed having really done something to make their ideals come true. The Punks evaluated personal relations, but were relatively indifferent to family concerns.

In regard to future orientation, the Controls mentioned more material goals and aspirations, like an own family, education, profession, house, etc. The Punks expected more negative things from the future, concerning both global issues and personal conditions. A pessimistic view of the future seems to be a logical consequence of the critique of the contemporary society. Lamy and Levin (1985) describe a world made up of "antivalues," when the dominant culture is regarded as repressive and obsolete.

Many Punks said they were living "only one day at a time." Also, they did not expect their ideals or their outer appearance to change very much during the next ten years. Wartenberg (1984) speaks of a search for "a never ending adolescence" by the punks (p.83), and Clarke et al. (1981) mention their outspoken "generational consciousness."

The Punks in our study felt that "becoming" a punk was a personal choice, and they did not admit to the influence of other people on this choice. It is probable, however, that the tense atmosphere and otherwise difficult relations in their parental home had an effect on their decision.

It is true that the family background of this punk sample does not not give the impression of being as shattered as it has been found in many other studies. However, the Punks had experienced their home atmosphere and the interaction between the family members as more conflictual and negative than the Controls. Authoritarianism, secretiveness, confinement, and condemnation were typical aspects of the families of the Punks. These may have been some of the reasons that made these adolescents turn against their families and toward new types of self-expression and values. The punk appearance and attitudes of the children undoubtedly, in turn, have the effect of increasing conflicts with the parents.

We had a second Control group, the Receivers, to observe how the symbolic expression by punks was received. Judging from the Receivers' guesses about what punks try to convey to others, punks do get their message through, at least to some extent. For instance, the Receivers guessed that individual freedom would be the most important value among the punks, and that a high standard of living and religion were the last options for them. From a theoretical and from a social standpoint, perhaps the most significant implication of these findings is that social deviance among adolescents need not be associated with aggressive anti-social behaviors.

But is the punk outfit an aggressive message? The answer is both yes and no. The Punks admitted that they wished to irritate and to look rebellious, but they did not claim that their intention was to look cross or to scare, although one could expect that from their appearance and from previous discussions (e.g. Hebdige, 1984, p. 86).

The Punks valued peace and were opposed to war, and claimed that they had taken more action against war and to promote peace than the Controls did. Both groups were opposed to individual violence. More Punks than Controls claimed that they had been targets of violence. However, the Punks themselves had not been guilty of any notable violence or of offences against law and authorities.

Tillman (1980) writes that the violent behavior of punks is not so much concrete participation in violent actions as an "attack through style." Through their outfit punks do not attempt to show personal aggression in the first place, but rather opposition against the evils, faults, and pitfalls of the present way of life, as they see them.

REFERENCES

Argyle, M. (1972). *The Social Psychology of Work.* Suffolk: The Penguin Press.

Bay, J. (1984). Dadada—is all I want to say to you. Om Punk i Danmark. In *Ungdomskultur: Identitet—motstand,* Fornäs, J., Lindberg, U. & Sernhede, O. (Eds.). Stockholm: Akademilitteratur. pp. 207-234.

Becker, H., Eigenbrodt, J., & May, M. (1983). Cliquen und Raum. Zur Konstituierung von Sozialräumen bei unterschiedlichen sozialen Milieus von Jugendlichen. *K'lner Zeitschrift fur Soziologie und Sozialpsychologie, Sonderheft 25,* 451-481.

Bortino, R. & Gilardi, A. (1989). L'image. In-formation et de-formation. *Psychologie Medicale, 21,* 723-724.

Brake, M. (1985). *Comparative youth culture: The sociology of youth subcultures in America, Britain and Canada.* New York: Routledge & Kegan Paul.

Brinkman, G. R., & Reinhard, H. G. (1989). Subcultural styles in adolescence. *Acta Paedopsychiatrica, 52,* 217-231.

Burr, A. (1984). The Ideologies of Despair: A Symbolic Interpretation of Punks and Skinheads' Usage of Barbiturates. *Social Science and Medicine, 19,* 929-938.

Clarke, J., Hall, S., Jefferson, T., & Roberts, B. (1981). Sub Cultures, Cultures and Class. In *Culture, Ideology and Social Process,* T. Bennett, G. Martin, C. Mercer, & J. Woollacott (Eds.). London: Billing & Sons.

Glick, P., DeMorest, J., & Hotze, C. A. (1988). Keeping your distance: Group membership, personal space, and requests for small favors. *Journal of Applied Social Psychology, 18,* 315-330.

Gold, B. D. (1987). Self Image of Punk Rock and Nonpunk Rock Juvenile Delinquents. *Adolescence, 22,* 535-544.

Grabner, H.(1985). Punks in der Wiener Gassergasse. Studie zur Lebenswelt jugendlicher "Aussenseiter". *Österreichische Zeitschrift fur Soziologie, 10,* 103-120.

Fornäs, J., Lindberg, U., & Sernhede, O. (Eds.) (1984). *Ungdomskultur: Identitet—motstand.* Stockholm: Akademilitteratur.

Hebdige, D. (1984). In Ras, stil och subkultur, J. Fornäs, U. Lindberg, & O. Sernhede (Eds.), *Ungdomskultur: Identitet—motstand,* pp. 71-108. Stockholm: Akademilitteratur.

Heinonen, M. (1980). Tiedustelu huumausaineiden käytöstä v. 1980. Helsinki *Sosiaali- ja terveysministeriön tutkimusosasto, Julkaisuja 7.*

Lamy, P. & Lewin, J. (1985). Punk and Middle-Class Values. A Content Analysis. *Youth & Society, 17*(2), 157-170.

Lehtonen, K. (1989). Does rock and roll suit the teacher? Rock music as a manifestation of youth culture. (Miten käy maikalta rock & roll? Rockmusiikki nuorisokulttuurin ilmentäjänä.) *Kasvatus, 20,* 504-511.

Nemirovskij, V. G. (1989). The attitudes of youth toward ideological trends abroad. (Otnoshenie molodezhi k zarubezhnym ideologicheskim techeniyam.) *Sotsiologicheskie-Issledovaniya, 16,* 93-95.

Nurmi, J.-E. (1983). Nuorten tulevaisuuteen suuntautuminen II: Tulevaisuuteen suuntautumisen psykologinen struktuuri ja siihen vaikuttavat tekijät 11-, 15- ja 18-vuotiailla nuorilla. Turku *Turun yliopisto: Psykologian tutkimuksia, 67.*

Rauste-von Wright, M. (1982). Life values of Finnish adolescents and their beliefs about the values of peers and adults. *Scandinavian Journal of Psychology, 23,* 201-205.

Roe, K. (1985). Swedish youth and music: Listening patterns and motivations. *Communication Research, 12,* 353-362.

Saari, S. & Majander,H. (1985). Seurantatautkimus mielenterveyden kehittymisestä. Helsinki: *Helsingin yliopisto: Psykologian laitoksen tutkimuksia, 2.* Yliopistopaino.

Sosioekonominen asemaluokitus. Ammattiasemaluokitus (1983). Helsinki: *Tilastokeskus. Käsikirjoja Nro 17. Yliopistopaino.* (Classification of scioeoconomic status. Professional status. The Statistical Centre of Finland.)

Stratton, J.(1985). Youth Subcultures and their Cultural Contexts. *ANZJS, 21*(2). 194-218.

Thompson, P. (1979). Youth Culture and Youth Politics in Britain. *Radical America, 13*(2), 53-65.

Tillman, R.H. (1980). Punk rock and the construction of "pseudopolitical" movements. *Popular Music and Society, 7,* 165-175.

Wartenberg, G. (1984). Perspektivlosigkeit und demonstrative Lebensstil-Suche - Der Junge Mensch im Spannungsfeld gesellschaftlicher Entwicklung. *Praxis der Kinderpsychologie, 33,* 82-88.

Widdicombe, S. & Wooffitt, R. (1990). 'Being' versus 'doing' punk: An achieving authenticity as a member. *Journal of Language and Social Psychology, 9,* 257-277.

Willis, P. (1990). *Common Culture: Symbolic Work at Play in the Everyday Cultures of the Young.* Bristol: Open University Press.

CHAPTER 11

IS WAR A CONSEQUENCE OF HUMAN AGGRESSION?

ROBERT HINDE

I am delighted to contribute to a volume to honor Professor Adam Fraczek. He has made great contributions to the study of aggressive behavior, and is the more to be honored because of the difficult circumstances in which his research was carried out. Having been his guest in Poland on more than one occasion, I feel a considerable personal debt to him.

This contribution is concerned with an area in which the concept of aggression is of very limited usefulness, namely the causes of international war. This may seem paradoxical, but it is as important to recognize the limitations of a concept as its area of maximum applicability.

There are countless definitions of aggression, and it would serve no useful purpose to review them here. But nearly all involve the infliction of harm by one individual upon another. When one individual strikes another, we label his behavior as aggressive. When one nation invades another, we use the same term. It is therefore easy to assume, and too often taken for granted, that individual aggressiveness is the cause of international war. War indeed falls within the definition of aggression,

ROBERT HINDE • MRC Group, Cambridge University, Madingley, Cambridge, CB3 8AA, England.

Aggression: Biological, Developmental, and Social Perspectives, edited by Seymour Feshbach and Jolanta Zagrodzka. Plenum Press, New York, 1997.

but that does not mean either that wars are caused by human aggressiveness, or that people fight in war because they are aggressive.

Nowadays, at least, the destructiveness and the waste of war are
generally recognized. With rare exceptions, politicians lead their countries to war when all else fails. War is not seen as a means to be preferred. And it is well established that, in war, most soldiers are afraid
most of the time. Furthermore, the bomb aimer who presses the bomb
release button, the artillery man who fires a field gun, the soldier aiming
at a presumed enemy a mile away, are not motivated by aggression.
They act as they do because that is their duty in the institution of war.
When individual aggressiveness is involved, it is more a consequence
of war than a cause. The reports of those who participated in the mas-
sacre of My Lai indicate that the aggressiveness that they felt was a product of fear and frustration caused by the war. In the recent terrible battles
accompanying the disintegration of Yugoslavia, individual aggressiveness has been apparent, but it stemmed from religious and ethnic preju-
dices legitimated by the state of war, and was not the cause of war.

War, therefore , must be seen as an institution, with a number of
constituent roles—soldier, general, politician, munitions maker, doctor,
backroom boy, and so on. What exactly do we mean by an institution
here? Marriage is an institution, with the constituent roles of husband
and wife. The behavior of husbands and wives is determined in part by
the rights and duties associated with those roles in the cultures in which
they live. Parliament is an institution with the roles of Prime Minister,
Ministers, Members, the voting public and so on. The behavior of each
incumbent in those roles is determined in part by the rights and duties
associated with it. In the same way, in war soldiers fight because it is
their duty to do so, doctors minister to the wounded because it is their
duty to do so, munitions workers turn out shells because it is their role
in the institution of war. If we are to understand war, if we are to minimize its incidence, we must therefore understand war as an institution.
This means that we must identify and attempt to counter the forces that
maintain war as an institution (see Hinde, Ed., 1991).

Before pursuing that, however, some issues concerning the nature
of war must be mentioned. War involves groups, and the aggressiveness
of a group is not simply the sum of aggressiveness of its members.
Group membership is associated with a tendency to see the in-group as
superior to the out-group, and the out-group is denigrated and even
seen as sub-human. Individuals may see it as proper to behave aggressively to other groups in defense of the values of the in-group. Any
perceived threat to the interests or values of the in-group can serve as
an instigator to aggression.

In a confrontation between groups, the internal dynamics of the group may escalate the tendencies toward violent action. The relative anonymity of individuals and the arousal produced by the group situation, may augment the motivation of group members. If aggressive behavior is valued by the group, individuals may seek out a target in order to show off their aggressive prowess to fellow group members, and thereby increase their own status within the group. Thus, assertiveness enhances aggressiveness.

Whether a confrontation or conflict of interests between groups leads to aggression may depend absolutely on the leaders. The hierarchically structured group may be more likely to show aggression if led by an individual with strong aggressive propensities.

While war involves groups, war differs from most inter-group aggression in at least two ways. First, war, or at least modern international war, involves a much greater degree of role differentiation than does conflict between groups. Second, war usually involves conflict between societies, each of which is complex and consists of many overlapping groups. Thus war embraces the issues of group aggression, but much else besides with individual aggressiveness playing a much smaller, and at most secondary, role. Furthermore, wars themselves are heterogeneous. Historically, the increase in complexity and diversity of the roles of those involved, the greater destructiveness of weapons and the multitudinous processes required for their manufacture, and the related increased involvement of the civilian population, have made a dramatic difference to the nature of war (Pogge von Strandmann, 1991). But their complexity means that leaders at every level must make decisions based on data that are incomplete and ambiguous, involving many factors simultaneously, including differences of opinion between sub-groups on their own side, and on the basis of committees of specialist advisors who may reach a consensus very different from the rational outcome of the integration of the different viewpoints of the participants (Janis, 198; Rabbie, 1989; Tetlock, et al, 1989).

We may now return to the forces that maintain war as an institution. These can be categorized under three headings:

1. *Continuously Acting, Everyday Factors.* Many of the metaphors used in everyday speech, such as "going over the top" and "getting dug in" are derived from war, and their use helps to make war acceptable. Fussel (1975) has analyzed the "high diction" that is used in war and tends to conceal its true reality. Thus a "friend" becomes a "comrade", "danger" becomes "peril", the "dead" becomes the "fallen", and so on. The Second World War had its own euphemisms: in the RAF to die was "to get the

chop". War Toys introduce children to the concept of war, and most films about war sanitize its violence and emphasize its nobility (Winter, 1991).

Women, who in general value peace more highly that do men (Smith, 1984), play a major part in peace movements, but seldom participate in the decision-making processes that determine whether or not war shall occur (Pulkkinen, 1989; Riddick, 1989). (There are of course exceptions here.)

Although the issues of everyday language or the films shown on television may seem trivial issues, they no doubt contribute to the cheerful optimism shown by many recruits going to war who are subsequently disillusioned by its reality (Brodie, 1990).

2. *Pervasive Cultural Factors.* Countries differ in status awarded to individual aggression and in the public view of the acceptability of war. Some countries have a long record of belligerence, others, like Switzerland, of neutrality. Sweden has changed its status over the centuries.

Religions also differ in their attitude to war. For some, the status of the warrior is the most honorable. Others are in theory pacifists, though pacifism is by no means always continued into practice. The early Christians were pacifists, and it was not until the fourth century that the conversion of Constantine was instrumental in causing Christians to accept militarism. St. Augustine founded a "just war" tradition that provided a moral justification for Christian participation in war and in recent years few church figures have stood up in opposition when their country went to war (Ramsey, 1968; Santoni, 1991). Indeed, Christian symbolism has been used to justify war. Sykes (1991) has illustrated the close relations between the Christian language of sacrifice and the readiness of soldiers to die in battle in the First World War. Similarly, Stern (1975) has recorded the way in which Nazi ideology made use of the religious concept of sacrifice in the Second World War.

The just war tradition became insignificant with the rise of modern nation states, so that between the seventeenth and the early twentieth centuries the right to go to war was almost unlimited. After the First World War, however, the League of Nations convenant and subsequent treaties limited the right to go to war, although the implied recognition that there were some circumstances in which it was permissible to go to war could be interpreted as support for the institution of war. More recently, the Charter of the United Nations has ruled that the use of force for settling international disputes should be the monopoly of the United Nations: unfortunately, lack of Great Power unanimity in the decades after World War II undermined the functioning of this agreement.

Not related to religion in its fundamental bases are devotion to one's own country, and belief in its superiority. Patriotism (love of one's country) and nationalism (belief in the superiority of one's own country) are powerful forces that encourage individuals to go willingly to war to make sacrifices, and even to give up their lives for their country. Patriotism and nationalism, discussed in more detail by Feshbach (1990), contribute to the willingness of individuals to go to war, make sacrifices, and even to give up their lives. It is likely that patriotism and nationalism depend, at least in some measure, on basic human propensities. As we have seen, individuals tend to believe that the group to which they belong is better than any out-group and to exaggerate the differences from them. Belonging to a group and promoting its interest is likely to be important to individuals in a variety of ways, and may be a consequence of natural selection (Krebs and Davies, 1981). Natural selection may have acted, either because membership of the group is of immediate advantage to the individuals concerned, or because individuals in the same group are likely to be genetically related. It has been suggested that humans have been adapted to treat as kin those with whom they associate most intimately and most frequently, and those who are similar to themselves (Johnson, 1986, 1989). In any case, the feeling of belonging to a group is augmented by similarity with other group members, and by a feeling of interdependence with them. These are just the issues exploited by nationalistic propaganda. Individuals are encouraged to see themselves as interdependent, resembling each other, and differing from the enemy, who is portrayed as evil and even subhuman. Propaganda also plays on human aggressiveness: this is, indeed, one place where individual aggressiveness may play a part, although an indirect one, in war. Group cohesiveness is also augmented by parades, flags, medals, and other symbols.

Human cognitive and linguistic capacities give flexibility to our behavioral propensities, and also enable us to reify them into principles which may become incentives for action even when that action is the detriment of the actor.

3. *War as an Institutionalized Set of Institutions.* The institution of war is far from simple. Indeed it is best seen as an institutionalized set of nested institutions, namely the military-industrial-scientific complex. Each member of this trio is, in fact, itself to be seen as a nested set of institutions, with innumerable inter-relations between them. Each institution is maintained by further forces, though common factors, and perhaps the major ones, are the career ambitions and inertia of the

individuals concerned. Each of these sub-institutions is further maintained by positive feedback consequent upon its own activity.

The military establishment, for instance, has considerable resistance to change, due in part to the career stability of its members. More important in the Cold War era was the manner in which military demands spurred on the arms race with government policies subordinated to the weapons that became available. Similarly, there is great inertia in the scientific member of the military/industrial/scientific complex. Governments tend to give considerable resources to defense contractors and to universities engaged in defense oriented research. Technology then spurs policy, and scientists, pursuing their research, often produce more than is requested.

The role of industry is even more important. Industrial firms become dependent on arms production, seek new markets for their current products and develop new weapons to stimulate further demand. The bureaucratic procedure involved in defense decision-making involves lack of accountability and not only produces bad decisions and wastes money but also perpetuates outmoded assumptions, and the growth of the arms industry produces economic pressures against reversal of the trend. Not only is the creation of industry for arms purposes accompanied by entrepreneurs and lobbyists who maintain pressure on the government to spend money on arms and to maintain or expand the industry, but also Trades Unionists do likewise with the aim of maintaining employment figures.

CONCLUSION

We see, then, that although making war can be described as an aggressive act, individual aggressiveness plays only a very limited role in either the causation of war or the behavior of the individuals involved. Where individual aggressive motivation is aroused, as occasionally in hand-to-hand conflict, it is more a consequence of war than a cause. Individual aggressive motivation also enters indirectly, by contributing to the effectiveness of propaganda used to elicit public support for war. There may also be an indirect effect of individual aggression in that, because the enemy is personified in propaganda, individuals support war policies as if they were in conflict with an individual.

For the most part, however, the behavior of individuals is seen as a consequence of their perceived duties in the roles which they occupy in the institution of war. This includes the behavior of the leaders who initiate war. The problem, therefore, is to specify the forces that maintain war as an institution. Some of these have been sketched briefly in this article. It will be noted that these depend in large measure on individual propensities other than aggressiveness—for instance, the tendency to differentiate between in-group and out-group, fear of strangers, assertiveness and/or acquisitiveness in leaders, politicians, or other individuals in setting the stage for and prosecuting the war. No doubt, individual qualities of leaders and politicians and their abilities to cope with special demands made upon them in crisis situations, also play a role.

REFERENCES

Brodie, M. (1990). *A World Worth Fighting For.* East Withering: Goody.

Feshbach, S. (1990). Psychology, human violence and the search for peace: Issues in science and social values. *Journal of Social Issues, 46,* 185-198.

Fussel, P. (1975). *The Great War and Modern Memory.* London: Oxford University Press.

Janis, I. L. (1982). *Victims of Groupthink: A Psychological Study of Foreign Policy Decisions and Fiascoes.* Boston: Houghton Mifflin.

Johnson, G. R. (1986). Kin selection, socialization, and patriotism: an integrating therapy. *Politics and the Life Sciences, 8,* 62-69.

Johnson, G. R. (1989). The role of kin recognition mechanisms in patriotic socialization: Further selections. *Politics and the Life Sciences, 8.*

Krebs, D. L., & Davies, N. B. (1981). *An Introduction to Behavioral Ecology.* Sunderland, Mass.: Sinauer.

Pogge von Strandmann, H. (1991). History and war. In R. A. Hinde (Ed), *The Institution of War.* London: Macmillan.

Pulkkinen, L. (1989). Progress in education for peace in Finland. In R. A. Hinde & D. Parry (Eds.), *Education for Peace.* Nottingham: Spokesman.

Rabbie, J. M. (1989). Group processes as stimulants of aggression. In J. Groebel & R. A. Hinde (Eds.), *Aggression and War,* pp. 141-55. Cambridge: Cambridge University Press.

Ramsey, P. (1968). *The Just War.* New York: Scribeners.

Ruddick, S. (1989). *Maternal Thinking.* London: The Women's Press.

Santoni, R. E. (1991). Nurturing the institution of war: Just war theory's 'justifications' and accommodations. In R. A. Hinde (Ed.), *The Institution of War.* London: Macmillan.

Stern, J. P. (1975). *Hitler: The Fuhrer and the People.* London: Fontana.

Smith, T. W. (1984). Gender and attitudes towards violence. *Public Opinion Quarterly, 48,* 384-96.

Sykes, S. (1991). Sacrifice and the ideology of war. In R.A. Hinde (Ed.), *The Institution of War.* London: Macmillan.

Tetlock, P. E. (1989). Methodological themes and variations. In P. E. Tetlock & J. L. Husbands, R. Jervis, P. C. Stren & C. Tilly (Eds.), *Behavior, Society and Nuclear War.* New York: Oxford University Press.

Winter, J. (1991). Imaginings of war: Some cultural support of the institution of war. In R. A. Hinde (Ed.), *The Institution of War.* London: Macmillan.

PART IV

THE FRUSTRATION–AGGRESSION HYPOTHESIS: A THEORETICAL REVISION AND AN OVERVIEW OF THE ROLE OF BIOLOGICAL, DEVELOPMENTAL, AND SOCIAL INFLUENCES

CHAPTER 12

ON THE DETERMINANTS AND REGULATION OF IMPULSIVE AGGRESSION

LEONARD BERKOWITZ

TWO VIEWS OF VIOLENCE

It has long been a virtual truism throughout the social sciences that people's actions result from their decisions, whether these are made consciously or unconsciously. Standard economics and the other decision sciences obviously take this idea for granted as they focus on how people choose among alternative courses of action by considering the costs and benefits of each. This decision assumption is also pervasive in contemporary sociology and social psychology (as can be seen, for example, in the great popularity of the Fishbein-Ajzen [e.g., Ajzen & Fishbein, 1980] theory of reasoned action). Psychoanalysis and psychodynamic conceptions of personality essentially also share in this view when they maintain that people's actions are virtually always carried out in deliberate pursuit of some conscious or unconscious goal.

Much more relevant to the topic of this paper, decision/choice views of human conduct are prominent in criminology, especially in

LEONARD BERKOWITZ • Department of Psychology, University of Wisconsin, Madison, Wisconsin 53706.

Aggression: Biological, Developmental, and Social Perspectives, edited by Seymour Feshbach and Jolanta Zagrodzka. Plenum Press, New York, 1997.

control theory analyses of crime (see, for example, Cornish & Clarke, 1986). The Wilson and Herrnstein (1985) interpretation of criminal misconduct is a good example. For these writers as for other control theorists, crime is best explained as a failure to restrain wrongful actions, often because the miscreants do not anticipate sufficiently negative consequences for this behavior in the long run. Wilson and Herrnstein regard many criminals as being impulsive in that they frequently "assign a very low value to distant rewards" and place greater emphasis on immediate gratifications (p. 380). Crimes of passion, they say, are "no more irresistible than cheating on one's income tax . . . [and] could have been suppressed by a greater or more certain penalty" (p. 56).

However, we also occasionally encounter other interpretations of human conduct that seem inconsistent with these assumptions of a deliberate choice. These other views basically maintain that people sometimes behave impulsively without making a decision, even at the unconscious level. The American Psychiatric Association's (1987) *Diagnostic and Statistical Manual of Mental Disorders, Third Edition–Revised* (DSM-III-R) provides several examples: The Attention-Deficit Hyperactivity Disorder is described as having a high degree of impulsiveness (p. 50), and the Intermittent Explosive Disorder is said to be characterized by "loss of control of aggressive impulses" so that there are "serious assaultive acts or destruction of property" (pp. 321-322). In both cases but especially in the latter one, the clear implication is that the behaviors at issue are impelled by some inner urge and carried out with relatively little thought.

Violent actions are, of course, especially likely to be regarded as impulsive and thoughtless, and several non-psychiatric authorities have argued that many violent crimes are of this nature. On the basis of his analysis of police-reported robberies in Detroit from 1962 through 1974, Franklin Zimring (1979, cited in Berkowitz, 1993a, p. 279) estimated that a good fraction of whatever killings had occurred in these crimes were accidental rather than instrumental to the furtherance of the perpetrators' aims. Something might have happened during the encounter in these instances that had stimulated the criminals to an unplanned and even unintentional level of violence. Richard Block (1977) has carried this line of thought even further in his analysis of Chicago homicides. Apparently unaware of Feshbach's (1964) important distinction between instrumental and hostile aggression, he employed similar concepts, maintaining that instrumental assaults were different from the more impulsive/expressive aggressive actions. For him, many robberies are generally instrumental in nature in that "the victim and the offender are both acting to maximize their benefits and minimize their costs in a dangerous situation" (p. 9). These robberies can also be regarded as an outgrowth of a deliberate decision. However, in line with Feshbach's (1964) notion of hostile aggression, Block maintained that there also is an impulsive/expressive aggression in which "there is no weighing of costs and benefits, only the desire to injure or kill" (p. 9). He proposed that many aggravated assaults fall into this category. Interestingly, both Zimring and Block contend that many aggravated assaults are similar in important respects to homicides. A life is not taken in the former case, they argued, only because firearms were not immediately available. At any rate, some observers have this kind of impulsive/expressive aggression in mind when they speak of violent attacks carried out in an outburst of rage.

This then, in simple form, is the issue of primary concern to us here: Given the widespread belief that humans choose to act as they do, and the very reasonable assumption that much of human behavior is indeed an outgrowth of a deliberate decision, whether this is made consciously or unconsciously, is it scientifically worthwhile to speak of an involuntary, impulsive act of aggression that is carried out with relatively little, if any, thought? And if so, how can impulsive/expressive attacks best be understood?

The answers to these questions are not only of interest to professional social scientists but also have broad social policy implications. Consider the controversy regarding the efficacy of gun controls. The eminent criminologist Marvin Wolfgang (1958) has suggested that lessening the availability of firearms would not lower the rate of homicides in U.S. society: "Few homicides due to shooting could be avoided merely if a firearm were not immediately present. . . . The offender would select some other weapon to achieve the same destructive goal" (p. 83). Wolfgang here contends that few, if any, murders are impulsive actions impelled by intense rage. Rather, for him, the killings result from a deliberate decision to slay the intended victim. Similarly, Wright, Rossi, and Daly (1983) have raised doubts as to whether there are many impulsive domestic murders arising from strong outbursts of passion. Pointing to a study conducted in Kansas City, they noted that "no fewer than 85% of all homicides involving family members had been preceded at some point in the past by some other violent incident sufficiently serious that the police were called in." This means, Wright, Rossi, and Daly argued, that the killings were typically "the culminating event in a pattern of interpersonal abuse, hatred, and violence that stretches well back into the histories of the parties involved" (p. 193). As they saw it, then, if a wife murdered her husband, this was because she had developed such a great hatred for the man that she had intended to kill him sooner or later, and then did so deliberately. From this perspective, there are relatively few instances in which an intensely angry person grabs

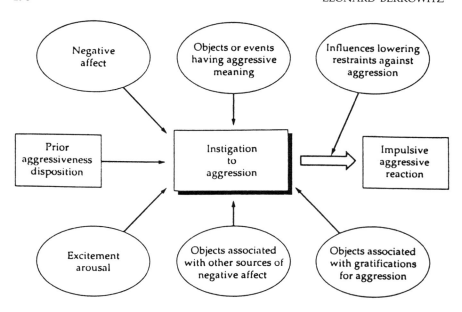

FIGURE 1. Several factors that can add to the strength of an ongoing instigation to aggression.

an available gun and impulsively fires at some offending party in an explosion of rage. According to Wolfgang and Rossi and his associates (as well as many others), if the gun had not been present, the would-be killer would have simply chosen another weapon to carry out her/his decision.

THE NATURE AND DETERMINANTS OF IMPULSIVE AGGRESSION

If Zimring (1979, cited in Berkowitz, 1993a) was correct in his interpretation of the Detroit robbery-murders (mentioned above), the criminals were engaged in instrumental aggression when they held up their victim, intending to hurt him/her at least by taking this person's money. But then some external influence had presumably occurred to suddenly intensify the robbers' aggressive urge and produce the extremely violent outburst. Of course, many things can have this kind of aggression-strengthening effect. Figure 1 taken from my 1993 aggression book (Berkowitz, 1993a) lists several factors that can add to the strength of an ongoing instigation to aggression. Because of space limitations, however, I will here focus on only two of these influences: decidedly unpleasant conditions that generate intense and agitated negative affect, and the sight of objects/events having an aggressive meaning. These (and other) influences could intensify whatever urge to aggression exists at the time, or perhaps even activate such an inclination, so that an available target is attacked more severely than was initially intended.

Over the years I have written frequently about these matters so that the present paper is, to some extent, a reprise of my earlier statements. However, it will also add to these previous analyses by having more to say about the operation of inhibitions and the way some cognitive processes can influence affective aggression.

DECIDEDLY UNPLEASANT, STRESSFUL CONDITIONS

Physical Pain

People sometimes attack others not because they have been offended or frustrated by these persons but only because they happen to be feeling very bad at the time. Pain-instigated aggression is perhaps the clearest manifestation of this aversively generated aggression. Thus, as I (Berkowitz, 1983, 1993a, b) and others (e.g., Hutchinson, 1983; Ulrich, 1966) have noted, in a great many experiments with nonhuman subjects, when two animals were cooped up together in a small chamber and exposed to noxious stimuli (such as physical blows, electric shocks, or intense heat), they frequently began to fight. Of course, this aggression is not an inevitable response to painful stimulation since many afflicted animals prefer to avoid or escape from the aversive situation rather than attack an available target (Hutchinson, 1983). Nevertheless, the studies also indicate that the pained animals are especially apt to assault the target when they do not know how to get away from the pain source. It is much as if the noxious occurrence activates *both* fight *and* flight tendencies, although one of these inclinations may mask the other urge on many occasions. Prior learning obviously can influence the relative strengths of these opposing tendencies. Learning about the likely consequences of an aggressive reaction is especially important. If the pain-induced assaults are repeatedly punished, they are less likely to occur openly in response to the aversive event, whereas the likelihood of further attacks is increased if the aggressive actions lead to a reduction in the noxious stimulation (see Hutchinson, 1983).

However, in this latter connection, it is important to recognize, as I (e.g., Berkowitz, 1983, 1993a,b) and others (e.g., Hutchinson, 1983) have proposed, that the pain-instigated aggression is *not* only a defensive reaction aimed merely at the elimination or lessening of the aversive stimulation. The assault can also be offensive in nature, an attempt to injure the intended target. An animal experiment by Knutson, Fordyce, and Anderson (1980, cited in Berkowitz, 1993a, p. 51) provides some of the evidence. The researchers here demonstrated that pain-elicited aggression can be reinforced by the cessation of the unpleasant event—but they also found that afflicted animals were inclined to fight even when they had not learned that their attacks could terminate the aversive occurrence.

Observations of humans experiencing physical pain suggest that these findings are not necessarily limited to the lower animal species and that there even are intriguing parallels in the results with humans and animals. Most notably, medical and psychological investigations of people suffering from intense pain (arising, for example, from severe episodic headaches or lasting injury to their spinal cords) have reported that many of these patients are frequently angry and/or hostile (see Berkowitz, 1993b). Although these reports obviously are far from conclusive and do not allow us to say whether the pain caused or was exacerbated by the anger/hostility, they do indicate that felt pain can promote aggression by humans as well as other animals. Furthermore, in humans as in animals, the likelihood of overt aggression increases as the pain becomes chronic and the afflicted organism finds there is no effective way of avoiding pain (Vernon & Ulrich, 1966; Pilowsky & Spence, 1976; Wilson, Blazer, & Nashold, 1976). There also are parallels in somewhat more complicated phenomena: The classical conditioning of pain-elicited aggression has been reported with both animal (e.g., Vernon & Ulrich, 1966) and human subjects, the latter by Adam Fraczek (1974) in a clever experiment.

However, going further than the animal research, several medical studies also provide suggestive information about the individual differences in the pain-aggression relationship. Many afflicted patients display little if any anger. According to some papers, those people who do become openly angry are apt to be generally "affectively disturbed" by their condition (e.g., Pilowsky & Spence, 1976; Wilson, Blazer, & Nashold, 1976). If these observations can be generalized, it would appear that anger and aggression result not from the pain sensations in themselves but from the felt distress or experience of suffering produced by the hurt. Indeed, I am now inclined to believe that an agitated negative affect is the fundamental root of affective aggression.

Other Forms of Physical Discomfort

A wide variety of physically uncomfortable conditions can generate this felt distress (or agitated negative affect), and thereby lead humans to anger and perhaps even overt aggression. Sampling from the available literature, research has shown that people can become angry and even hostile to innocent bystanders when they are exposed to such aversive conditions as foul odors, irritable cigarette smoke, disgusting scenes, information about a forthcoming threatening event, and unpleasant temperatures (see Berkowitz, 1983; also Carlson & Miller, 1988). And again, as in many of the animal studies, in much of this research the exhibited anger and aggression could not reduce or eliminate the aversive stimulation.

The aggressive consequences of unpleasant temperatures have received closer attention than any of the other physically uncomfortable conditions, largely because of Craig Anderson's systematic investigations (see Anderson, 1989; Anderson et al., 1995; Anderson et al., 1996). Although laboratory experiments have not consistently found that unpleasant heat leads to overt assaults on an available target (Anderson, 1989), there is fairly good evidence that people exposed to uncomfortably hot and cold temperatures are very apt to develop angry feelings and hostile thoughts (Anderson et al., 1995; Anderson et al., 1996). What is also pertinent to the present paper, some of Anderson's findings indicate that when the unpleasant temperature does prompt an open attack, this is especially likely to be seen in the suffering persons' *initial* reaction to the available target (Anderson, personal communication, 1995). Bothered (and perhaps agitated) by the heat, they might impulsively react in a hostile manner to someone nearby, but then, realizing their hostility is not warranted, might restrain themselves in their later, continued interactions with that individual.

Research by Berkowitz, Cochran, and Embree (1981) adds to this picture of aversively stimulated aggression by indicating that physical discomfort, in humans as well as animals, sometimes generates a desire to hurt others. The women university students in their experiments kept one hand in water that was either painfully cold or at a more comfortable room temperature as they evaluated a fellow female student's solutions to several assigned problems. The subjects could provide these evaluations by delivering either rewards (nickels) or punishments (noise blasts) to the supposed worker. Cross-cutting this variation, half of the women in each condition were informed that whatever punishment they administered was likely to *hurt* the problem-solver, whereas the others

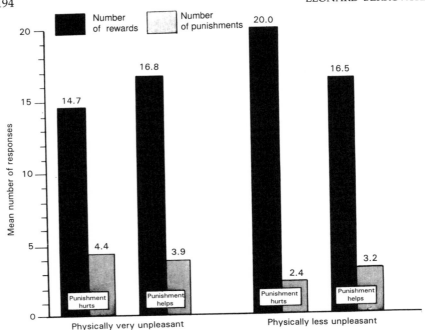

FIGURE 2. Number of rewards and punishments to "worker" as a function of aversiveness of situation and whether punishment will hurt or help the "worker."

were led to believe the punishments might actually *help* the other person by motivating her to do better.

As Figure 2 indicates, the subjects were generally reluctant to punish their fellow students, especially when their hands were in the more comfortable water. In the *less* unpleasant condition the women told that punishment would be harmful generally delivered the fewest punishments and most rewards. This unwillingness to hurt clearly was much weaker when the subjects were exposed to the decidedly unpleasant water. Here, as the figure shows, those believing they could injure the other person gave her the most punishments and the fewest rewards. Their suffering apparently increased their desire to hurt the other woman even though the pain they inflicted could not get them out of the unpleasant condition any sooner.

Social Stress

In my view the present argument can also be extended to the strain theories of crime causation initially advanced by Robert Merton (1957) and later adapted by other theorists such as Richard Cloward and Lloyd Ohlin (1960). Although these formulations are clearly incomplete as a general analysis of all crime, they can help account for some types of antisocial actions (see Lilly, Cullen, & Ball, 1989). Strain theories basically contend that poorly socialized people in those groups that are frustrated by the barriers preventing them from reaching the economic goals emphasized by U. S. society are apt to develop antisocial motivations including inclinations to violence. I incorporate this reasoning into my own formulation by assuming that frustrations generate an instigation to aggression primarily because they are decidedly unpleasant (Berkowitz, 1989). In essence, this conception suggests that the social disjunctions identified by strain theorists contribute to aggressive/antisocial tendencies because they are unpleasant and thus frequently generate agitated negative affect.

Economic distress obviously can be extremely aversive and so, not surprisingly, several investigators have reported that poverty and unemployment are associated with high levels of violent crime. Thus, it has been found that increases in unemployment in the U. S. between 1948 and 1985 were linked to jumps in homicide rates (Devine, Sheley, & Smith, 1988), that poverty-stricken areas of this country tend to have relatively high homicide rates (e.g., Williams & Flewelling, 1988), and that unemployed young men are more likely than their gainfully employed peers to engage in wife battering (Howell & Pugliesi, 1988, cited in Berkowitz, 1993a, p. 270).

The present thesis goes well beyond economic conditions, however, and holds that many different kinds of aversive conditions—including personal stress—can promote violence.

Consistent with this proposition, studies conducted in Israel found that increases in the number of highly salient threats to that country's security predicted a subsequent rise in the national homicide level (Landau & Pfefferman,1988). The rapid changes in Israeli society from 1950 to 1981 along with inflation and unemployment could also be viewed as social stresses that were positively related to the country's homicide rate in this period (Landau & Raveh, 1987).

Social stresses at the individual level are also linked to interpersonal violence. When Murray Straus and his colleagues (Straus, 1980; Straus, Gelles, & Steinmetz, 1980) asked a representative sample of U.S. adults about the stresses in their lives during the previous year (such as whether they had moved to a different neighborhood or town, whether someone close had died, whether a family member had health or behavior problems, and so on), they found that both male and female respondents were more likely to report having abused their children the greater was the number of stressors they had experienced. And further-more, the greater the number of stressful events that were felt by any one couple, the higher was the rate of both verbal and physical aggres-sion in that couple.

Putting these and other findings together, it could well be that (1) any one decidedly unpleasant event tends to activate, among other things, a temporary urge to attack an available target, and (2) repeated aversive experiences give rise to a fairly strong readiness to react ag-gressively to aggression-related stimuli. In either case, whether the per-son is disturbed by one or many stressful events, there's some chance that he or she may then react with an impulsive act of overt verbal or physical aggression if the situation is right. Our next problem, then, is to identify the kinds of situations that can facilitate aggression by those who, for one reason or another, are disposed to be aggressive.

THE IDEAS LINKED TO SITUATIONAL FEATURES

Almost from the beginning of my research career, I have empha-sized the way external stimuli having an aggressive meaning can heighten the intensity of whatever aggression a person is disposed to carry out. I had initially interpreted this kind of effect in classical con-ditioning-association terms, suggesting that the external stimulus func-tions as a CS to elicit associated ideas and motor reactions (cf. Berkowitz, 1964, 1974). In light of the current preference for cognitive theorizing, however, I now speak of this phenomenon using cognitive concepts and talk of the external object or event as a prime that activates semanti-cally-related thoughts, feelings, and motor tendencies (cf. Berkowitz, 1984, 1993a).

Violent scenes. Whatever terminology is employed, aggressive mov-ies are a good example of external events that can heighten the chances of aggression-related ideas, feelings, and inclinations. If the viewers do not have any thoughts incompatible with aggression as they watch oth-ers fighting or assaulting someone, they could well get hostile ideas and might even have a stronger aggressive urge than they otherwise would have experienced (Berkowitz, 1984, 1993a; Bushman & Geen, 1990).

My experiments in this area also have demonstrated that people with certain aggression-related characteristics are especially likely to draw aggression from those who are aggressively disposed at that time. In these particular studies the participants were first deliberately pro-voked by the experimenters' accomplice posing as a fellow student, then watched a six-minute-long prize fight scene in which the protagonist received a bad beating, and soon afterwards were given an opportunity to express hostility towards the provocateur. According to one study (see Berkowitz, 1964, pp. 109-110), this annoying "student" was attacked most strongly after the violent film when he was said to be member of the university's boxing team (boxing was an official university sport in those years) rather than a speech major. The target's semantic connection with the prize fight scene, and/or with fighting generally, apparently heightened his aggressive cue value, thereby resulting in his drawing stronger aggression from his antagonists. In a somewhat related manner, other research (e.g., Geen & Berkowitz, 1966, cited in Berkowitz, 1993a, pp. 220-221) showed that the angering person is also likely to be attacked fairly strongly after the violent scene if he has the same name as the victim of the witnessed fight. Here the provocateur-target's association with the *victim* of the observed aggression tended to increase his aggressive cue value, as if he was linked to rewarded aggression.

Weapons. Basically akin to the effects of watching violence, the sight of a weapon can also prime aggression-related ideas (see Anderson et al., 1996) and perhaps even violent action tendencies. If people seeing a gun or even knife are sufficiently uninhibited at the time, the weapon's mere presence might then stimulate them to become more aggressive than they otherwise would have been and or than they had initially intended.

My original experiment reporting such an aggression-heightening influence of firearms (Berkowitz & LePage, 1967) has attracted some criticism, and there have been several failures to replicate the original findings. However, later research has generally supported the Berkowitz-LePage results (cf. Turner, Simons, Berkowitz, & Frodi, 1977), and in a number of European nations as well as in the U.S. (see Berkowitz, 1993a). As just one example of a non-U.S. experiment, Frodi (1975) showed that Swedish high school boys administered significantly more electric shocks to a fellow student (as a supposed evaluation of his work) when weapons were close by than when they saw a baby bottle and pictures of a nursing mother or when no neutral objects were nearby on the work table. And moreover, some of the research in this area (such as, but not only, Frodi's just mentioned experiment) indicates that the sight of a gun can prime aggressive tendencies even in people who are *not* angry at the time.

This is not to say that a weapon's presence will always lead to increased aggression. I have long noted, and the priming concept also makes this clear, that the nearby firearm or knife must have an aggressive meaning for the beholders if there is to be an aggressive priming; the weapon will not promote hostile thoughts and aggressive inclinations if those seeing it associate guns with recreational hunting or sport or, at the other extreme, think of firearms as morally repugnant and/or anxiety-provoking. Then too, Turner and Simons (1974, cited in Berkowitz, 1993a, pp. 422-424) have demonstrated that the sight of a gun does not produce increased aggression in those with a high level of "evaluation apprehension," i.e., who wish to make a good impression on the other persons who can learn of their actions. Generally speaking, many people know that our society usually disapproves of aggressive behavior, and so, they typically tend to refrain from exhibiting hostility when they want strangers to think well of them. Having such a concern at a given time, they might well inhibit whatever aggressive inclinations are activated at that moment by a weapon's presence.

The point here, of course, is that a weapon's meaning encompasses not only its use, what the object can do, but also whether this use will bring favorable or unfavorable outcomes. Carrying this theme even further, yet another experiment showed that the consequences of a weapon's use can determine whether its presence strengthens or weakens aggressive inclinations. In this investigation (Berkowitz & Frodi, 1977) the mere sight of an object that had previously been employed in rewarded aggression led to the greatest number of physically different punishments that were given to another individual, whereas the "weapon's" presence led to the lowest number of these different punishments when this object's use had previously been disapproved. Evidently, guns can heighten aggressive proclivities to the extent that they are associated with successful rather than punished aggression.

Miomir Zuzul (cited in Berkowitz, 1993, pp. 74-75) has extended this last mentioned point further by showing that even relatively subtle cues indicating disapproval for aggression can dampen the "weapons effect." In his experiment 6-year-old Croatian schoolchildren were shown either real weapons, toy guns, or no weapons at all after an adult had told a story implying that this grownup had either a positive or negative attitude toward aggression or had no attitude one way or another on this matter. At the end of this story, some of the children were frustrated by being forbidden to engage in an attractive activity, whereas the others were not so thwarted. Finally, all of the youngsters were allowed half an hour of free play as they were watched by observers (who were unaware of the children's experimental condition).

Figure 3 reports the number of aggressive acts (mainly non-playful pushing and hitting) recorded for the frustrated children in each condition. (The same trends were exhibited by the nonthwarted youngsters although there were no significant condition differences.) As the figure indicates, the grownup's indication of disapproval for aggression evidently tended to stifle their aggression in the following free play period.

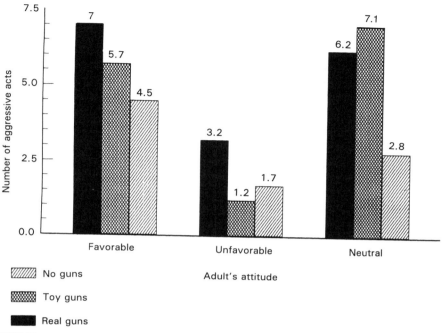

FIGURE 3. Influence of adult's attitude toward aggression on children's aggressive reactions to sight of weapons.

However, if the adult had established either a positive or neutral "atmosphere" toward aggression, the children who had seen either the real or toy guns were generally much more assaultive towards their peers than were their "controls" who hadn't been shown any weapons. The "weapon effect" is most likely to become apparent, in other words, when there are few if any restraints against aggression in the situation.

All in all, the mere presence of weapons can increase the chances that people will display open hostility, especially if these persons assign a positive aggressive meaning to the weapons, are disposed to become aggressive at the time, and also do not possess strong inhibitions against aggression in that setting. These lastmentioned provisos are relevant to some of the doubts that have been expressed about the frequency of the weapons effect in natural situations. When Kleck and McElrath (1991) analyzed national crime data from 1979 to 1985, they found that the presence of a gun in a criminal encounter had apparently lessened the likelihood that an open physical attack would be made in the situation. Arguing that the laboratory demonstrations of a weapons effect should not be generalized to the "real world," the investigators concluded that the offenders' deadly weapons actually had served to decrease the chances of a violent outburst by enhancing their ability "to terrify, to coerce compliance with [their] demands" (p. 673). We should note, however, that Kleck and McElrath had intentionally confined their research sample to incidents in which the participants were not acquainted (such as robberies of strangers) and thus excluded cases in which the participants were apt to be strongly emotionally aroused (such as cases of domestic violence). This suggests that both the robbers and the victims in the Kleck-McElrath sample had carefully weighed the costs and benefits of the alternative actions possible in the situation and had decided to behave in such a way as to minimize future punishment. However, it is quite possible that there would not be the same careful restraint if the participants were highly aroused at the time and were not aware of any punishment cues. Not thinking of the likelihood of suffering great punishment for any violence they displayed and strongly disposed to attack their opponent, the sight of a gun could well intensify their aggressive urge.

INHIBITING THE AGGRESSIVE IMPULSE

The discussion up to now has basically made two related proposals: First, that a variety of external influences can strengthen or perhaps even activate aggressive inclinations, and second, that as a result, the affected persons might act in ways they had not consciously intended. This kind of analysis obviously is not universally accepted, even within the social sciences, and for a number of reasons. I will here address only one type of objection: The fact that angered people often restrain their assault on their target before they severely injure, or kill, the offender.

Some observations made by Baumeister and Heatherton (1996) in their analysis of "self-regulation failure" are illustrative. Pointing out that "Most people do stop short of lethal violence even when they are extremely angry," these psychologists believe that "People could control their behavior if they wanted to do so." For Baumeister and Heatherton, those who strike out at another in intense rage are unlikely to have "lost control." Rather, these writers maintain, the aggressors have "acquiesced" in their absence of self-restraint. They presumably did not want to control themselves. To buttress their reasoning, the writers refer to what happened when the British achieved control over Malaysia. Malaysians apparently had long believed that serious provocations could easily lead to uncontrollable aggression, and presumably as a consequence, there were many instances of people "running amok" in attacking their enemies. However, Baumeister and Heatherton say, when the British "instituted severe penalties for running amok, the practice diminished substantially, indicating that the young men could control it [their aggression] after all." These psychologists then concluded that "the notion of irresistible impulses" is not only "weak and dubious as a scientific hypothesis" but also serves to justify and perhaps even encourage assaults on others.

Baumeister and Heatherton may be right in arguing that the "notion of irresistible impulses" can be used to justify certain instances of criminal assaults. What I do question here, though, is their contention that the idea of impulsive, uncontrolled aggression is "weak and dubious as a scientific hypothesis."

The preceding research review made a number of references to inhibitions and restraints so it should be clear that the concept of impulsive aggression is certainly not incompatible with an acceptance of the role of inhibitory processes. It was stated repeatedly that the effect of situational, aggression-enhancing influences depends upon the strength of the restraints against aggression in the immediate situation. Thus, the sight of external aggression-related stimuli such as weapons is unlikely to lead to an overt attack on an available target when there is a good possibility that any aggression will be punished.

We have still more evidence of how the threat of punishment often reduces antisocial conduct in a research review of the effectiveness of sentencing commissioned by the National Academy of Sciences. This review indicated that the certainty of punishment for various crimes was much more important than the severity of the punishment in deterring this criminal behavior (see Berkowitz, 1993a, p. 319). The British policy against the Malaysian practice of running amok mentioned by Baumeister and Heatherton undoubtedly raised the probability that these wild assaults would be punished, and thus increased the Malaysian youths' self-restraint.

We should recognize, however, that the threat of punishment is not always effective in dampening aggression. The ultimate penalty, capital punishment, evidently is not a good deterrent to murder. Suggesting this, when investigators have compared the homicide rates in regions (U.S. states or entire countries) that execute convicted killers with demographically matched regions (states or countries) not carrying out capital punishment, they typically have not seen any indications that the threat of execution restrains many would-be murderers (see Berkowitz, 1993a, pp. 320-321). One possible reason for this, of course, is that the punishment is by no means certain. Some murderers do get away with their crimes. In recent years only about 7 in 10 homicides brought to the attention of the police resulted in arrests, and of these only about 70 percent led to convictions (see Berkowitz, 1993a. p. 323). But in addition, in a great many instances the lethal violence stems from conflicts between people who know each other (although there has been an increase in the proportion of cases in which a stranger is slain), and it is quite likely that many of the persons involved in these conflicts were highly enraged at the time of the killing (Berkowitz, 1993a, pp. 277-279). If so, the killers might not have thought of the possible long-term consequences of their assault but only struck at their antagonist in anger with whatever weapon was available. Far from being dubious, then, the present line of reasoning is supported by empirical findings in the homicide statistics.

Another aspect of the present formulation should also be addressed: This analysis assumes that inhibitory processes as well as instigatory ones can operate in a largely automatic manner. When people are disposed to attack someone, the strength of their aggressive inclinations are presumably affected automatically not only by the aggression-related stimuli in the situation, as I have been proposing, but also by inhibition-generating situational features that are linked to the punishment of aggression. And moreover, both the activated aggression-enhancing and aggression-inhibiting processes can vary in strength, from very weak to very strong.

This is not the place to cite the many theoretical accounts of self-regulation that assume the automatic operation of inhibitory/control mechanisms. However, I would like to note the family resemblance between the present formulation and Neal Miller's (1948) stimulus-response analysis of displacement. As was once well known, Miller's model attempted to account for the target of displaced aggression in terms of such concepts as the conflict between approach and avoidance tendencies and stimulus generalization. Extending other research findings, he postulated that both the strength of the tendency to perform a goal-oriented response (in this case, to inflict injury) and also to avoid performing the action (that is, to inhibit one's aggression because of the possibility of punishment) increased the closer the organism came to the goal (here, the closer the organism came to the perceived angering source). Assume we have a variety of possible targets an aggressively disposed person might attack, and that these possible targets vary in their degree of psychological association with the angering source. The closer the aroused person comes to the provocateur the stronger will be the urge to aggress, but any inhibitions against aggression stemming from fear of punishment will also be stronger. Since the avoidance gradient (inhibition) is often steeper than the approach/attack gradient, in many cases when the angry person meets the angering source the in-hibitory tendency will completely suppress the aggressive inclination. Nevertheless, because the approach/attack gradient extends further than the avoidance/inhibitory gradient, when the provoked person faces an-other target, one having an intermediate degree of linkage to the anger-ing source, the approach/attack tendency could well be considerably stronger than the inhibitory tendency so that this associated person may now receive a displaced open attack. Both the instigatory and inhibitory tendencies are quite weak when the angered person encounters someone psychologically very far removed from the angering source, and if any overt aggression takes place, it theoretically will only be fairly mild.

One of the few experiments designed to test this analysis of dis-placed aggression (Fitz, 1976) has yielded supporting results. Because of its considerable relevance, I will describe this experiment in some detail. Each real subject, a male undergraduate, thought he was participating along with three other male fellow students (actually the experimenter's confederates) in an investigation of the effects of evaluations on creativ-ity. The subject was also led to believe that two of his partners were friends with similar personalities. We will call these two persons P and P's Friend. The third student was a stranger to them all.

As the experiment got under way three experimental conditions were established: a non-angered control group and two deliberately pro-voked conditions. In the latter two cases each subject's initial perform-ance was deliberately belittled by P in an insulting manner. For the next phase every subject was then told he was to evaluate the three other students' "creative free associations" to stimulus words. These evalu-ations were to be delivered in the form of unpleasant noises sent to each "worker"; the more intense the noise the evaluator delivered, the more unfavorable was his assessment of the "worker's" creativity. However, before the supposed evaluations got under way, the two angered con-ditions were differentiated: Half of the provoked men were also in-formed that there would be yet another phase of the study in which P (the provocateur) would evaluate their work on a later task by giving them electric shocks (Anger-High Fear), whereas the remaining subjects were started on their evaluations without being given this latter infor-mation (Anger-Low Fear).

The subject then listened to each of the other "workers'" responses on their task, with the order in which each "worker" was heard being systematically varied, and delivered a noise blast as his evaluation of each response. Figure 4 reports how much more intense was the average noise the angered men administered to each of the three targets above the mean intensity that was delivered to each target by the non-angered subjects.

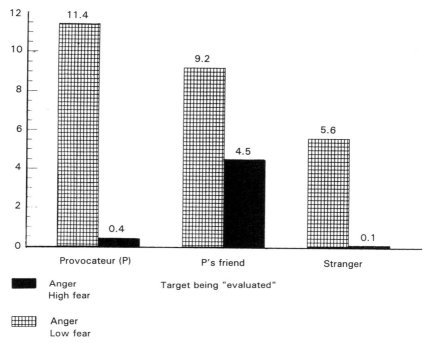

FIGURE 4. Increase in "evaluation" noise intensity above that provided to some target in non-angered control condition.

The data for the angry but unafraid men reveal the generalization gradient postulated by Miller's conflict model: The provocateur (P) received the most unpleasant evaluation relative to what P was given by the "controls," the target associated with him (P's Friend) received the next most unfavorable assessment, and the increase in noise intensity to the stranger was lower still. By contrast, the angry men led to be fearful of P's retaliation show the aggression displacement predicted by Miller: Their evaluation of both the stranger and P was at about the same level as that delivered by the non-angered controls, but they were much harsher to the person associated with P, his friend. Where they apparently had tended to inhibit their aggression toward the potentially dangerous P, they evidently were less reluctant to punish the man linked to him and were harsher to him than to the stranger. This displaced aggression in keeping with the theoretical model indicates that it certainly is not implausible to suggest that the subjects' actions had been influenced in a fairly automatic manner by the stimuli in the situation.

It is possible to extend Miller's stimulus-response analysis further to deal with the form of the overt aggression displayed by aversively aroused persons. Again imagine a two dimensional space, with the X axis referring to psychological closeness to the perceived source of the unpleasantness (the target). This time, however, the Y axis has to do with the nature of the overt aggression occurring, and ranges upward from the most indirect forms of aggression (such as, perhaps, only thoughts and fantasies) to indirect but open verbal aggression, then direct verbal aggression, and finally to direct physical aggression capable of doing serious injury. Here too we can think of the approach/attack gradient slopping upward as the provoked individual approaches the target. The stronger the aggressive urge, the higher will be its level along the Y axis, meaning the more direct and more serious will be the open aggression that is carried out. However, in this particular model the operation of inhibitions serves to deflect the attack gradient downward, with the degree of deflection being in proportion to the strength of the inhibitions against aggression. As a consequence, a relatively weak inhibition might interfere with a direct fatal attack (if there is any restraining effect at all) but will allow all of the forms of aggression at lower Y levels to occur. Stronger inhibitions presumably will prevent more direct forms of aggression from appearing overtly but, theoretically, will not restrain the more indirect, verbal and fantasy reactions at lower Y levels.

This particular formulation obviously remains to be tested. However, the theoretical implications of both this and Miller's conflict model are what is most important for us now. These analyses show that involuntary, automatic influences need not operate in an all-or-nothing manner, whatever the critics of the present type of reasoning might suppose. Inhibitions can vary in strength from one situation and one occasion to another because of the stimulus conditions that are present. Angry people might show a great, or lesser, restraint in their assaults on an antagonist without these strong, or weak, inhibitions necessarily being the outcome of a deliberate decision.

COGNITIONS IN AFFECTIVE AGGRESSION

Several of my recent discussions of affective aggression (e.g., Berkowitz, 1990) have referred to the theorizing spelled out here as a "cognitive-neo-associationistic" formulation because it recognizes the role of cognitive as well as associationistic processes. Up to this point the present paper has focused on the latter, associationistic processes because of its concern with the more impulsive aspects of aggression. However, cognitive processes clearly have a very important influence on affective and even impulsive aggression and I should say something (admittedly too little) about some of the ways in which cognitions contribute to this behavior.

HOSTILE APPRAISALS AND ATTRIBUTIONS

For all of my emphasis on the role of painful or otherwise stressful circumstances in generating aggressive inclinations, we probably are most likely to become aggressive when we think we have been deliberately wronged by someone (Berkowitz, 1993a, pp. 86-88). Our appraisal of this person's actions as being improper or even deliberately malevolent arouses our ire and can provoke an aggressive urge. What is most relevant to us here, though, is that decidedly unpleasant conditions can give rise to this kind of hostile appraisal, as Anderson and his associates (1995) have pointed out. On showing in one experiment that many of the subjects who were exposed to uncomfortably high temperatures developed angry feelings and hostile ideas, the Anderson team suggested that unpleasant heat could lead to hostile interpretations of other people's ambiguous behaviors. I go even further here and propose that the full variety of aversive conditions discussed in this paper can also increase the chances that one will appraise another's ambiguous actions in a hostile manner.

Of course, there undoubtedly are individual differences in how readily these negative ideas about others are generated. Some people are easily provoked to violence because they are generally quick to interpret other people's actions as threatening or a deliberate affront. Dodge and Coie (1987, see Berkowitz, 1993a, pp. 149-150) have highlighted the role of these hostile attributions in their important study of aggressive schoolboys. The investigators first used teachers' ratings to identify some youngsters as being easily angered (these were termed reactive aggressors), whereas other boys were selected as being inclined to employ aggression only instrumentally (for example, to bully and dominate others). When all of the children were shown videotaped interactions between two other youngsters, all portraying one boy knocking down the other's blocks, these two groups of children differed significantly in their interpretations of why this had happened—but only if the actor's motivation had been unclear. In this ambiguous setting, the easily angered, reactive aggressors were especially likely to believe the victim's blocks had been knocked down deliberately. They were also more likely than the instrumentally oriented boys to then say that they themselves would react aggressively to such an occurrence. These findings probably hold for many other easily provoked persons, adults as well as children: They too may be quick to lose their tempers because they tend automatically to interpret other people's ambiguous actions as being motivated by hostile intent.

ATTENTION DIRECTION

The direction of a person's attention can also affect how she or he responds to an aversive event. So far I have been proposing that a good many impulsive assaults arise because a strong aggressive urge is activated in that situation, often along with a weakening of inhibitions against aggression. An arousal-produced narrowing of attention can contribute to such a lowering of restraints. Research has demonstrated that strong emotion arousal tends to reduce the range of cues to which one pays attention (Christianson, 1992; Easterbrook, 1959). Strongly aroused people are apt to focus on the main features of the situation confronting them to the neglect of matters that are relatively peripheral for them at the time. Someone who is extremely angry, then, as Baumeister and Heatherton (1996) also note, could well concentrate his attention on the person who had provoked him and the wrong he believes he had suffered and totally disregard other considerations such as the possibility of being punished for aggression. He thinks only of attacking his tormentor, not of any negative consequences this might bring.

Where the focusing of attention on the source of one's displeasure can increase the likelihood of open aggression, under some conditions attention to one's unpleasant feelings at the time might well lead to greater restraints against socially disapproved conduct. A series of experiments carried out in my laboratory (see Berkowitz, 1990; Berkowitz, 1993a; Berkowitz & Troccoli, 1990) suggests this could happen because the awareness of the negative feelings, perhaps when these are somewhat unexpected, prompts more elaborate and more analytic thinking. To the extent that this heightened analytic thinking does come about, the distressed persons might then pay more attention to the wide variety of information that is available in the situation. They might also become more conscious of whether other people nearby are responsible for their displeasure so that, realizing these others are indeed innocent, they do not displace their aggressive urges onto them.

Two experiments by Berkowitz and Troccoli (1990) point to some such process at work. In the first of these, undergraduate men were induced to be either depressed or happy, after which half of them were distracted by a brief irrelevant assignment, whereas the others were asked to rate their present feelings so that they were highly aware of their mood. Right after this, all of the participants were asked to evaluate a fellow student's performance on another task by giving him points worth money. There was a significant feelings attention by mood interaction in the amount of these "rewards" that were provided: When the men's attention had been turned away from themselves, their moods influenced their expressed judgments; those who were depressed gave reliably fewer points to the worker than those who were happy. But on the other hand, when their attention was drawn to their feelings, their mood at the time did not reliably affect how many points they delivered to the worker. It is as if these latter people, who were highly conscious of how bad they felt, had become aware they should not take out their unhappiness on the other person.

The second Berkowitz-Troccoli experiment shows these results are not restricted to depressed moods. The male subjects in this later investigation were given a physical activity to carry out which was decidedly uncomfortable in half of the cases, and again, some of the men were led to be highly aware of their discomfort by asking them to rate their feelings. Immediately after this, they listened to a brief autobiographical statement supposedly made by another man and gave their impressions of his personality. A multiple regression analysis was then carried out testing whether the experimental variations interacted with the subjects' self-rated felt discomfort in predicting how many bad qualities the men assigned to the target person. As can be seen in Figure 5, such a significant interaction was obtained: Again, when the subjects' attention was turned away from themselves, the worse they felt, the more unfavorable was their impression of the target. By contrast, those who were highly conscious of their discomfort seemed to "lean over backwards" in their judgments; the greater their felt displeasure, the *fewer* was the number of bad qualities they attributed to the target.

All in all, the feelings attention in these studies apparently gave rise to a relatively careful consideration of what was socially appropriate under the given circumstances and, consequently, produced a heightened self-restraint. However, attention to one's feelings probably will not always have such an effect. The target person in these experiments clearly was not the source of the subjects' displeasure. Thinking more about what was going on, they realized they should not blame others for their distress and evidently sought to be fair in their judgments. But on the other hand, in a very different situation people who are highly aware of themselves and their bad feelings conceivably might become even more hostile towards an available target—when (a) it is not at all clear

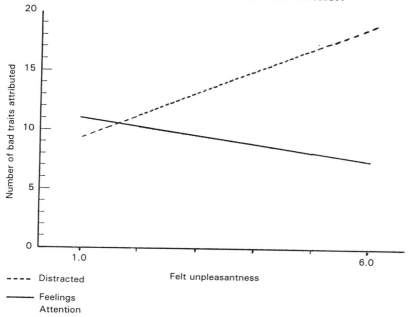

FIGURE 5. Relationship between negative feelings and expressed negative judgment as a function of attention to feelings.

to them that this person should not be blamed, and (b) they are not motivated to be accurate in their judgments.

This brief overview of some of the ways in which cognitive factors can influence affective aggression does not mean that I believe cognitive processes are relatively unimportant in the determination and regulation of these emotional responses. Indeed, I call the ideas summarized here a "cognitive-neo-associationistic" approach because I believe an adequate account of affective aggression must employ both cognitive and associationistic concepts and propositions. Cognitions obviously can play a major role in determining how highly aroused persons behave. Nevertheless, even when cognitive processes operate, they often work in a fairly automatic and involuntary manner so that the aroused individuals do not stop to think and decide what they should do.

REFERENCES

Ajzen, I., & Fishbein, M. (1980). *Understanding attitudes and predicting social behavior.* Englewood Cliffs, NJ: Prentice-Hall.

Anderson, C. A. (1989). Temperature and aggression: Ubiquitous effects of heat on occurrence of human violence. *Psychological Bulletin, 106,* 74-96.

Anderson, C. A., Anderson, K. B., & Deuser, W. E. (in press). Examining an affective aggression framework: Weapon and temperature effects on aggressive thoughts, affect, and attitudes. *Personality and Social Psychology Bulletin.*

Anderson, C. A., Deuser, W. E., & DeNeve, K. M. (1995). Hot temperatures, hostile affect, hostile cognition, and arousal: Tests of a general model of affective aggression. *Personality and Social Psychology Bulletin, 21,* 434-448.

Baumeister, R. F., & Heatherton, T. F. (1996). Self-regulation failure: An overview. *Psychological Inquiry,* in press.

Berkowitz, L. (1964). Aggressive cues in aggressive behavior and hostility catharsis. *Psychological Review, 71,* 104-122.

Berkowitz, L. (1974). Some determinants of impulsive aggression: Role of mediated associations with reinforcements for aggression. *Psychological Review, 81,* 165-176.

Berkowitz, L. (1983). Aversively stimulated aggression: Some parallels and differences in research with animals and humans. *American Psychologist, 38,* 1135-1144.

Berkowitz, L. (1989). The frustration-aggression hypothesis: Examination and reformulation. *Psychological Bulletin, 106,* 59-73.

Berkowitz, L. (1990). On the formation and regulation of anger and aggression: A cognitive-neo-associationistic analysis. *American Psychologist, 45,* 494-503.

Berkowitz, L. (1993a). *Aggression: Its causes, consequences, and control.* New York: McGraw-Hill.

Berkowitz, L. (1993b). Pain and aggression: Some findings and implications. *Motivation and Emotion, 17,* 277-293.

Berkowitz, L., Cochran, S., & Embree, M. (1981). Physical pain and the goal of aversively stimulated aggression. *Journal of Personality and Social Psychology, 40,* 687-700.

Berkowitz, L., & Frodi, A. (1977). Stimulus characteristics that can enhance or decrease aggression: Associations with prior positive or negative reinforcements for aggression. *Aggressive Behavior, 3,* 1-15.

Berkowitz, L., & Troccoli, B. T. (1990). Feelings, direction of attention, and expressed evaluations of others. *Cognition and Emotion, 4,* 305-325.

Block, R. (1977). *Violent crime.* Lexington, MA: Lexington Press/D.C. Heath.

Carlson, M., & Miller, N. (1988). Bad experiences and aggression. *Sociology and Social Research, 72,* 155-157.

Christianson, S.A. (1992). Emotional stress and eyewitness memory: A critical review. *Psychological Bulletin, 112,* 284-309.

Cloward, R. A., & Ohlin, L. E. (1960). *Delinquency and opportunity: A theory of delinquent gangs.* Glencoe, IL: Free Press.

Cornish, D. B., & Clarke, R. V. (1986). *The reasoning criminal: Rational choice perspective on offending.* New York/Berlin: Springer-Verlag.

Easterbrook, J. A. (1959). The effect of emotion on cue utilization and the organization of behavior. *Psychological Review, 66,* 183-207.

Feshbach, S. (1964). The function of aggression regulation of aggressive drive. *Psychological Review, 71,* 257-272.

Fitz, D. (1976). A renewed look at Miller's conflict theory of aggression displacement. *Journal of Personality and Social Psychology, 33,* 752-732.

Fraczek, A. (1974). Informational role of situation as a determinant of aggressive behavior. In J. deWit & W. W. Hartup (Eds.), *Determinants and origins of aggressive behavior* (pp. 225-230). The Hague: Mouton.

Frodi, A. (1975). The effect of exposure to weapons on aggressive behavior from a cross-cultural perspective. *International Journal of Psychology, 10,* 283-292.

Hutchinson, R. R. (1983). The pain-aggression relationship and its expression in naturalistic settings. *Aggressive Behavior, 9,* 229-242.

Kleck, G., & McElrath, K. (1991). The effects of weaponry on human violence. *Social Forces, 69,* 669-692.

Landau, S. F., & Pfeffermann, D. (1988). A time series analysis of violent crime and its relation to prolonged states of warfare: The Israeli case. *Criminology, 26,* 489-504.

Landau, S. F., & Raveh, A. (1987). Stress factors, social support, and violence in Israeli society: A quantitative analysis. *Aggressive Behavior, 13,* 67-85.

Lilly, J. R., Cullen, F. T., & Ball, R. A. (1989). *Criminological theory: Context and consequences.* Newbury Park, CA: Sage.

Merton, R. K. (1957). *Social theory and social structure, rev.ed.* Glencoe, IL: Free Press.

Miller, N. E. (1948). Theory and experiment relating psychoanalytic displacement to stimulus-response generalization. *Journal of Abnormal and Social Psychology, 43,* 155-178.

Pilowsky, I., & Spence, N.D. (1976). Pain, anger and illness behaviour. *Journal of Psychosomatic Research, 20,* 411-416.

Straus, M. (1980). Social stress and marital violence in a national sample of American families. *Annals of New York Academy of Science, 347,* 229-250.

Straus, M., Gelles, R. J., & Steinmetz, S. (1980). *Behind close doors: Violence in the American family.* New York: Anchor/Doubleday.

Turner, C. W., Simons, L. S., Berkowitz, L., & Frodi, A. (1977). The stimulating and inhibiting effects of weapons on aggressive behavior. *Aggressive Behavior, 3,* 355-378.

Ulrich, R.E. (1966). Pain as a cause of aggression. *American Zoologist, 6,* 643-662.

Vernon, W., & Ulrich, R. E. (1966). Classical conditioning of pain-elicited aggression. *Science, 152,* 668.

Williams, K. R., & Flewelling, R. L. (1988). The social production of criminal homicide: A comparative study of disaggregated rates in American cities. *American Sociological Review, 53,* 421-431.

Wilson, J. Q., & Herrnstein, R. J. (1985). *Crime and human nature.* New York: Simon and Schuster.

Wilson, W. P., Blazer, D. G., & Nashold, B. S. Jr. (1976). Observations on pain and suffering. *Psychosomatics, 17,* 73-76.

Wolfgang, M. E. (1958). *Patterns in criminal homicide.* Philadelphia: Univ. of Pennsylvania Press.

Wright, J. D., Rossi, P. H., & Daly, K. (1983). *Under the gun: Weapons, crime, and violence in America.* New York: Aldine.

CHAPTER 13

THE PSYCHOLOGY OF AGGRESSION: INSIGHTS AND ISSUES

SEYMOUR FESHBACH

INTRODUCTION

A traveler visiting the United States will be cautioned about entering particular areas in our urban centers, especially at night. Even if he does not find himself the direct object of assault, he might well be the victim of a stray bullet, fired during the course of a drive-by shooting or an exchange of gunfire between rival gangs. He may discover that violence is not restricted to the evening or to inner city streets, and be struck by television reports of vandalism, extortion, physical attack, guns, and knives and other indices of aggression in the public schools.

Violence, of course, is not confined to the United States, and is not unknown to the traveler at home where he lives. Scapegoating of and physical attacks on foreigners in his own land may be common occurrences, as are spouse abuse and child abuse. At times he becomes concerned about commuting to work because of bomb explosions in buses and train stations set by dissident groups. He is also disturbed by the

SEYMOUR FESHBACH • Department of Psychology, University of California, Los Angeles, 405 Hilgard, Los Angeles, California 90095-1563.

Aggression: Biological, Developmental, and Social Perspectives, edited by Seymour Feshbach and Jolanta Zagrodzka. Plenum Press, New York, 1997.

frequency with which his younger son gets into fights with his peers and the attendance by his older son at sporting events at which fighting often takes place between players and between spectators. His place of employment is also a source of distress because the employees are angry about deterioration in working conditions and reductions in medical allowances and other benefits.

And when he turns to television temporarily to escape from these daily stresses, he finds that watching television news, while absorbing, also adds to his discomfort. It seems that nations everywhere are beset by ethnic discord or conflicts with their neighbors. But he is especially disturbed by the form of aggression that takes place. Limbs are severed, women are raped, and defenseless innocents (even infants) are slaughtered.

It is clear that human aggression, including its most violent manifestations, is not restricted to early historical periods or to particular peoples and cultures. There may well be less social and moral acceptance of aggression in contemporary society than in ancient times or the nineteenth century. Nevertheless, aggression in its various forms remains a major social problem. Whether as a social problem or as a salient facet of human behavior, the understanding of the mechanisms mediating aggression presents an important challenge to psychologists and biologists engaged in the study of behavior. The problem of aggression is also addressed in important ways by other disciplines—e.g., sociology, history, political science, economics. However, our concern in this volume has been with the contributions of psychologists and biologists to our understanding of aggressive phenomena.

Within the domain of psychology and biology, there have been a multitude of issues that have been extensively investigated by researchers. No single volume can do justice to the extensive literature on aggressive behavior. However, each of the chapters offers special insights and, in most instances, new data, bearing on some facet of aggressive behavior. In this concluding chapter, I shall attempt to place each of these individual contributions into a broader context. In addition, I shall consider theoretical and empirical issues that I believe to be important that either have not been examined by students of aggression or that, in my judgment, require clarification and sharpening. To this end, it will be helpful first to consider historical developments in the study of aggression.

EARLY APPROACHES TO THE STUDY OF AGGRESSION

Until the publication in 1939 of the "frustration-aggression" volume by John Dollard and his colleagues at Yale (Dollard, Doob, Miller,

Mowrer, Sears, 1939), the predominant theoretical approach to the understanding of aggressive phenomena was that of psychoanalysis. The Freudian conception of aggression was similar in many respects to that of biological instinct theory but also had features unique to psychoanalytic theory. Following the expressions of hostility and the destruction and enormous toll in lives that took place in World War I, Freud elevated the construct of aggression to that of a basic primal, instinctual impulse , at a level with libidinal impulses. Aggression joined libido as one of the drives that comprised the system of unconscious, instinctual motivations that Freud labeled the "id." Freud conceived of aggression as a motivation that early in development was largely directed outwardly but became increasingly directed inwardly, ultimately eventuating in death; hence, the label "Thanatos" for aggressive drive to contrast with "Eros," his label for libidinal impulses.

The combination of aggressive and libidinal impulses enabled psychoanalysts to "explain" a great many phenomena. ranging from oedipal conflicts, to humor, to paranoia, to war. However, the psychoanalytic model did not readily lend itself to explanations of the variations in aggressive behavior. While psychoanalytic theory took cognizance of variability in the strength of the aggressive instinct, in the socialization experiences of the child and in the strength of inhibitory factors, psychoanalysis did not provide a systematic account of the antecedent factors influencing aggression. It remained for frustration-aggression theory to provide a framework for the investigation and analysis of the antecedents of and individual differences in aggression.

The frustration-aggression approach, like that of psychoanalytic theory, proferred a drive model of aggression. However, it differed in proposing a functional link between aggression and particular kinds of experiences. This link was quantitatively described such that the degree of aggression was hypothesized to be a direct function of the degree of frustration. This formulation had a major heuristic consequence and lent itself to a wide range of empirical investigations. One could experimentally manipulate frustrating situations and assess the degree and form of aggressive behaviors that ensued. One could explore particular socialization experiences, and determine the extent to which individual differences in the degree of frustration entailed in these experiences were related to individual differences in aggressive attitudes and behavior. The heuristic value of the frustration-aggression hypothesis was not limited to studies at the individual psychological level but facilitated the analysis of social class, cultural and societal differences in aggression.

Although the frustration-aggression hypothesis had and continues to have great value, its initial formulation—while having the virtue of a powerful theoretical hypothesis—was overly stated. It was subject to a number of different kinds of criticisms and had to be modified. In its strongest formulation, the frustration-aggression hypothesis entailed two contestable propositions: a) If frustration, then aggression; that is, frustration always results in aggression (direct or inhibited); b) If aggression, then frustration; that is, aggression is always preceded by frustration. A third problem has to do with the definition of aggression which, in terms of the frustration-hypothesis, is an instigation or motivation to inflict pain. Issues arise concerning possible differences in the functions of various aggressive behaviors. This problem area overlaps with proposition (b) since the functions of aggression are, to a considerable degree, determined by the antecedents of aggression.

The critiques and modifications of the frustration-aggression hypothesis provide a useful context in which to consider the contributions to this volume and related issues in aggression research. The three broad concerns regarding the frustration-aggression hypothesis (the effects of frustration, the antecedents of aggression, the meaning and functions of aggressive acts) are related and most of the contributions bear on two or all three of these concerns. Nevertheless, because they provide a helpful organizational framework, each of these issues will be considered separately.

THE MEANING AND FUNCTIONS OF AGGRESSION

Both the Freudian and the frustration-aggression model of aggression lump together the emotional response of anger, the instrumental use of aggression to achieve a nonaggressive goal such as food or sex or money or dominance, and the motivation or drive to inflict injury. These categories of aggression should be conceptually distinguished and, where possible, empirically distinguished, even though they often overlap (Feshbach, 1964). William James(1917) argued many years ago for the constructive use of anger as in moral rearmament, and Averill (1982) has shown that the experience of anger infrequently results in aggressive acts. Nor does an aggressive act have to be accompanied by anger or the desire to hurt. A child may use aggressive force to obtain a desired toy from another child, without being angry at or wishing to hurt the other. Similarly, a criminal may use aggressive force solely to obtain the victim's money. However, as research reported in this volume indicates, these mechanisms are often interwoven.

INSIGHTS FROM ANIMAL RESEARCH

Fonberg, as reported in the chapter by Zagrodska and Fonberg, distinguishes between emotional, emotional-instrumental, and purely instrumental aggression. However, she notes that purely instrumental aggression may not be so common in animals. Zagrodska and Fonberg then go on to demonstrate that predatory aggression, which would appear to be purely instrumental in nature, is not a simple food seeking response. Thus the destruction of the ventromedial part of the amygdala of cats, preselected as mouse-killers, eliminates predatory behavior but not food intake. The cats even prefer eating meat from a bowl to eating a mouse. They further show that predatory attack persists while food intake decreases with destruction of the dorsomedial part of the amygdala. Similarly, destruction of the ventro-posterior medial region of the hypothalamus does not impair mouse killing but totally inhibits mouse consumption.

The question arises as to why predatory attack persists in these situations if the aggression is not reinforced by eating of the prey. It is not that the animal is enraged when killing the prey. Zagrodska and Fonberg note that the ability to carry out a predatory attack is unrelated to the level of affective aggression, that predatory attack apparently does not engage the rage system. Karli's research also conveys the difference between predatory aggression and the more defensive affective aggression, differing not only in the context in which they are elicited and in features of the response but also in areas of the brain by which they are respectively evoked by stimulation. However, predatory aggression and territorial aggression appear to be related in the rat in that they are both enhanced by electrical stimulation of the hypothalamus and both abolished by lateral lesions of the hypothalamus.

The question remains of the factors that maintain the predatory attack independent of food consumption. Zagrodska and Fonberg suggest that taste and play with the mouse may be reinforcing for the rat. Perhaps it is the cessation of activity by the prey when it is injured or killed. Resolution of the question of what reinforces or sustains the attack behavior in these animals may have important implications for human aggression. The possibility is raised, as Fraczek and others have suggested, that the performance of the aggressive response alone may be intrinsically rewarding.

This is not to deny the central importance of the consequences of the aggressive response—whether or not it is rewarded or punished, or approved or disapproved. However, one might add to the three functional categories of aggression—anger, instrumental and hostile (drive) a fourth, namely more or less innate stimulus>aggressive response links. It is certainly the case, as Berkowitz has so well documented, that particular stimuli in the environment (notably "aggressive" stimuli such as guns) increase the probability of an aggressive response. These stimulus-response connections do not have the automaticity that is observed when a male stickleback fish invades the territory of another male, or when a male robin espies the red breast of another male. Also, the associations that have been studied at the human level are clearly learned. Still the possibility remains that certain stimuli tend to evoke an aggressive response, and that performance of an aggressive response is intrinsically rewarding.

OFFENSIVE AND DEFENSIVE AGGRESSION

A major distinction made in animal studies of aggression, and one that may well have profound implications for human aggression, is the difference between offensive and defensive aggression. This distinction is rarely made in studies of human aggression. Yet, it is fundamental to the research reported by Zagrodska and Fonberg, Karli, and Shaikh and Siegel. We have already alluded to the research indicating that different brain sites mediate predation and defensive aggression. Moreover, Shaikh and Siegel, in a series of studies, demonstrate how the action of these different brain sites are differentially affected by amygdaloid stimulation and administration of a particular biochemical, substance P. Whereas amygdaloid stimulation facilitates defensive rage behavior, it suppresses predatory attack behavior. Administration of substance P blocks both of these amygdaloid effects. This is not say that both forms of aggression cannot occur in the same situation or that they cannot be modified through learning.

The question arises as to what implications, if any, these studies distinguishing offensive (predatory) and defensive aggression in animals have for the understanding of human aggression. While this distinction, so fundamental to animal research, has its human analogue, language usage and the complex cognitive and social factors mediating human aggression (to which Karli alludes) prevent a simple generalization to the human level. Instrumental aggression without anger would be roughly analogous to predatory aggression. Still, in the case of humans, instrumental aggression is usually intraspecies while predatory aggression is interspecies. When humans kill animals for food, it is generally not considered aggressive in the same sense as killing a witness to insure their silence, or assaulting someone to steal their money. Even killing animals for sport would not be viewed by many individuals as a form of aggression. From a scientific perspective, it could be included within the construct of aggression if its antecedents and correlates were similar to those of behaviors that either through consensus or empirical study are considered as aggressive.

Even more complex problems arise in establishing for humans the equivalent of defensive aggression in animals. The expression of anger by humans is presumably the analogue of defensive aggression. However, the range and kinds of stimuli that evoke anger in human is quantitatively and qualitatively different from those that elicit the rage reaction and defensive aggression in animals. For animal species other than humans. defensive aggression is a response to a manifest physical threat. For humans, the threat can be psychological as well as physical, social and environmental as well as personal, and is further a function of how the potential threat is cognitively perceived.

In addition, at the human level, the concept of defensive aggression has a different connotation. Attacking someone who has made one angry by an insulting comment is not viewed as defensive aggression. While attackers may feel that they are defending their honor, the behavior is functionally different from utilizing physical aggression to defend against a physical attack. The latter behavior is considered as defensive aggression, whether or not it is mediated or accompanied by anger. Society sharply distinguishes between an aggressive act which is unprovoked and a defensive aggressive act which is a response to a provocation and is appropriate to the degree of threat entailed in the provocation.

Although society makes this distinction, studies of human aggression usually cluster these two types of aggression. For example, in the Feshbach (1970) and the Parke and Slaby (1983) reviews of the child socialization literature, there is an absence of studies relating child rearing practices to defensive aggression in the sense of appropriate defensive aggressive reactions to an aggressive assault, There is, of course, a very rich literature linking early experiences and socialization to aggressive behavior in children and adolescents.

It may prove to be the case that children who manifest high defensive aggression also manifest high offensive aggression. Nevertheless, the possibility ought to be considered that there are individual differences in the readiness to and frequency with which one defends oneself when attacked or threatened, and that variation in defensive aggression reflects a different dimension than variation in offensive aggression. The differentiation made by Dodge and Coie (1987) between reactive and proactive aggression and work by Pulkkinen (1987) provide some empirical support for the utility of a distinction between defensive and offensive aggression in humans.

To further complicate the comparison between animal and human defensive and offensive aggression, social norms as to what is normative and appropriate have a powerful effect on determining manifestations of aggression. If society decrees that a son is obligated to retaliate against one who has defamed his family name, then responding with aggression is an act of conformity, and failure to aggress would be an act of nonconformity. Aggression in these circumstances is an instrumental act, the goal being societal approval and avoidance of shame. However, this form of instrumental aggression would appear to be functionally different than instrumental aggression where the goal is to obtain personal, material rewards. One would expect differences in the personality and child-rearing practices that are associated with these two forms of instrumental aggression.

CONTINUITIES AND DISCONTINUITIES BETWEEN ANIMAL AND HUMAN AGGRESSION

It is evident that the dynamics of human aggression are much more complex than the dynamics of animal aggression. This is not to say that animal research on aggression is irrelevant to the understanding of human aggression. There clearly are continuities between social behavior in animals and in humans that are illuminated by evolutionary theory, sociobiology and brain research. Karli enumerates several areas in which neurobiological research with animals bears on aggressive behavior in humans. These include emotional responsiveness and the differentiation between anger mediated and instrumental aggression, the conditions fostering impulsiveness and the effects of anxiety and of early learning on aggression. Other pertinent research areas are the cognitive and affective effects on aggression of familiarization and of the consequences of aggressive acts—i.e., whether they result in success, defeat, or punishment. Also, an area of inquiry highly relevant to human manifestations of aggression, and one that has been much more extensively studied in animals than in humans, is the modulating role of competing affective states of attachment and social comfort. Parenthetically, the evidence indicating that different brain sites mediate anger and instrumental aggression suggests that while attempting to reduce human violence through biochemical interventions that block the arousal of anger may have some influence on anger mediated aggression, the incidence of instrumental aggression will be largely unaffected.

The complex and often subtle interplay between biological and social determinants of aggression is well documented in Brain's discussion of the effects of alcohol on aggression. The consumption of alcohol has frequently been linked to acts of aggressive behavior. The question is the nature of the mechanism or mechanisms that mediate this linkage. Early experiments with rats (Conger, 1949) and cats (Masserman, 1946), pairing electric shock with a goal box containing food and then determining the effects of alcohol on the approach behavior of the animal, led to the view that alcohol exerted its effects through reducing anxiety. However, as Brain documents, subsequent research on the physiological effects of alcohol and the role of social and contextual variables indicates that the effects of alcohol are variable and not readily attributed to any single process or mechanism. Brain indicates that in terms of its biological effects, alcohol is an extremely nonspecific drug that affects a number of physiological functions. These functions are not specifically linked to aggressive behavior. Thus, chronic alcoholism has a femininizing effect, resulting from the fact that alcohol stimulates estrogen rather than testosterone secretion. If the latter had been the case, one might contend that alcohol could increase aggression through stimulating secretion of the male hormone, testosterone. Further, as Brain notes, alcohol has a complex effect on motivation. While alcohol has been shown to increase defensiveness in mice, moderate and high doses generally reduce fighting and threat in animals due to the sedative effect of alcohol. The effects of alcohol on motivation may be mediated by cognitive impairments resulting from alcohol intake. These disturbances in cognitive functioning influence the perception of and the production of social cues and can directly result in maladaptive social behaviors. Finally, the effects of alcohol, especially in humans, are markedly influenced by social context. Brain points out that expectancy effects of drinking can be as strong as the direct effects of alcohol itself. Brain's chapter reinforces Karli's conclusions regarding the continuities and discontinuities between animal and human aggression.

THE XYY CHROMOSOME

Karli, in addition to discussing the issues entailed in generalizing from animal aggression research to human aggression, cautions more generally against predominant biological explanations of human aggression. He cites the unusual interest in the XYY chromosome as an example of the tendency to misinterpret the role of biological determinants of aggression. The extraordinary excitement and research attention that was generated by the discovery of the XYY chromosomal abnormality should provide an illuminating chapter in the sociology of scientific inquiry. A finding that some prisoners had an extra Y chromosome elicited the interest of research laboratories throughout the world.

To explore the possible contribution of genetic and other biological influences to criminal and to aggressive behaviors is a reasonable enterprise. To view a biological structure as possibly being "the" key to understanding human violence and criminal behavior indicates that even trained scientists are susceptible to the "genetic fallacy." Biological structures, including genes, function in an environment, and their effects are as much dependent upon that environment as they are upon that structure. In the case of social behaviors as complex as aggression and criminality, it becomes especially important to take cognizance of Karli's reminder that the human is not only a biological individual but also a social actor and a self-reflective and deliberating creature.

It happens that the results of the more than one thousand studies of the relation of the XYY chromosome to social behavior indicate that the relation between this chromosomal deviation and deviations in social behavior is, at best, marginal. In an extensive review of this research (Witkin et al., 1976), it was concluded that there appears to be a slight relationship between presence of the XYY chromosome and criminality but none with aggressiveness or violence. Even if a significant correlation had been obtained between this chromosomal abnormality and individual aggression, one would not gainsay the importance of experiential, cultural and other social factors. To rephrase the argument, the problem with the XYY research enterprise was not the effort to discover a relationship between a biological variable and human aggression, but the implicit, and sometimes explicit belief that the XYY chromosome, like Lombroso's protuberances of the skull, was the basis of human aggression or human criminality. To the extent that theory guided the XYY research, it seemed to take the form of an illogical four step analogical reasoning sequence: (1) Men are more aggressive than women; (2) maleness is determined by an XY while femaleness is determined by an XX chromosome; (3) An extra Y chromosome adds additional maleness to the individual; (4) Additional maleness results in additional aggression, The core of the fallacy lies, of course, in the third proposition. The deeper lesson of the XYY episode is that approaches scientists take to the study of human aggression and their views concerning the causes of aggression may be a reflection of their value systems as well as of research findings.

IF AGGRESSION, THEN FRUSTRATION

The Frustration-Aggression volume conveyed the impression that the only or primary antecedent of aggressive behavior was frustration. The authors of the volume readily acknowledged the criticism that the role of learning in the development of aggressive behavior had not been addressed. Inasmuch as these authors were all eminent members of the Yale Learning Theory group, one can assume that the failure to address the role of learning was a consequence of their interest in the antecedents and expression of aggressive drive—or in their language, the instigation to aggression.

The acquisition of aggressive responses through learning has been well established (Feshbach, 1970, Parke & Slaby, 1983). There have been primarily two learning mechanisms that have been emphasized in the aggression research literature—the acquisition of aggressive responses through direct reinforcement, and the acquisition of aggressive responses through the modeling of aggressive behavior. A technical issue in a number of these studies arises in regard to the role of reinforcers. Do reinforcers function primarily as incentives for the performance of aggressive responses in particular social contexts or do they serve to strengthen the connection between particular stimuli or social contexts and an aggressive response. This issue aside, what is critical about research on the learning of aggression is the demonstration of the power of reward on the acquisition and performance of aggressive behavior. Aggression, for social learning theorists, is one of a variety of instrumental behaviors available to the organism in striving to achieve some desired goal.

SOCIAL LEARNING AND AGGRESSION

It is of interest that while a number of the contributions bear on the social learning of aggression, none offer either a simple reinforcement or straightforward modeling interpretation of their findings. Björkqvist, in a prior study, found that identification is an an important variable in determining the effects of a model. Sons who had a poor relationship with a physically aggressive father were less aggressive than sons who had a positive relationship with a physically aggressive father. Presumably, the positive relationship facilitated identification with the father and the acquisition of the father's values and modes of behavior. In his investigation of the relationship between father's, mother's, and son's and daughter's aggression reported in this volume, Björkqvist finds evidence of modeling effects that vary with the similarity between the child's and parent's gender, and with the social context in which aggression is reported. When the aggressive behavior takes place at home, boy's aggression is more strongly correlated with that of the father than with that of the mother. While girl's aggression correlated somewhat more with that of the mother than of the father, the difference was small. Surprisingly, when the aggression is with peers, aggression in both boys and girls was much more strongly correlated with mother's than with father's aggression. One might conjecture that social relationships are seen to be gender typed so that the children take their cues for appropriate behavior in interacting with peers from the mother than from the father. It also may be that the children have much more opportunity to observe their mother than their father in social interactions, the frequency with which a particular behavior is observed being an important factor determining the degree to which a behavior is modeled. Additional research is needed to obtain data bearing on these and other possible interpretations of the data.

MULTIDETERMINANTS OF AGGRESSION

The Kirwil study highlights the multiplicity and complexity of factors that influence the development of aggression. The study focuses on an intriguing familial situation—namely, a lack of congruence beween parental approval of aggression and their child's initial level of aggression, Two and a half years later, the aggressive behaviors of many of the children have moved in the direction of the parental value while the aggressive behavior of others remains discordant with the parental value. Kirwil then addresses the question of familial attitudes and behaviors that distinguish the families of children whose aggression changed from those of families of children whose aggression remained similar to the level displayed two and a half years previously. She finds evidence of socialization flexibility in parents with nonaggressive values whose children had decreased in aggression while the family patterns of parents with non-aggressive values whose children sustained their aggressiveness tended to be chaotic and lacked systematic responsiveness to the child's behavior. In the case of families with aggressive values and initially non-aggressive children, the parents of those children whose level of aggression increased over the two and half year time span tended to be less well educated and less oriented to behavioral control. These data reflect the variety of situational and direct and indirect learning factors that influence the development of aggression.

If one looks at the families of the two groups of children who were aggressive at the later time period—those who sustained their aggressiveness from the earlier period and those who increased their aggressiveness—we find some similarities but also differences. The differences suggest different paths to the same outcome of aggressive behavior. A question of interest that is not addressed in this chapter by Kirwil, which is concerned with changes in aggression, are the factors mediating the initial discordance between the values of the family and the behavior of the child who ultimately moves in the direction of the family's values. We understand why the cohesiveness and good communication of families with nonaggressive values led to a decline in their children's aggressiveness. But why were the children aggressive to begin with? The answer might simply be temperament. However, early experiences and other aspects of the family structure and socialization practices might also play a role.

The longitudinal study carried out by Caprara and his associates is concerned with the utility of aggression and several other indices of affective and social behavior as predictors of scholastic achievement and social adjustment manifested four years later. While the study does not directly address the development of aggression, the findings indirectly bear on the instrumental utility of aggression. Children's aggression at ages 7-9 proved to be positively correlated with peer rejection at ages 11-14. This finding is not surprising. However, it does indicate that aggression, which has been demonstrated to be a stable behavior over time (Olweus, 1979), is associated with negative consquences. Undoubtedly, as Patterson (1982) and others have demonstrated, parents and peers may also be engaging in behaviors that reinforce the aggressive response. Nevertheless, the question arises as to why noxious consequences such as peer rejection and punishment by parents and school authorities do not offset and override the reinforcers that the child may be receiving. We know that the timing of the reinforcer is a critical variable. However, while there may be a time gap between the punishment and the aggressive response which reduces the influence of the outcome, peer responses of acceptance and rejection are fairly immediate. To understand the persistence of aggressive behavior, one needs to examine other dynamic elements in the social situation besides rewards and punishments that may be influencing the aggressive behavior. Thus, the child who is rejected because of his or her aggression may experience pain and frustration that foster anger and hostility. Cognitive changes may occur in the attributions the child makes regarding other's motives and attitudes (Dodge & Coie, 1987). These cognitions may then mediate the instrumental outcomes of the child's aggressive acts and serve to regulate the child's behavior.

The importance of utilizing a multiprocess approach in the analysis of aggressive behavior is underlined in the Eron, Guerra, and Huesmann chapter. Eron has long been associated with a social learning interpretation of aggressive behavior. Later work with Huesmann led to the incorporation of cognitive schemas in the social learning analysis. In this study which focuses on demographic variables, stress and frustration are added to the mix of factors influencing aggression, although the social learning model is maintained in that aggressive responses to frustration and stress are viewed as having been acquired through modeling or direct reinforcement. It is of interest that neighborhood violence stress had a significant effect on aggression in all three ethnic groups in the study sample. This finding suggests that defensive aggression may be contributing to the aggressive behaviors of the children. Since there is variability in the extent to which children in a poor and crime-ridden neighborhood experience violence stress, it may be that differences on the violence stress measure reflect the child's cognitive apprehensions and attributions rather than the actual degree of violence exposure.

Also of interest are the findings that the effects of poverty are mediated though neighborhood violence stress and life events stress. Economic privation in itself predicted aggression in only one of the three ethnic groups studied. Another difference between the ethnic groups in the pattern of variables correlated with aggression was the negligible correlation obtained for African-American children between aggressive behavior and aggressive normative beliefs. These differences point to the multiplicity of variables influencing aggressive behavior, and remind us that the pattern of these variables may differ as a function of ethnicity and other demographic factors.

INSTRUMENTAL AGGRESSION, BIOLOGY AND WAR

Certainly the most destructive, if not the most egregious, form of human aggression is war. War has been traditionally seen as a manifestation of the human aggressive instinct, rooted in our evolutionary heritage. In the famous interchange of correspondence between Einstein and Freud (Nathan & Norden, 1968), Einstein queries Freud as to the roots of the apparent human predilection for war, and the possibilities of altering this highly destructive human behavior. For Freud, war is a manifestation of the instinctual aggressive drive. exacerbated by the role of leaders and other social factors. Interestingly, Freud does not see sublimation—that is, the expression of aggressive impulses in a socially acceptable form—as do other psychoanalysts (Glover, 1933; Strachey, 1957), as the solution to Einstein's question. Rather, he feels changes, difficult to achieve, are required in two areas of human functioning. The first change entails the enhancement of human intellectual functioning. If humans were more rational, they would be better able to find and agree upon alternative solutions to national or ethnic conflicts. However, rationality is not sufficient since in some situations, it may be concluded that it is in the national self-interest to promulgate a war. Freud felt a psychological deterrent was necessary. And that deterrent was Eros; that is the enhancement of positive feelings towards other ethnic and national groups.

Freud's recommendations may have merit, whether or not his views concerning the instinctual basis of war are viewed as sound. Hinde offers a very different analysis of the bases for war. The very title of his chapter is provocative namely, is war a consequence of human aggression? Hinde is, of course, not questioning the fact that war entails an aggressive act. Rather, he rejects the notion that war is the expression of individual aggressive drives, whether or not instinctually derived. Wars, according to Hinde, may not be caused by human aggressiveness, nor do people fight in war because they are necessarily aggressive.

My own research (Feshbach, 1987) provides consistent support for Hinde's assertion concerning the relationship between individual aggression and war. In a series of studies, various indices of individual aggression proved to be negligibly or weakly correlated with militaristic, hawkish views concerning armaments and war. Individual hostility or physical aggressiveness were poor predictors of attitudes toward war. A much stronger correlate of the readiness to engage in war are nationalistic attitudes reflecting the importance of national dominance and power. War is an action in which pacific as well as aggressive individuals engage. It is a form of group aggression that bears little relationship to individual aggressiveness.

For Hinde, war is a form of instrumental aggression involving groups and is a highly institutionalized behavior. Hinde details for us the institutionalized roles that individuals occupy in the course of implementing a military action. The physician who attends to the wounded, the pilot who drops a bomb on the enemy below, the infantryman who fires from his foxhole in the direction of an enemy he may not even see, are all fulfilling the obligations of a role. Their success in fulfilling that role is largely or completely independent of their aggressiveness or hostile feelings. For Hinde, and for a great many other behavioral scientists, to reduce the incidence of war, one needs to address the social and cultural factors that support the institution of war rather than focus on the reduction of individual aggressive tendencies.

It should be noted that this instrumental view of the basis of war that Hinde puts forth (and which I happen to share) has some problems. These are intimated in the chapter itself. Thus Hinde refers to the tendency of in-group members to see the in-group as superior, and to denigrate the out-group. These perceptions can, of course, be strongly influenced by experience. However, it is possible to argue on the basis of evidence from social psychological studies of in-group, out-group relations, that there is a dynamic tendency for in-groups to place a higher value on themselves and to devalue out-groups (Tajfel, 1982). Hinde, himself suggests that patriotism and nationalism may depend in part upon basic human tendencies. This kind of dynamic does not insure that the groups will be aggressive toward each other— avoidance and dominance-submission are alternatives. However, it greatly facilitates in-group aggression directed toward the out-group. Shaw and Wong (1989) offer a sociobiological argument to the effect that in-group preferences and domination of out-groups maintain and augment the in-group's gene pool. The assumption here is that there is greater similarity between the gene pools of members of the same ethnic group, including nations that are not ethnically diverse, than between members of different ethnic groups. According to this account, wars, while not inevitable, are closely linked to human biological proclivities. Within this framework, the difference between war as an instrumental behavior whose function is to preserve and enhance the group's gene pool and war as an instinctual response of in-groups to out-groups becomes rather subtle.

Greatly complicating the issue of war in modern times is the distinction between a "defensive" war and an "offensive" war. Whereas in earlier historical periods, there were few sanctions—and sometimes even admiration—for nations that expanded their land and economic power through the successful waging of war, modern rules of international conduct prohibit the waging of an offensive war. Unfortunately, few nations admit to initiating an offensive war. National leaders have a remarkable capacity to perceive or to invent threats by other nations. And while some weapons are clearly defensive in nature, most weapons can be used for either offense or defense. Because it has become so difficult to distinguish between the instrumental use of war for defensive versus offensive purposes, it would seem appropriate to pursue Hinde's suggestions to focus on the cultural and social factors that maintain the institution of war, defensive or offensive.

IF FRUSTRATION, THEN AGGRESSION

Still another criticism of the strong form of the frustration-aggression hypothesis was the implication that the instigation to aggression was an inevitable consequence of frustration. Both theory and data indicated that frustration led to a number of reactions such as creativity.

There were several problems with the first proposition. It was noted that frustration can result in a variety of behaviors such as problem solving, avoidance, depression, and resignation, other than aggressive responses. There were those (predominantly psychoanalytically oriented), who argued that even when these alternative reactions to frustration were dominant, the instigation to aggress was still evoked, albeit inhibited or repressed or expressed in a disguised form. This latter possibility is impossible to test empirically since if no evidence of direct or indirect aggression is found following frustration, one can always argue that the search for manifestations of aggression was incomplete. A more useful approach is to determine the conditions under which frustration leads to an aggressive or to an alternative outcome.

ALTERNATIVE RESPONSES TO FRUSTRATION

We shall not attempt to review here the extensive literature on problem solving responses to frustration, the conditions under which frustration facilitates or interferes with learning and performance, regressive responses to frustration, frustration and learned helplessness, and other nonaggressive reactions to frustration. Whether or not one contends that frustration will evoke aggression in some form, it is evident that the response to frustration can be strongly influenced by learning. As Karli notes in his paper, animal aggression is strongly influenced by experiences of success versus defeat. Studies with children demonstrate that aggressive responses to frustration are significantly affected by reinforcement and nonreinforcement or punishment of the response (Davitz, 1952).

The chapter by Feshbach, Feshbach, and Jaffe on gender differences in the relationship between aggression and depression indirectly bears on the issue of alternative responses to frustration. There is, of course, a substantial research literature on gender differences in aggression and gender differences in depression. Males are more likely than females to respond to provoking, frustrating situations with aggression. The very fact that aggressive responses are less frequent in females implies that they are reacting to these frustrating stimuli with some response other

than aggression. The research indicating that women are more susceptible to depression than men suggests that one of the alternative responses to aggression being elicited in women by frustration is
depression.

The source of these gender differences is a matter of debate. One
can emphasize biological, temperament factors; one can focus on differences in socialization and reinforcement histories. Biological and learning
influences are not mutually exclusive. With regard to the findings of the
Feshbach, Feshbach, and Jaffe study, the role of experiential factors is
more apparent. The initial gender difference in the relationship between
aggressive and depressive tendencies, and the changes over time in the
strength of this relationship, can be most readily accounted for by hy-
pothesizing that male and female responses to frustration are differentially reinforced.

While there are differences in the conditions that elicit aggression
and depression, there is also a substantial overlap in the kinds of situations that evoke an aggressive response and the kinds that evoke a depressive response. Given this overlap, one would expect to find a
correlation between aggressive and depressive response tendencies.
However, Feshbach, Feshbach, and Jaffe suggest that this correlation
should be attenuated in young boys because, in comparison to girls, their
aggressive responses are differentially reinforced. The findings for the
younger age group were consistent with this hypothesis. The decrease
in the relationship between aggressive and depressive tendencies that
occurred with the older age girls can be attributed to changes in the
kinds of painful experiences to which girls are exposed with increasing
age. For girls, social relations become especially important, and experiences of social acceptance and social rejection, more salient. Social rejection is more likely to lead to depression than aggression, especially in
populations in which aggression is discouraged.

COGNITIONS, FRUSTRATION, AND AGGRESSION

Apart the issue of alternative responses to frustration, questions
arose regarding the defining properties of frustration and whether particular kinds of frustration were especially likely to evoke anger and aggression. It was argued that frustration of more central ego motives such
as self-esteem was more likely to elicit aggression than frustration of
hunger, or comfort or other bodily related motives (Maslow, 1941). A
closer examination of the construct of frustration led to the proposal that
frustration entailed interference with an expected positive outcome or
reward rather than interference with the outcome per se (Berkowitz,

1960). Thus, the failure to receive a requested salary increase is not frustrating if there was no expectation that the request would be approved. The reformulation of frustration in terms of expectancies facilitated the interpretation of seeming paradoxes such as increased aggression by an ethnic group following the implementation of public policies leading to positive economic and social changes for members of the group. Despite these positive changes, group members may be frustrated and angry if the stated public policy had led to "rising expectations" which were not met.

The role of cognition in the revisions of the frustration-aggression hypothesis was not restricted to the introduction of expectancy into the definition of frustration. Perceived attributes of the frustrating situation were shown to be significant determinants of the degree of anger and aggression elicited (Nickel, 1974, Pastore, 1952). These attributes include such cognitions as perceived intentionality of the frustrating act, perceived responsibility of the actor, and perceived justice of the act. Tripping over someone's foot elicits less anger if it is perceived as accidental rather than as a consequence of a deliberate, intentional effort to trip one. An infant, dropping an expensive vase to see it shatter, elicits less anger and aggression than an adult committing the same act because the infant is perceived as less responsible than the adult. A C grade on an examination elicits less anger, even if an A was anticipated, if the C grade is perceived by the recipient as merited than if the grade was felt to be unjustified.

These and related cognitions determine whether a stimulus event innocuous in itself, may evoke feelings of anger and hostility. The multicolored short hair and the earrings and clothes of the Punks studied by Lagerspetz take on significance as stimuli that may elicit aggression by virtue of the attributions that are made regarding the intent and responsibility of the wearer. The punk is seen as intentionally defying social expectancy to conform in manner and dress. More important, the deviation in appearance is perceived as symbolic of a more fundamental deviation from social conventions. Some of these perceptions are inaccurate. The Punks in Lagerspetz's sample are not as individually aggressive as they are often perceived to be. While they do get into difficulties with the law, they are not arrested for acts of violence. They tend to be opposed to individual and to group violence. However, their message of rebelliousness or nonconformity is accurately perceived by others. Punks may also evoke aggression by violating important values regarding drug usage and work habits. Individuals who are perceived as being able to work and being capable of choosing not to take drugs (attribution of responsibility) and who deliberately deviate from work and drug usage expectancies (attribution of intentionality) are likely to elicit an aggressive reaction.

One can argue whether punk behavior should be included under the umbrella of aggressive acts. However, an important message of the Lagerspetz study is that social deviance need not be associated with aggressive, antisocial deviance.

NEGATIVE AFFECT, AGGRESSIVE SYMBOLS, AND AGGRESSION

The cognitive revisions of the frustration-aggression hypothesis greatly enhanced our understanding of the antecedents of aggressive behavior. However, while cognitive mediating variables are important determinants of an aggressive response to frustration, they may not be necessary determinants. To the extent that there is continuity between animal and human aggression, one would expect that various conditions of competition, threat, and frustration would tend to elicit anger and aggressive responses with the only cognitive mediation being that of simply apprehending the stimulus.

Berkowitz, in an impressive series of studies, demonstrates the "thoughtless" nature of aggressive responses to a range of frustrating stimuli. In doing so, he introduces an important change in the frustration-aggression hypothesis, expanding the range of antecedent stimuli so that the hypothesis is reworded as "noxious stimuli>aggression." These noxious stimuli include physical pain, unpleasant heat, depression, and, most probably, social and personal stresses. Berkowitz, in these experimental demonstrations and in his review of the literature on crime and violence, reminds us that many aggressive acts are impulsively carried out and not directed to any instrumental goal, their only object being to inflict pain. The threshold for aggression is lowered in individuals who are under stress and discomfort, A parent who is in a bad mood because of problems at work may irrationally strike a child who committed a minor misbehavior and then regret his impulsive aggressive reaction. The increase in child abuse that is associated with unemployment can hardly be attributed to intentional, justified, and responsible acts of frustration by the child.

Berkowitz further demonstrates how irrational elements can influence aggressive behavior through the situational presence of external stimuli that have an aggressive meaning. Some examples of such stimuli are the presence or picture of a weapon, a name paired with an aggressor or object of aggression, and a movie scene of a fist-fight. The effects of these extraneous stimuli are mediated through more or less automatic cognitive priming mechanisms that activate "semantically-related thoughts, feelings, and motor tendencies." Berkowitz notes that these stimuli may not have an aggression enhancing effect if there are inhibitory factors associated with them.

Berkowitz does not argue that individual aggression is necessarily under the sway of irrelevant noxious states or irrelevant aggressive symbols. As Karli has noted, humans, unlike animals, have the capacity for self-reflection. And Berkowitz also demonstrates that awareness of and attention to noxious feelings can eliminate their aggression-evoking effects.

SOME CONCLUDING COMMENTS

The contributions to this volume reflect the the advances that have taken place in our understanding of aggressive phenomena since the early biological and psychoanalytic postulation of an aggressive instinct. Human aggression is not a unitary phenomenon dependent upon one major source. Rather, there are different categories of aggression with different functions and antecedents. The brain anatomical and neurochemical studies of animal aggression provide a bridge to human aggression while, at the same time, helping us be cognizant of the differences between the factors entailed in animal and human aggression resulting from the greater cognitive capacities of humans. There are analogues between the automaticity of aggressive responses to releasing stimuli that have been studied by ethologists and the "weapons" and related priming effects studied by Berkowitz. But humans have the capacity to modulate these effects and humans have the capacity to take into account the motivations of one who frustrates them.

We have a much better understanding since Freud of the role of learning in the acquisition of aggressive behavior and are obtaining a better grasp of the interaction between learning, biological, and experiential factors of frustration and threat. As psychologists we have tended to focus on individual antecedents of aggression but more recently have begun to interrelate social and cultural antecedents with individual factors as we address gender, ethnic, and national differences in aggressive behavior. However, major gaps remain in our understanding of particular facets of aggression and, especially, in our ability to control and reduce the incidence of aggression.

There is the problem of the persistence of aggression without obvious reinforcement. There are a number of possible interpretations that one can offer to account for this persistence. The aggressor may find satisfaction in the infliction of pain; aggression may become functionally autonomous of any instrumental outcome and be intrinsically rewarding; aggression in some individuals may be temperamentally rooted reactions to particular stimulus events. Much more research is needed to document any of these hypothesized mechanisms. Aggressive drive, in the sense of engaging in directed behavior whose goal response is destruction or the infliction of pain (Feshbach, 1964), is not well understood unless one assumes that the drive is innate.

We are beginning to address the emergence of aggressive scapegoat behavior in preadolescent youth, especially boys, but have not yet linked the group factor with individual factors contributing to scapegoat behavior. More generally, our research and theory provides a better basis for understanding individual acts of aggressive behavior than the aggressive acts which individuals carry out as members of a social group. Is the gang member who commits a violent act simply conforming to group norms or is he or she also disposed to be aggressive? Why do gangs carry out high-risk violent acts that offer so little in the way of concrete rewards? One can offer explanations in terms of pride, self-esteem, and retaliation, but the question remains of the provocation of the retaliatory sequence and how violence becomes associated with pride and self-esteem.

Similar questions can be raised with regard to violent acts committed as members of larger entities such as nations, ethnic groups, and religious groups. Why are some individuals willing to leave their homes, sacrifice material gain, and risk their lives to participate in some national, ethnic, or religious struggle? What are the factors that cause and maintain ethnic enmities? How can we help resolve these enmities and provide stable alternatives to violence as a mechanism for coping with conflict? Important challenges remain for investigators of human aggression.

REFERENCES

Averill, J. R. (1982). *Anger and aggression: An essay on emotion.* New York; Springer-Verlag.
Berkowitz, L. (1960). Repeated frustrations and expectations in hostility arousal. *Journal of Abnormal and Social Psychology, 60,* 422-429.
Conger, J. J. (1949). An analysis of the effect of alcohol upon conflict behavior in the white rat; Ph.D. dissertation. Yale University, New Haven.
Davitz, J. (1952). The effects of previous training on post-frustration behavior. *Journal of Abnormal and Social Psychology, 47,* 309-315.
Dodge, K. A., & Coie, J. D. (1987). Social-Information processing factors in reactive and proactive aggression in children's peer groups. *Journal of Personality and Social Psychology, 53,* 1146-1158.

Dollard, J., Doob, L. W., Miller, N. E., Mowrer, O. H., & Sears, R.R. (1939). *Frustration and aggression.* New Haven: Yale University Press.

Feshbach, S. (1964). The function of aggression and the regulation of aggressive drive. *Psychological Review, 71,* 257-272.

Feshbach, S. (1970). Aggression. In P. H. Mussen (Ed.). *Carmichael's manual of child psychology.* New York: Wiley

Feshbach, S. (1987). Individual aggression, national attachment and the search for peace: Psychological perspectives. *Aggressive Behavior, 13,* 315-325.

Glover, E. (1933). *War, Sadism and Pacifism: Three Essays.* London: Allen and Unwin.

James, W. (1917). The moral equivalent of war. In, *Memoirs and studies.* London: Longmans.

Maslow, A.H. (1941). Deprivation, threat and frustration. *Psychological Review. 48,* 364-366.

Masserman, J.H., & Yum, K.S. (1946). An analysis of the influence of alcohol on experimental neurosis in cats. *Psychosomatic Medicine, 8,* 36-52.

Nathan, O., & Norden, H. (1968). *Einstein on peace.* New York: Schocken Books.

Nickel, T. W. (1974). The attribution of intention as a critical factor in the relation between frustration and aggression. *Journal of Personality, 42,* 482-492.

Olweus, D. (1979). Stability of aggressive reaction patterns in males: a review. *Psychological Bulletin, 86,* 852-875.

Parke, R. D., & Slaby, R. G. (1983). The development of aggression. In P. H. Mussen (Gen. Ed.) & E. M. Hetherington (Vol. Ed.), *Handbook of child psychology: Vol 4, Socialization, personality and social development* (4th ed.). New York: Wiley, 547-641.

Pastore, N. (1952). The role of arbitrariness in the frustration-aggression hypothesis. *Journal of Abnormal and Social Psychology, 47,* 728-731.

Patterson, G. R. (1982). *Coercive family process.* Eugene, Oregon: Castalia Press.

Pulkkinen, L. (1987). Offensive and defensive aggression in humans: A longitudinal perspective. *Aggressive Behavior, 13,* 197-212.

Shaw, P. R., & Wong, Y. (1989). *Genetic seeds of warfare. In evolution, nationalism and patriotism.* Boston: Unwin Hyman.

Strachey, A. (1957). *The unconscious motives of war.* London: Allen & Unwin.

Tajfel, H. (1982). *Social identity and intergroup relations.* New York: Cambridge Press.

Witkin, H. A., Mednick, S. A., Schulsinger, F., Bakestrom, E., Christianses, K. O., Goodenough, D. R., Hirschhorn, K., Lundsteen, C., Owen, D. R. Philip, J., Rubin, D. B., & Stocking, M. (1976). Criminality in XYY and XXY men. *Science, 196,* 547-55.

INDEX